The Bible Speaks Today

Series Editors: J. A. Motyer (OT)
John R. W. Stott (NT)

The Message of Genesis 1 – 11

The dawn of creation

D0179086

Titles in this series

The Message of Genesis 1 – 11

The dawn of creation

David Atkinson
Fellow and Chaplain, Corpus Christi College,
Oxford

Inter-Varsity Press
Leicester, England
Downers Grove, Illinois, USA

Inter-Varsity Press
38 De Montfort Street, Leicester LE1 7GP, England
P.O. Box 1400, Downers Grove, Illinois 60515, USA

First published 1990
Reprinted 1991, 1993

British Library Cataloguing in Publication Data
Atkinson, David, *1943–*
   The message of Genesis 1–11.
   1. Bible O.T. Genesis – Critical studies
   I. Title   II. Series
   222.1106
UK ISBN 0–85110–676–5

Library of Congress Cataloging in Publication Data
Atkinson, David John, *1943–*
   The message of Genesis 1–11: the dawn of creation/David
   Atkinson.
      p. cm. – (The Bible speaks today)
   Includes bibliographical references.
   ISBN 0–8308–1229–6
   1. Bible. O.T. Genesis I–XI – Commentaries. I. Title.
   II. Series.
BS2825.3.A85   1990
222'.1106–dc20   90–36736
                                                        CIP

USA ISBN 0–8308–1229–6
USA ISBN 0–87784–925–0 (set of The Bible Speaks Today, paperback)

Typeset by AKM Associates (UK) Ltd, Southall, London
Printed in England by Clays Ltd, St Ives plc

*Inter-Varsity Press, England, is the book-publishing division of the Universities and Colleges
Christian Fellowship (formerly the Inter-Varsity Fellowship), a student movement linking
Christian Unions in universities and colleges throughout the United Kingdom and the Republic of
Ireland, and a member movement of the International Fellowship of Evangelical Students. For
information about local and national activities write to UCCF, 38 De Montfort Street, Leicester
LE1 7GP.*

*InterVarsity Press, USA, is the book-publishing division of InterVarsity Christian Fellowship,
a student movement active on campus at hundreds of universities, colleges and schools of nursing in
the United States of America, and a member movement of the International Fellowship of
Evangelical Students. For infomation about local and regional activities, write Public Relations
Dept., InterVarsity Christian Fellowship, 6400 Schroeder Road, P.O. Box 7895, Madison, WI
53707–7895.*

*Distributed in Canada through InterVarsity Press, 860 Denison St., Unit 3, Markham, Ontario
L3R 4H1, Canada.*

General preface

The Bible Speaks Today describes a series of both Old Testament and New Testament expositions, which are characterized by a threefold ideal: to expound the biblical text with accuracy, to relate it to contemporary life, and to be readable.

These books are, therefore, not 'commentaries', for the commentary seeks rather to elucidate the text than to apply it, and tends to be a work rather of reference than of literature. Nor, on the other hand, do they contain the kind of 'sermons' which attempt to be contemporary and readable without taking Scripture seriously enough.

The contributors to this series are all united in their convictions that God still speaks through what he has spoken, and that nothing is more necessary for the life, health and growth of Christians than that they should hear what the Spirit is saying to them through his ancient – yet ever modern – Word.

J. A. MOTYER
J. R. W. STOTT
Series Editors

To Adèle, my Mother

and

to the memory of John, my Father

Contents

Author's preface

Throughout all my work on this study I have been torn between a mixture of deep apprehension on the one hand and an overwhelming sense of wonder on the other. The apprehension has come from pondering what on earth there is left to say: Genesis 1 – 11 really says it so much better than most of its commentators in any case! To try to say anything about such great themes as 'creation', 'evil', 'death', 'grace', 'judgment', 'hope' – indeed, life, the universe and everything – within the confines of a book of this length – is that not to play the fool?

Yet these chapters of Genesis evoke wonder: wonder at the majesty of God in his creative power, loving mercy, terrible judgment and life-giving hope. And I have found that sense of wonder deepened as I have worked on this book. Genesis 1 – 11 is really an overture to the rest of the Bible, and I pray that in playing it over again, in this form, something of the majesty and love of the God who makes himself known in the Christ of the whole Bible will be heard.

Some of this material found its way into some weekly expository Bible readings I was invited to give at Wycliffe Hall. Some of it was used again as the basis of some meditations in a spirituality class at Mansfield College, Oxford. I have profited much from the reactions of those who joined in both groups, and from the wise comments on a first draft from colleagues and from my former teacher, Alec Motyer. The Annual Retreat of the Society of Ordained Scientists – which as its name implies is a group of practising scientists who are in addition ordained ministers in the church – also provided me with fruitful conversations.

I should give a word about my approach. These chapters, as is well known, are the subject of much scholarly debate concerning their origins and authorship. The belief for a long time that they came from the pen of Moses was, to a large extent, displaced last century in the minds of many scholars. They came to the view that there are several strands of literature, from different sources and different times, now edited together in the text which we have in our Bibles. In the last twenty years or so considerable work has been done on the text and it is fair to say that there is still much that is unclear. Even if it is agreed that Genesis uses many sources, it is hard to be clear where the boundaries are. Furthermore, there has been a renewed emphasis on approaching the text in the edition in which we now have it in our Bibles, as a literary whole. Whatever views some of us have about the author or authors and editors, the fact remains that it is this text in its canonical form which Christian people have from the beginning received as the opening chapters of their Bibles. It is this text as a whole which the writers of the New Testament had before them. It is this text through which the divine Word comes to us.

While I have therefore derived much help from commentaries which reflect the whole spectrum of scholarly views about Genesis (and also from the magnificent series of sermons by Helmut Thielicke, *How the World Began*), I have approached the text, as it were, through the eyes of its final editor – whoever that may have been, and whenever his work was done.

My father, through his life, his love and his preaching, helped me understand our life of faith. It is to his memory, and to my mother, that I am pleased to dedicate this book.

DAVID ATKINSON

Bibliography

Augustine, *Confessions*, especially Books XI – XIII.

K. Barth, *Church Dogmatics* (Eng. tr., T. & T. Clark, 1935–).

R. J. Bauckham, 'First Steps to a Theology of Nature', *Evangelical Quarterly*, vol. 58/3, 1986, pp. 229ff.

R. J. Bauckham, 'The Genesis Flood and the Nuclear Holocaust', *Churchman*, 1985, no. 2, pp. 146 ff.

H. Blocher, *In the Beginning* (IVP, 1984).

D. Bonhoeffer, *Creation and Fall* (SCM, 1959).

M. Buber, *I and Thou* (1937; tr. by W. Kaufmann, T. & T. Clark, 1970).

J. Calvin, *A Commentary on Genesis* (Banner of Truth edition, 1965).

U. Cassuto, *A Commentary on the Book of Genesis. Part 1: Adam to Noah* (Eng. tr., Magnes Press, 1961).

D. Clines, 'The Significance of the "Sons of God" episode (Genesis 6.1–4) in the context of the Primeval History (Genesis 1 – 11)', *Journal for the Study of the Old Testament*, 1979, pp. 33ff.

D. Clines, 'Theme in Genesis 1 – 11', *Catholic Biblical Quarterly*, vol. 38, 1976, pp. 483ff.

D. Clines, 'The Theology of the Flood Narrative', *Faith and Thought*, vol. 100, no. 2, 1972–73, pp. 128f.

J. Hick, *Evil and the God of Love* (Macmillan, 1966).

C. F. Keil and F. Delitzsch, *Biblical Commentary on the Old Testament*, vol. 1 (Eerdmans reprint, 1971).

D. Kidner, *Genesis* (Tyndale Press, 1967).

J. Moltmann, *God in Creation* (Eng. tr., SCM, 1985).

J. Moltmann, *The Power of the Powerless* (Eng. tr., SCM, 1983).

J. Moltmann, *The Future of Creation* (Eng. tr., SCM, 1979).

A. R. Peacocke, *Science and the Christian Experiment* (OUP, 1971).

A. R. Peacocke, *Creation and the World of Science* (OUP, 1979).

11

A. Phillips, *Lower than the Angels* (Bible Reading Fellowship, 1983).

M. Polanyi, *Knowing and Being* (Routledge, 1969).

J. Polkinghorne, *One World* (SPCK, 1986).

J. Polkinghorne, *Science and Creation* (SPCK, 1988).

J. Polkinghorne, *Science and Providence* (SPCK, 1989).

M. W. Poole and G. J. Wenham, *Creation or Evolution: a False Antithesis?* (Latimer House, 1987).

A. Richardson, *Genesis 1– 11* (SCM, 1953).

E. A. Speiser, *Genesis*, The Anchor Bible (Doubleday, 1964).

Angela Tilby, *Let There be Light: Praying with Genesis* (Darton, Longman and Todd, 1989).

H. Thielicke, *How the World Began* (Eng. tr., James Clarke, 1964).

W. H. Griffith Thomas, *Genesis: A Devotional Commentary* (Eerdmans, 1946).

K. Thomas, *Man and the Natural World: changing attitudes in England 1500–1800* (Penguin, 1983).

T. F. Torrance, *Space, Time and Incarnation* (OUP, 1969).

G. J. Wenham, *Genesis 1 – 15*, Word Biblical Commentary (Word Books, 1987).

C. Westermann, *Genesis 1 – 11: a Commentary* (1974; Eng. tr., SPCK, 1984).

C. Westermann, *Creation* (Eng. tr., SPCK, 1974).

Margery Williams, *The Velveteen Rabbit* (Heinemann, 1922).

G. von Rad, *Genesis* (Eng. tr., SCM, 1961).

1:1 – 2:3
1. Majesty and mystery

In the beginning God created the heavens and the earth. ²The earth was without form and void, and darkness was upon the face of the deep; and the Spirit of God was moving over the face of the waters.

³And God said, 'Let there be light'; and there was light. ⁴And God saw that the light was good; and God separated the light from the darkness. ⁵God called the light Day, and the darkness he called Night. And there was evening and there was morning, one day.

⁶And God said, 'Let there be a firmament in the midst of the waters, and let it separate the waters from the waters.' ⁷And God made the firmament and separated the waters which were under the firmament from the waters which were above the firmament. And it was so. ⁸And God called the firmament Heaven. And there was evening and there was morning, a second day.

⁹And God said, 'Let the waters under the heavens be gathered together into one place, and let the dry land appear.' And it was so. ¹⁰God called the dry land Earth, and the waters that were gathered together he called Seas. And God saw that it was good. ¹¹And God said, 'Let the earth put forth vegetation, plants yielding seed, and fruit trees bearing fruit in which is their seed, each according to its kind, upon the earth.' And it was so. ¹²The earth brought forth vegetation, plants yielding seed according to their own kinds, and trees bearing fruit in which is their seed, each according to its kind. And God saw that it was good. ¹³And there was evening and there was morning, a third day.

¹⁴And God said, 'Let there be lights in the firmament of the heavens to separate the day from the night; and let them be for signs and for seasons and for days and years, ¹⁵and let them be lights in the firmament of the heavens to give light upon the earth.' And it was so. ¹⁶And God made the two great lights, the greater light to rule the day, and the lesser light to rule the night; he made the stars also. ¹⁷And God set them in the firmament of the heavens to give light upon the earth, [18]*to rule over the day and over the night, and to separate the light from the darkness. And God saw that it was good.* [19]*And there was evening and there was morning, a fourth day.*

[20]*And God said, 'Let the waters bring forth swarms of living creatures, and let birds fly above the earth across the firmament of the heavens.'* [21]*So God created the great sea monsters and every living creature that moves, with which the waters swarm, according to their kinds, and every winged bird according to its kind. And God saw that it was good.* [22]*And God blessed them, saying, 'Be fruitful and multiply and fill the waters in the seas, and let birds multiply on the earth.'* [23]*And there was evening and there was morning, a fifth day.*

[24]*And God said, 'Let the earth bring forth living creatures according to their kinds: cattle and creeping things and beasts of the earth according to their kinds.' And it was so.* [25]*And God made the beasts of the earth according to their kinds and the cattle according to their kinds, and everything that creeps upon the ground according to its kind. And God saw that it was good.*

[26]*Then God said, 'Let us make man in our image, after our likeness; and let them have dominion over the fish of the sea, and over the birds of the air, and over the cattle, and over all the earth, and over every creeping thing that creeps upon the earth.'* [27]*So God created man in his own image, in the image of God he created him; male and female he created them.* [28]*And God blessed them, and God said to them, 'Be fruitful and multiply, and fill the earth and subdue it; and have dominion over the fish of the sea and over the birds of the air and over every living thing that moves upon the earth.'* [29]*And God said, 'Behold, I have given you every plant yielding seed which is upon the face of all the earth, and every tree with seed in its fruit; you shall have them for food.* [30]*And to every beast of the earth, and to every bird of the air, and to everything that creeps on the earth, everything that has the breath of life, I have given every green plant for food.' And it was so.* [31]*And God saw everything that he had made, and behold, it was very good. And there was evening and there was morning, a sixth day.*

[2:1]*Thus the heavens and the earth were finished, and all the host of them.* [2]*And on the seventh day God finished his work which he had done, and he rested on the seventh day from all his work which he had done.* [3]*So God blessed the seventh day and hallowed it, because on it God rested from all his work which he had done in creation.* (1:1 – 2:3)

1. Majesty

The poem of beauty and grandeur which forms the opening chapter of our Bibles is a hymn of praise to the majesty of God the Creator. That is not to say that it was necessarily written as a hymn of worship. Rather, that countless believers through the ages have found that this chapter evokes praise. Through its structured harmonies our hearts are tuned to the music of the heavens, and our minds are lifted to contemplate God as the source and sustainer of all that is. This chapter invites us to bow in humility before his creative Word. It shows us our own place within the panorama of God's purposes for the whole of his creation.

Here there is *majesty*. The writer's heart and mind are moved in praise to God, in whose purposes lie the secrets of this world. Like the psalmist, who worships the King, all glorious above, we are caught up into this writer's doxology:

> Bless the LORD, O my soul!
> O LORD my God, thou art very great!
> Thou art clothed with honour and majesty,
>> who coverest thyself with light as with a garment,
> who hast stretched out the heavens like a tent,
>> who hast laid the beams of thy chambers on the waters,
> who makest the clouds thy chariot,
>> who ridest on the wings of the wind,
> who makest the winds thy messengers,
>> fire and flame thy ministers.[1]

The explicit setting for much of chapters 1 to 11 of Genesis is the land of Mesopotamia. Genesis 2:10–14, for example, is set in an area close to the rivers Tigris and Euphrates, the area that came to be known as Babylon, and that we now know as Iraq. Genesis 11:1–9 refers to the land of Shinar, another name for the same area. It is no surprise, therefore, to find that the themes of Genesis 1 – 11 in general, and the pattern of the poem of Genesis 1 in particular, are very similar in some ways to Mesopotamian creation stories. The *Epic of Atrahasis*, for example, written about 1600 BC, tells a story of the creation of the world, and moves from it to an account of a great flood. A much later Babylonian work, the *Enuma Elish*, also has an account of the creation.

The *Enuma Elish* begins with the divine spirit and with a primeval chaos. Its main purpose is to glorify the chief Babylonian god, Marduk, who defeats the watery chaos monster, Tiamat. Light

---

[1] Ps. 104:1–4.

emanates from the gods, and then the firmament, dry land, luminaries and eventually humankind are created. The gods then rest and celebrate. Such stories may well, of course, have been known to the people of God. But despite some similarities, how very different from the Mesopotamian myths is the creation poem of Genesis 1. Gordon Wenham writes: 'The author of Genesis 1 . . . shows that he was aware of other cosmologies, and that he wrote not in dependence on them so much as in deliberate rejection of them.'[2]

Whereas the *Enuma Elish* talks about many gods, Genesis proclaims a majestic monotheism: there is one God. Whereas in the Babylonian stories the divine spirit and cosmic matter exist side by side from eternity, Genesis proclaims God's majestic distinction from everything else which in sovereign power he creates, and which depends on him for its existence. Whereas in Near Eastern mythology the sun, moon, stars and sea monsters are seen as powerful gods, Genesis tells us that they are merely creatures. (Genesis even avoids the usual Hebrew words for 'sun' and 'moon', perhaps in case they could be misconstrued as deities, and talks simply about the greater and lesser lights.) Whereas in the Mesopotamian myths light emanates from the gods, in the Genesis narrative, God creates light by the power of his word. So although Genesis shares with the Babylonian stories a similar pattern, its theological message is very different. Genesis 1 sings the praise of the majestic Creator of all. It speaks of his life-giving power. It also gives a profound significance to human life. Whereas in the Middle Eastern myths human beings seem only to have a walk-on part – they are there to supply the gods with food – in Genesis 1 the creation of human life is a high point in the narrative. It is God who provides food for men and women.

One can imagine what a rock of stability this chapter would have provided for the people of God when faced with the lure of pagan myths around them. Exiles of the people of God during their time in Babylon, for example, may have been tempted to fall in with the ideas of their conquerors. Genesis 1 calls them back to the worship of the one sovereign majestic Lord, who, in the transcendent freedom of his creative Word, is the source of all things, all life, all creatures, all people.

In the words of Gerard Manley Hopkins' poem, 'The world is charged with the grandeur of God'. Or as the psalmist put it:

> O LORD, how manifold are thy works!
> In wisdom hast thou made them all;
> the earth is full of thy creatures.

[2] Wenham, p. 9.

May the glory of the LORD endure for ever,
may the LORD rejoice in his works.[3]

There is majesty here, and there is *mystery* also.

2. Mystery

In contrast to Genesis chapters 2 and 3, where the tone is more
intimate, the context more homely, and the centre of attention is
on human relationships, Genesis 1 stands detached in rugged simplicity and grandeur – as majestically distant as the glorious mountain ranges of the Rockies stand in comparison with my back
garden. And as the Rockies convey to their observers a sense of
awesome mystery, so Genesis 1 preserves and points us to the
mysteries of creation. There is much about the world we live in
which we do not and cannot understand. The writer does not
attempt, or want, to *explain* creation. With reverence, he wants to
catch us up into its wonder. He is not concerned with the question
'How did God do it?' He would not, I think, have been terribly
interested in our debates about the time-scale of evolution, or the
physics of the First Three Minutes. Those are not the questions he
is asking. And when we ourselves bring such questions to the text,
we are disappointed. We perhaps want to know how it is that the
sun and moon (1:14–16) are created after the light (1:3). The writer
is not so stupid as to be unaware that there is a problem. He leaves
us with the mystery. He simply tells us without explanation that
the divine light is not dependent on the luminaries of the sun and
moon. Why are we not told that God created the waters, but just
that his Spirit is moving over them (1:7)? Did God create the
darkness as well as the light (1:4)? We want to know. The author
does not say. Surely deliberately, he does not get into such 'How
to' questions. He is concerned with something else. He is safeguard-
ing and proclaiming something of the unsearchable mystery of
God. We mistake the purpose of this chapter if we expect it to
answer all the questions we, with the benefit of modern science,
want to ask about creation. 'Creation', in any case, does not come
within the domain of science: it is not a scientific category. Whatever science may propose concerning the origin of the universe and
the Big Bang, many thousand million years ago, no scientific result
could establish whether or not this was 'Creation'.

As we shall see, there is no reason to find conflict between the
theology of this chapter and the important tasks of scientific
research. Some of the themes of this chapter undergird and inspire

[3] Ps. 104:24, 31.

17

the very possibility of science. But there are necessarily limits to what science can observe and quantify. And we must learn from this author not only that some of our questions may for ever, this side of heaven, remain unanswered, but also to allow ourselves to be caught up into creation's wonder and mystery.

Faith moves beyond empirical knowledge. In this chapter we are brought in touch with a faith which holds on to us when the world around us is mysterious and uncertain. In a sense, faith is what God gives us to hold us in our uncertainties. That, too, has been a source of strength to the people of God throughout their history. How strengthening must the power of this chapter have been to them when they were tempted to believe that God had abandoned them, when they could discern no meaning or purpose in their predicament, when, for example, weeping by the waters of Babylon,[4] they had given up hope of ever seeing home again, and when they found it all too easy to believe the taunts of their accusers, 'What does your faith in God amount to now?' There is a faith that will hold you even in the dark, if it is a faith in God the Creator of all. He is the source of your life. You, too, have a place within his creative purposes. Let the deep faith of this Genesis author lift your heart and mind again to the majesty and mystery of God.

3. Order and contingence: the assumptions of science

All of us from our earliest days are delighted with patterns. We make patterns in the sand, we look for patterns in the stars. We find delight in crystals and snowflakes, in number series and repeated pictures on wall-paper. Science exists because of patterns. It is a way of searching for and giving expression to the regular patterns we believe that nature follows.

One of the most striking features of Genesis 1 is its pattern. The story is structured around the theme of one week of six days leading to a seventh. The regular refrain moves the story along: *there was evening and there was morning.* The gradually increasing complexity of what God creates, beginning with the formless empty waste (1:2), and ending with human beings, male and female in his image (1:27), gives a sense of deepening order and meticulous structure. God is bringing order and form into his world. Indeed, the pattern of days illustrates the progression from 'preparation to accomplishment' (Griffith Thomas) or from 'form to fullness' (cf. D. Kidner).

The story is told as three stages of 'separation'.

---

[4] Ps. 137:1.

1. In Day 1, God separates the light from the dark (1:4). We can set this in parallel with Day 4, in which God makes the light-bearers, the sun and the moon, to *rule over* the day and the night (1:16–18).

2. In Day 2, God separates the waters of the firmament of the heavens from the waters under the heavens (1:7). This can be set in parallel with Day 5, in which God makes the birds to fly across the heavens (1:20) and the sea monsters and fish to swarm in the seas (1:21).

3. In Day 3, God separates the dry earth from the seas and gives fertile vegetation. This can be set in parallel with Day 6 in which God makes animals, domestic and wild, to inhabit the earth, and human beings, male and female, to *have dominion over* all other living creatures.

The first three days set the context; the parallel last three days bring it to life. Three sets of separations; three sets of 'rulers'.

The author is concerned with order, and with pattern. He is also concerned with putting things in categories. He describes the vegetation and the animals in groups (*according to their kinds*, vv. 11, 21, 24, 25). The principle of reproductive fertility is built into creation itself, as we see in verses 11–12 where the plants are said to yield seed, and fruit trees have fruit in which is their seed. We see it also in verse 22, where God's blessing enables animal reproduction. This author is interested also in the purposes of the created order: the sun and moon *to rule* (1:18); mankind to *have dominion* (1:26).

Here is a mind that is not far from the interests of science. Indeed, the whole enterprise of science rests precisely on the assumption of an ordered world in which pattern can be discovered and categories established. The ordered rationality of the created world, deriving from the transcendent rationality of the creative Word, is a basic assumption – not usually expressed in those terms – of natural science. There would be no science at all without an ordered world.

Alongside order, we must also speak of contingence. By that we mean: things do not have to be the way they are. If the order of the world were a *necessary* order that could be uncovered by logical reasoning from a philosopher's armchair, there would be no science. But the world's order is contingent. God could have made it otherwise. And to find out the way it is, we have to investigate it. We need to explore. It is the contingence of the world's order, dependent on God and derived from God, that underlies the inescapable need for experiment and discovery. It drives the scientist out of his armchair and into the laboratory.

Genesis 1, then, emphasizes here the transcendence of the Creator, and the implication that the 'natural' order of the world is a dependent, derived and contingent order. Far from conflicting with science, therefore, the theological stance of the author of this chapter provides insight into two of the basic conditions on which the scientific enterprise depends: order and contingence.

A third condition, without which there could be no science, is that our human minds can, at least partly, understand the world outside them. There is a correspondence between the rational minds of human beings and the rational order of the physical world.

Arthur Peacocke in his book *Science and the Christian Experiment* writes this:

> The realization that our minds can find the world intelligible, and the implication this has that an explanation for the world process is to be found in mental rather than purely material categories, has been for many scientists who are theists . . . an essential turning point in their thinking. Why *should* science work at all? That it does so points strongly to a principle of rationality, to an interpretation of the cosmos in terms of mind as its most significant feature. Any thinking which takes science seriously must, it seems to me, start from this . . . There is clearly a kinship between the mind of man and the cosmos which is real, and which any account of the cosmos cannot ignore.[5]

Peacocke is asking: Why should science work at all? His answer is that the ordered world which we observe and the ordering processes of our scientific minds are both part of the same world. There is a Mind behind the world order and from which our thinking processes derive. The fact that science works seems to Peacocke (and to many others) to support the view that God's existence makes sense.

The correspondence between our minds and the world we observe is part of the expression of 'God's image', to the meaning of which we shall turn our attention a little later.

4. God created

a. Out of nothing

In the beginning, we are told, God *created* (1:1a). The Hebrew word *bārā'*, translated 'create', always has God as its subject when it occurs in the Old Testament. The writer of Genesis 1 sometimes uses a different word (translated 'made'). Thus God *made* (*'āśâ*) the firmament (1:7); God *made* the two great lights (1:16); God *made* the beasts of the earth (1:25). But alongside this there is the

---

[5] Peacocke, *Science and the Christian Experiment*, p. 133.

more special word reserved for the sort of creating God does – the word *bārā'*. In this chapter it is used six times: God *created* the heavens and the earth (1:1); God *created* the great sea monsters (1:21); and (three times) God *created* man as male and female (1:27). God rested from all his work which he had done in creation (2:3).

Although the word *bārā'* when used elsewhere in the Old Testament does not necessarily mean creation out of nothing, that is certainly the implication here. Wenham writes: 'there is a stress on the artist's freedom and power', and he goes on to quote W. H. Schmidt saying that *bārā'* preserves the idea of 'God's effortless, totally free and unbound creating, his sovereignty'.[6]

We have here God's transcendent freedom to bring into being things that do not exist. In contrast to the Babylonian idea that matter existed alongside God from eternity, it seems likely that the Genesis author wants to stress that God created all that is out of nothing. There is nothing that co-exists eternally with God. Is not this the story that other biblical writers tell?

In the Old Testament, for instance, the psalmist calls on all the heavens, sun, moon and stars to praise the Lord, 'for he commanded and they were created',[7] and in Proverbs 8, the wisdom of God – the principle of all creation – was there 'before the beginning of the earth'.[8] In the New Testament that creative wisdom of God is embodied in the incarnate Word of God of whom it is said:

Without him was not anything made that was made.[9]

All things were created through him and for him.[10]

From him and through him and to him are all things.[11]

The world was created by the word of God, so that what is seen was made out of things which do not appear.[12]

It is important to see that what God creates is something distinct from himself. This chapter has no place for *pantheism* – the idea that 'God' is another name for 'everything'. It is true that God 'indwells' the world, and the world has its being 'in God', but God remains God, and in transcendent distinction from what he has made.

It is important also to notice that elsewhere in the Bible, the word *bārā'* is used in the context of salvation. The unique word for God's creative activity is much more commonly used of his

---

[6] Wenham, p. 14.   [7] Ps. 148:5.   [8] Pr. 8:22–27.   [9] Jn. 1:3.
[10] Col. 1:16.   [11] Rom. 11:36.   [12] Heb. 11:3.

liberating and saving actions in history.[13] The God who makes things is the God who also makes things new.[14] The God who we see in Genesis 1 is the Creator of all, we learn from a broader biblical picture is also the redeemer, sustainer, re-creator, and the one who brings all things to completion. God's creative activity in history is not only the preservation of what he has made; it is a continuous, creative engagement with his world, leading it forward to its future glory.[15]

b. 'The heavens and the earth'

God created the heavens and the earth (1:1b) – or as the Nicene Creed puts it: 'all that is, seen and unseen'. The phrase 'heaven and earth' describes everything that is not God – it means, first of all, *totality*. But it may be that in this separation of all that is into heavens and earth, the unseen and the seen, we are here, as else- where in the Bible, being reminded that there is within creation a lower, visible, earthly reality and a higher, invisible and heavenly reality. And God is Creator of all.

'Heaven' sometimes stands for the sky. More often 'heaven' refers to a higher world, of angels, of God's throne, of God's glory. Heaven is 'God's place'. So in speaking of the 'heavens' as well as the 'earth' (mankind's place), Genesis is reminding us that creation is 'open to God'. God's creation is not a closed system of natural causes; it is an 'open system'. There may be much within the created world which we cannot sense, cannot weigh and measure, cannot put in a test tube; there may be more things in heaven and earth than are dreamed of in our philosophy; but the Lord God made them all. There is a created spiritual world, just as there is a created material world. And as Deuteronomy 29:29 reminds us, 'The secret things belong to the LORD our God; but the things that are revealed belong to us and to our children for ever.'

Perhaps this was in Chesterton's mind when Syme asks,

> Shall I tell you the secret of the whole world? It is that we have only known the back of the world. We see everything from behind, and it looks brutal. That is not a tree, but the back of a tree. That is not a cloud but the back of a cloud. Cannot you see that everything is stooping and hiding a face? If only we could get round in front . . . [16]

But sometimes glimpses of the 'front' can be seen: there are

---

[13] *Cf.* Is. 43:1ff.   [14] Is. 43:19.
[15] *Cf., e.g.,* Rom. 8:18–22; Eph. 1:10; Rev. 21:5; Mt. 19:28.
[16] G. K. Chesterton, *The Man Who was Thursday.*

glimpses of heaven from earth. In his book *A Rumour of Angels*, Peter Berger uses the lovely phrase 'signals of transcendence'.[17] He means that there are pointers within the world of 'earth' to the hidden things of 'heaven'. We need to be open to seeing such signals of transcendence, glimpses of heavenly glory, in our world and in ourselves and in one another. For all that is made, heaven and earth, comes from the hand of God. In our world which overemphasizes material and 'earthly' values, which so often understands human life only in terms of material factors such as body chemistry or economic cost effectiveness, we need to remember that we are creatures of a God who made the heavens as well as the earth. Our world is open to him.

But more than that: the 'heavens' and the 'earth' can and will come together. 'Heaven' can reach down to earth, and the things of earth will be caught up into the place of God. And it is in our humanity that they meet: the place where, in God's purposes, heaven and earth are united. As the New Testament makes most clear, we can, at one and the same time be 'in chains' and 'in the heavenly places in Christ Jesus'.[18] For it is in Christ the Mediator that God enters 'our place', and by a gift of his grace, takes humanity into God. And it is in him, the Cosmic Christ, that God's purposes for the whole of creation will come to fulfilment:

> For [God] has made known to us in all wisdom and insight the mystery of his will, according to his purpose which he set forth in Christ as a plan for the fullness of time, to unite all things in him, things in heaven and things on earth.[19]

In telling us that God created the heavens and the earth, the author is saying that this universe is open to God, open to new possibilities, open to being transformed into the kingdom of his glory.

There is more, always, to the world we live in than is observable to the human eye, or scientific exploration. We need not be surprised when our provisional statements of uniformity – what we call 'laws of nature' – are sometimes apparently set aside, or transcended by special acts of God. The God whose ordering of the world makes science possible is a God who is also free, as he wills, to let the supernatural be seen.

---

[17] P. Berger, *A Rumour of Angels* (Penguin, 1969). [18] Eph. 6:20; 2:6.
[19] Eph. 1:9–10.

c. 'Without form and void'

There are two ways of translating the opening verses of the Bible. We could read them like this: 'When God set about to create the heavens and the earth – the world being then a formless waste, with darkness over the seas and only an awesome wind sweeping over the water – God said, "Let there be light".' As with the thunderous ' . . . and there was *light*' of Haydn's oratorio *Creation* bursting forth with creative energy and glory, so this reading emphasizes the brightness of God's light. The other reading, which most of the older versions of the Bible follow, speaks much more directly – as we have done earlier – of God creating the heavens and the earth (1:1), and then of what Calvin translates literally as 'confused emptiness'.

Without form and void (1:2a), Calvin's 'confused emptiness', is a phrase which we find echoed also in Jeremiah 4:23, and similarly in Isaiah 34:11. Both places underline the dreadful sense of waste and chaos, like a trackless desert, where God's creative word is not bringing order. Here in Genesis it indicates that in the beginning the created world lacked order and shape. It contrasts sharply with the developing order with which the rest of the chapter is concerned.

In the Academy in Florence stands Michelangelo's sculpture of St Matthew. It is unfinished. The inscription points out how the sculptor is about to cut away the stone from around the figure that he has perceived inside the marble block.[20]

So here creation, shapeless and formless, awaits the artistic creativity and ordering of the Creator's hand.

The 'formless waste' is also described as a *darkness . . . upon the face of the deep* (1:2) – and some hear echoes here of the Babylonian chaos monster, Tiamat, and perhaps also of 'Leviathan' who surfaces in Psalm 74:14. Are there echoes, too, of 'the raging of the sea' of which the psalmist writes in Psalm 89:9? In fact, the 'sea' and the 'deep' often carry a sense of disorder, of terror, almost of a power set over against God. This makes all the more poignant God's dividing of the sea for his people to cross, and of our Lord's stilling of the waves with his authoritative word: 'Be still.' But however frighteningly stormy 'the sea' remains for us, we must not read into Genesis the idea of 'the deep' as an alien force with which God has to struggle (as in some Mesopotamian myths). No, 'the deep' itself is part of God's creation. Even the dark deep is but a stage on the way towards a fully finished world. The earth is

[20] M. Polanyi, *The Study of Man* (University of Chicago Press, 1958), pp. 35f.

without form, but God, we read, is giving it form. The deep is covered in darkness, but God will command the light. The fearful sea will be contained. The frightening chaotic 'deep' will be brought to order. There is a separation of the waters; coastlines and river beds become part of the picture. Tracks are being made in the deserts. The storm is being reined in.

And when in verse 6 God makes a firmament (or 'expanse') separating the waters from the waters, we see a God who is making space for an inhabitable world. God is making space for an earth, open to heaven, in which plants and trees can grow and animals and human beings can have their life and livelihood.

We need to pause here. Not only are we invited to reflect on God's transcendent freedom to bring into being what he wills, to bring form out of what is formless, and to give order where there is disorder, shape and pattern and beauty to what is as yet a waste, but we need to do more. We need to take in that this is what 'creation' means. It is God's work to make things ordered and beautiful. This is the way God is. God brings into being things that are not. God brings life where there is no life. 'God' is not simply 'Nature'. God is the one who brings nature into being, and constantly renews its life.

That is yet another word of comfort and hope to people whose experience is marked by chaos, by ugliness, by disorder, by 'confused emptiness': God is the sort of God who comes into confusion and makes things new. He hovers over your darkness and says, 'Let there be light.' People of God: take heart!

There is a further aspect to this, too. All that is derives from the hands of God. As we shall see more clearly from later chapters of Genesis, it is fatally easy to spoil what God has made, to cause disruption again where there should be order. But there is nothing, however spoiled, that does not owe its existence to God. Everything we see, everything we handle, every creature we meet, every person who crosses our path, is a gift from the Creator's hands, to be treasured, honoured, treated with respect.

It is from this conviction that we need to begin in trying to develop a Christian mind on many of our contemporary environmental and social questions. Our concerns for pollution; our motivation to avert the ecological crisis; our anger at terrorism and our hatred of war; our delight in beauty and our support for the arts; our fighting against the depersonalizing trends of so much of modern ideology and for social and economic justice in the world; our longing to learn how to love our neighbours better – all these themes, which rightly fill the pages of much recent Christian writing, need all to be traced back to their beginnings. And their beginnings are to be found in the God who makes all things, and

25

who makes all things new.[21] Our deep human concerns for making things better is itself a reflection of the character of God.

> Worthy art thou, our Lord and God,
> to receive glory and honour and power,
> for thou didst create all things,
> and by thy will they existed and were created.[22]

d. Through Spirit and word

An 'awesome wind' (1:3) was sweeping over the water. The Hebrew word means both 'wind' and 'spirit', and is here rightly understood as the creative Spirit of God. The picture is that of a mother eagle stirring up her nest, fluttering over her young, bringing what is immature into more active life. (The same word is used in Dt. 32:11.) Derek Kidner comments, 'In the Old Testament, the Spirit is a term for God's outgoing energy, creative and sustaining.'[23] He refers to Job 33:4: 'The spirit of God has made me, and the breath of the Almighty gives me life.' God is as intimately involved in his creation as a mother bird is in intimate touch with her young. The motherhood of God is seen in this creativity – bringing creation to birth. A similar feminine metaphor for God's creativity can be seen in the way 'Wisdom', the principle of creation, is depicted in feminine terms in the Book of Proverbs (8:1, 22).

The Spirit's life gives life. As the psalmist wrote of all God's creatures:

> When thou takest away their breath, they die
> and return to their dust.
> When thou sendest forth thy Spirit, they are created.[24]

The Holy Spirit, we may infer, is 'poured out' on all God's creation. As Calvin – almost alone among past theologians – believed: 'It is the Spirit who, everywhere diffused, sustains all things, causes them to grow, and quickens them in heaven and in earth.'[25] And, as Moltmann argues, the Spirit 'creates the community of all created things with God and with each other, making it that fellowship of creation in which all created things communicate with one another and with God, each in its own way.' '*In* him we live and move and have our being.'[26]

All this means that alongside the strong theme we have already

---

[21] Rev. 21:5. [22] Rev. 4:11. [23] Kidner, p. 4. [24] Ps. 104:29–30.
[25] J. Calvin, *Institutes*, I.xiii.14; *cf.* Moltmann, *God in Creation*, pp. 10f.
[26] Acts 17:28.

explored of God's transcendent freedom over his creation, this chapter also opens up the theme of God's immanent indwelling with and in his creation. The Cosmic Spirit is a spirit of creativity, of wholeness, of community. Through him God indwells all his creation, and through him the 'open system' of earth is opened to 'heaven'. And here again we are reminded of a process. God's immanent presence within his world is part of the process of change through which he is bringing all things from one degree of glory to another, until all are brought to their completion in Christ. Our world is not closed, static, petrified, changeless. It is open, dynamic, infused with the life of the Spirit, in whose life there is liberty.[27]

The immanence of God indwelling his world must affect the way we think of space. We have sometimes been taught to think of space as a sort of 'receptacle' into which God 'comes down' in the birth of Jesus, and from which Jesus 'ascends' again to the Father after the resurrection. Of course, such spatial imagery is part of the biblical story, and is often the most appropriate symbolism for speaking (as we have ourselves) of God's relation to the world. But this 'receptacle' notion of space owes more to Newton's picture of a mechanistic universe, from which God is banished to the role of the Clockmaker who merely wound the whole thing up and has now left it to tick, than it does to the Bible. The Bible indicates a more 'relational' notion of space.[28] God's relationship with his world is one of dynamic and creative interaction. The birth of Jesus, and his ascension are not the comings and goings of God into and out of our space. No, they rather show God's dynamic and intimate relationship with his world, unveiled in Jesus' birth, and veiled again at the ascension. We need to hold on to this stress on God's immanent relationship with his creation. Otherwise we may fall into the 'deism' which makes God so transcendently separate from his creation that he is effectively lofted out of touch with our world and our lives.

Within the animating work of the Spirit, there are some moments when new things are commanded into being by God's Word. We have seen how Genesis sometimes uses the word 'made' but that alongside this it also uses the special theological word translated 'create'. Interwoven between the processes of making and the steps of creating, we find a litany of divine commands: *And God said* (1:3, 6, 9, 11, 14, 20, 24, 26, 29). What is not there is called into being by God's Word. Everything that exists can trace its origin to the fact that it has been commanded into being by God. So here, as earlier, we need to affirm again God's transcendence to save us from the sort of 'panentheism' which so stresses God's indwelling

[27] *Cf.* 2 Cor. 3:17.   [28] *Cf.* Torrance, *Space, Time and Incarnation.*

27

that it forgets his holy and sovereign distance.

This chapter thus brings together the creative, intimate, animating Spirit of God, and the creative, penetrating, commanding Word of God. The Spirit and the Word belong together.

Elsewhere in the Bible, the closeness of Spirit and Word is illustrated. The Messianic King depicted in Isaiah 11 is one on whom 'the Spirit of the Lord rests' and one who rules with 'the rod of his mouth'.[29]

And of us Christian people, who are God's new creation,[30] the New Testament writes of our birth 'by the Spirit'[31] and, in another place, 'through the Word'.[32] In us, as in creation, the work of the Spirit through the Word brings life where there is no life, brings the possibilities of growth and fulfilment where before there was only waste. God's creative relationship with his world is one of intimacy and yet of commanding power.

If we live only by the Word, our faith can become a rational, cold dogmatic system – more of a philosophy than a way of life; if we live only by the Spirit, we have no clear, objective vane to test which wind is blowing, and the joy of life can remain directionless and immature. May God help us to live in relation to our Creator who made us and sustains us by his Word and by his Spirit.

e. 'According to their kinds'

Both vegetation and living creatures are given the power to reproduce. *And God said: 'Let the earth put forth vegetation, plants yielding seed, and fruit trees bearing fruit in which is their seed, each according to its kind, upon the earth.' And it was so. The earth brought forth vegetation, plants yielding seed according to their own kinds, and trees bearing fruit in which is their seed, each according to its kind* (1:11–12). *God created the great sea monsters and every living creature that moves, with which the waters swarm, according to their kinds, and every winged bird according to its kind* (1:21). *And God said, 'Let the earth bring forth living creatures according to their kinds: cattle and creeping things and beasts of the earth according to their kinds* (1:24).

Ours is not a 'ready-made' world. There is a principle of newness, of creativity, built into it.

The picture is of an *emerging* creation. In one of Tintoretto's pictures, birds and sea creatures are depicted as streaming forth from the Creator's hands, and within that stream of life there is creative power. Within each distinctive strand of living creatures,

---

[29] Is. 11:2, 4.   [30] 2 Cor. 5:17.   [31] Jn. 3:6.   [32] Jn. 1:1–3.

there is the power for new life. The fruits have seeds in them; the swarming life of the waters, the flocks of birds in the sky, the animals on dry land all have the power of reproduction. They are all empowered to hand on the Creator's gift of life.

Fertility, development, and we may wish to say evolutionary capacity, are all gifts of God. At the end of *The Origin of Species* Charles Darwin writes: 'There is grandeur in this view of life, with its several powers, having been originally breathed by the Creator into a few forms or into one . . . '.

Whatever we may think of Darwin's biology, and certainly not crediting him with a Christian faith (though he once held Christian views, he abandoned them quite rapidly), and whether or not we concur with those who think that all life descended from one primordial form, we, with Darwin, must place all our scientific theorizings under this primary statement: 'breathed by the Creator'.

The word 'evolution' has a strange effect on people. It can create panic in some Christian minds who believe that it must necessarily mean a denial of God's work of creation. Others, however, look through books on Genesis wondering whether the word will even be mentioned, and if it is not, the writer can be written off as an obscurantist hiding his head in the sand! We need to be careful, because the word 'evolution' is sometimes used to mean different things. It can be used as a shorthand for the biological processes by which species change and develop. As such, evolution is a scientific theory, open to the techniques of verification and falsification which should be applied to any scientific theories. Most scientists believe that some form of evolutionary theory is the most consistent explanatory hypothesis for the phenomena of biological development and diversity that is available. Nevertheless we do well to heed what G. A. Kerkut wrote as long ago as 1960 at the end of his biological monograph *The Implications of Evolution* (and many others have also said the same):

There is a theory which states that many living animals can be observed over the course of time to undergo changes so that new species are formed. This can be called the 'Special Theory of Evolution' and can be demonstrated in certain cases by experiments. On the other hand there is the theory that all the living forms in the world have arisen from a single source which itself came from an inorganic form. This theory can be called the 'General Theory of Evolution' and the evidence that supports it is not sufficiently strong to allow us to consider it as anything more than a working hypothesis. It is not clear whether the changes that bring about speciation are of the same nature as

29

those that brought about the development of new phyla. The answer will be found by future experimental work and not by dogmatic assertions that the General Theory of Evolution must be correct because there is nothing else that will satisfactorily take its place.[33]

Some writers use the word 'evolution' in a further sense, however, to mean more than biological processes. It becomes a shorthand for 'evolutionism' which is really a philosophical world-view about the nature of reality. Evolutionism suggests that the biological theories of evolution are sufficient to explain everything about the living world. But this is to confuse 'description' with 'explanation'. Biological theories may well help us understand our biology by describing biological processes. But they cannot explain, give a full account of the meaning and purpose, of such processes. To illustrate this let us use the analogy of a watch.[34] Let us imagine we find a watch in a field, and have never seen one before. What would we make of it? We may be able to describe its workings, understand its physics and chemistry, marvel at its intricacy. But we will never explain it *as a watch*, unless we know what watches are *for* – and that is something neither physics nor chemistry can tell us. And as Dostoevsky's 'Grand Inquisitor' says at one point: 'The mystery of human life is not only in living, but in knowing why one lives.' Evolutionism offers little to answer that.

There is a further danger of evolutionism, also. There is often a tendency to fall into the error of 'reductionism', which reduces all the other dimensions of life down to the biological, or even further, to the physics and chemistry on which biology depends. All other phenomena – the psychological, social, moral, intellectual, spiritual dimensions to life – are then explained in terms of biology, physics and chemistry. This partly involves the fallacy of reducing the whole to the sum of its parts; it is partly the error which comes from recognizing only those parts which our particular way of looking can see. At its worst, reductionism is like saying that a sunset is *only* electromagnetic radiation, or a violin concerto *only* the scraping of the hairs of one animal over the gut of another! In the area of biological science, it reduces all of life to biochemistry, and ultimately to physics. The sad end of this reductionist line is most eloquently but pathetically expressed by Nobel Laureate Jacques Monod. In *Chance and Necessity*, Monod's exploration of the meaning of life on the basis of molecular biology, he is driven by his philosophical beliefs to write: 'The ancient covenant is in

[33] G. A. Kerkut, *The Implications of Evolution* (Pergamon Press, 1960), p. 157.
[34] This analogy is suggested by A. McIntyre, among others.

pieces; man at last knows that he is alone in the unfeeling immensity of the universe, out of which he emerged only by chance.'[35]

But in such a statement, Monod had moved way beyond biology; he has moved beyond evolution. This is a statement of faith: faith in no god.

Clearly, if 'evolution' is lifted out of the sphere of biological hypothesis where it is open to scientific investigation, and is elevated to the status of a whole world-view of the way things are, then there is direct conflict with biblical faith. But if 'evolution' remains at the level of scientific biological hypothesis, it would seem that there is little reason for conflict between the implications of Christian belief in the Creator and the scientific explorations of the way which – at the level of biology – God has gone about his creating processes.

All this, however, is to go beyond our text. Genesis is not to be read as a textbook of biological science. The author rather wants constantly to lift our minds up to the creative power of God. What mysteries of biology which generations of scientists have been exploring, are hidden under the simple phrase 'according to their kinds'!

f. 'He made the stars also'

If large areas of debate within biology are obscured by the phrase 'according to their kinds', how much more is hidden behind that greatest of all understatements: *He made the stars also* (1:16).

The ancients were, of course, fascinated by the stars. The Babylonians became the master astronomers of their day, developing quite sophisticated observational and computational skills particularly for their interest in planetary motion. Egyptian, Babylonian, and later Greek and Roman astrologers all developed schemes of relating stellar movements to earthly needs – mostly within a faith which regarded the stars as gods.

The fascination of the ancients was nothing compared to the mysteries of astronomy opened up by Galileo's telescope. In 1609 he saw the craters on the moon. The 'Copernican revolution' was the discovery that the sun did not go round the earth. To the five planets known to the ancients (Mercury, Venus, Mars, Jupiter and Saturn – they did not of course know that the Earth was a planet), astronomers could add the discovery in 1781 of Uranus, in 1846 of Neptune and in 1930 of Pluto. Then of course, in our lifetime, many new discoveries have been made. Views of the history of the universe have had to be modified again and again. If we think in

---

[35] J. Monod, *Chance and Necessity* (Eng. tr., Collins, 1971), p. 167.

terms of the current consensus, we are faced with a universe billions of years old. It has dimensions of almost incomprehensible magnitude. There are 100,000 light years across our own galaxy. There are two million light years to the Andromeda galaxy – one of our near galactic neighbours – which means that what we now observe is Andromeda as it was two million years ago. There are apparently something like one hundred billion other galaxies, moving apart in the sort of way we would expect if they had all come from a mighty explosion about ten thousand million years ago.

All this was unknown to Galileo, let alone the author of Genesis 1!

For all time, the skies have had a tremendous power to evoke wonder – often in the ancient world leading to the worship of the stars. It was against this that the people of Israel were warned, when they saw the sun, moon and stars and all the host of heaven, not to be drawn away to worship and serve them.[36] The true worshipper of God knew that it was the glory of God which the heavens are telling, and his handiwork which the firmament proclaims.[37] It is God who 'spread out the skies'.[38] The majesty and sovereignty of God were especially seen in the stars. Job 9 points us to the God who commands the sun, seals up the stars, stretched out the heavens and trampled the waves of the sea: he 'made the Bear and Orion, the Pleiades and the chambers of the south; [he] does great things beyond understanding, and marvellous things without number'.[39] Later he asks, 'Can you bind the chains of the Pleiades, or loose the cords of Orion?'[40] To Isaiah the stars induce a wondering reverence: 'Lift up your eyes on high and see: who created these? He who brings out their host by number, calling them all by name.'[41] 'We know God', says Calvin, 'who is himself invisible, only through his works. . . . This is the reason why the Lord, that he may invite us to the knowledge of himself, places the fabric of heaven and earth before our eyes, rendering himself, in a certain manner, manifest in them.'[42] The majesty and mystery of God, seen 'through his works', was surely part of the faith of the author of Genesis 1. He would no doubt have concurred with the psalmist: 'When I look at thy heavens, the work of thy fingers, the moon and the stars which thou hast established; what is man that thou art mindful of him . . . '.[43] He could have used the stars as a picture of God's almighty power by describing the awesome wonder which a starlit night evokes. But he makes his point another way, perhaps deliberately to detract from the idolatry of the stellar cults. The majesty of God is proclaimed by contrast with the

---

[36] Dt. 4:19. [37] Ps. 19:1. [38] Jb. 37:18. [39] Jb. 9:7–10.
[40] Jb. 38:31. [41] Is. 40:26. [42] Calvin, *Genesis*, p. 59. [43] Ps. 8:3–4.

comparative insignificance of all this stellar glory. He simply says, 'He made the stars also.'

5. The place of human beings (1:26–31)

The steady progression of the first twenty-five verses of chapter one comes to a high point in verse 26. Using a majesterial plural, the author brings us to the creation of human beings: *'Let us make man in our image, after our likeness.'*

One of the remarkable facts about the universe, which has come to light with recent work on the physics of the Big Bang, is its striking specificity. The balance needed between many different factors in the early development of the universe we know was so delicate that, just a small change here or there, and this universe would not exist. The earliest time envisaged after the singularity of the Big Bang is the Planck time (10^{43} seconds), when – it is thought – all the matter of the universe was compressed within a tiny sphere the size of the point of a needle. From then, the gigantic expansion of the universe into the world we experience has followed a highly specific path. If the ratios of sub-atomic particles had been different in a very small degree from what they were, there could have been no development of nuclei heavier than helium, which are necessary for the development of life.

And if the balance between explosive expansion and gravitational contraction had been different, the world we know could not have been born. The actual path the universe has taken is highly specific for the emergence of life.

It is only on a planet of a certain size on a nearly circular orbit, at a certain distance from the sun, that life could have evolved.[44] As Peter Hodgson put it: 'The more this evolution is studied, the more we realize that it is immensely improbable that we should be here at all.' He quotes Freeman Dyson: 'As we look out into the universe and identify the many accidents of physics and astronomy that have worked together to our benefit, it almost seems as if the universe must in some sense have known that we were coming.'[45]

Some scientists call the idea that the universe has taken just that path which leads to the possibility of human life, the 'anthropic principle'. For us to be here required what John Polkinghorne calls very 'fine tuning of the cosmic knobs'.[46] This is, in real sense, *our* world.

Strangely, therefore, the ancient world's picture of a man-centred

[44] P. E. Hodgson, 'The Desecularisation of Science', in W. Oddie (ed.), *After the deluge* (SPCK, 1987).

[45] F. J. Dyson, *Scientific American* 225.25 (1971).

[46] Polkinghorne, *Science and Creation*, p. 22.

universe, which was abolished by Copernicus' discovery that the sun did not go round the earth, is now being redrawn in a different perspective by the discoveries of the physics of cosmology.

We must pause here, though, with a note of caution. Impressive and important as the anthropic principle is we must not read this back into the mind of the Genesis author. Indeed, he himself would give us reason to pause on another count also. For, although the creation of human beings comes as a high point in the Genesis narrative, all the rest of Genesis 1 is there as well. We have all too often been tempted to think that all the rest of creation simply and only exists for us. But, as C. Westermann rightly comments:

> The simple fact that the first page of the Bible speaks about heaven and earth, the sun, moon and stars, about plants and trees, about birds, fish and animals, is a certain sign that the God whom we acknowledge in the Creed as the Father of Jesus Christ, is concerned with all of these creatures, and not merely with humans. A God who is understood only as the god of humankind is no longer the God of the Bible.[47]

Christian interpretations of verse 28, '*Have dominion . . .* ' have too often wrongly understood the rest of creation as being there solely for our benefit. Indeed the American historian Lynn White, Jr., went so far as to describe Western Christianity as 'the most anthropocentric religion the world has seen', and he blamed the medieval church's teaching on mankind's dominion for the horrors of modern pollution. As Keith Thomas shows, however, not all historians agree with that judgment, and argues that side by side with an emphasis in the medieval church on mankind's right to exploit inferior species was a doctrine of human stewardship and responsibility.[48] However, the church's record has not been altogether unambiguous, and it is true that much of the ecological crisis of our day can certainly be laid firmly at the door of human self-centredness.

In his fascinating book *The Turning Point*, Fritjof Capra puts it well:

> Excessive technological growth has created an environment in which life has become physically and mentally unhealthy. Polluted air, irritating noise, traffic congestion, chemical contaminants, radiation hazards, and many other sources of physical and psychological stress have become parts of everyday life for most of us. These manifold health hazards are not just incidental

[47] Westermann, *Genesis 1 – 11*, p. 176. [48] K. Thomas, pp. 22f.

byproducts of technological progress; they are integral features of an economic system obsessed with growth and expansion, continuing to intensify in high technology in an attempt to increase productivity.[49]

In addition to these health hazards, Capra rightly points us to possibly far more dangerous aspects of our present culture: the upset to the ecological processes which sustain our natural environment and thus the very basis of our physical existence. It is human selfishness disguised as 'productivity', 'efficiency' or 'competitiveness' which places short-term economic gains before long-term concern for the well-being of the planet we and our grandchildren are to inhabit. But Genesis 1 reminds us that the rest of God's creation – and we human beings also – are there *for him*. There is a community of creation, and each part is brought to its potential and fulfilment only in correspondence with other parts, as each stays in line with God's creative purposes for it.

To be sure, the creation of men and women is followed in Genesis 1:28 with a command to *'have dominion over'* the fish and the birds and every living thing. But what does this dominion mean?

Sometimes this text is inappropriately used to back up ideas of male headship and female subordination, but that cannot be found here. Quite clearly the 'dominion' is granted to the human creature God has made, both male and female.

As we shall see in a moment, we need to understand the sort of dominion human beings are to exercise in the light of their status as God's representative, *in the image of God* (1:27). Chapter 2 of Genesis will open up for us a picture of mankind as the estate manager, cultivating and protecting God's Garden. So it is as God's representatives, and in the light of God's creativity, that men and women are to *have dominion*. It cannot therefore be a lordly and exploitative domination, but a responsible stewardship, a facilitating servanthood, which recognizes that all things derive their existence from God's hands. We do well to read Genesis 1:28 in the light of the way we have described God's creative energy. He is the bringer of order out of chaos, and also is the preserver and sustainer of his world. Human 'subduing' of creation is a sharing in all these aspects of the divine task.

If human beings are seen as 'kings over nature', and that is perhaps implied in the command to 'rule over' the rest of creation, that may only be understood in the light of the kingly rule of God, committed to the welfare of his subjects, and serving their needs

---

[49] F. Capra, *The Turning Point* (Fontana, 1982), p. 249.

with benevolence. He is, so to speak, the 'Servant King'. We are also to be 'preservers' and 'sustainers' of the world, so that God's purpose of a community of creation in mutual interdependence can be achieved. In chapter 2, the animals are seen as man's companions. So our rule must, as Moltmann put it, be a 'rule of peace'. We are also, to change the metaphor, to act as 'midwife' to the groaning creation,[50] bringing new life and the possibilities of life to birth. Sadly, 'subdue' has sometimes been read only as 'dominate', and has cast human beings in the role not of facilitating servants, but of exploitative lords.

Having expressed this caution, we must now come back to the great importance and significance which this chapter gives to human beings. Out of the whole range of creatureliness, God calls forth one species to be special. And the specialness of human beings is described in terms of the 'image' and 'likeness' of God.

6. The divine image (1:26–27)

It would take us a very long time to discuss the many different interpretations there have been of the phrase 'in the image of God'. Whole books have been written; disputes have emerged as to whether 'image' and 'likeness' are synonyms or refer to different aspects of human life and faith; Catholics and Protestants have had different approaches; Lutherans, Barthians, Niebuhrians all take different lines.

Perhaps this diversity is, on second thoughts, not all that surprising. For what the phrase 'image of God' is pointing to is this question: What does it mean to be authentically human? Without any dispute, the phrase 'image of God' has something to do with our humanness, and it is the whole complexity of being human, the diversities and distinctivenesses of what it is to be a human being in this world, which leads different writers to highlight different aspects of our nature.

Some commentators understood the word 'image' in a very physical sense. If God were to come among us within the constraints of this physical world, he would be a human being. Others contrast a human's upright stature with that of other animals, and suggest that this points to our distinctiveness within the animal world. Many writers explore the meaning of various of the moral, rational and spiritual qualities of human beings, and suggest that 'the image of God' is another way of describing morality, or rationality, or a capacity to relate to God. Yet others link the phrase with the words which follow in the biblical text about 'having

---

[50] Cf. Rom. 8:22.

dominion', and they believe that the image of God is expressed in our human dominance over, and creativity in, the rest of the physical world. One theologian in particular, Karl Barth, expounds the divine image in terms of the words 'male and female', believing that sexual complementarity is the clue. Yet another thinks that what marks out human beings from every other creature, and links us to God, is our capacity for self-awareness and for reflective self-consciousness. God is the supremely 'self-aware' one: to be in his image is to be aware of ourselves as his creatures.

In a sense, like the parable of the blind men trying to describe an elephant simply by touch, each only feeling one small part, all these aspects of what it is to be human have truth in them. All of them, in some sense, shed light on the meaning of 'the divine image'. But there are several things more to be said.

Many of these approaches to 'the divine image' concentrate on some *capacity* in human beings to be or to do certain things. The focus is on something *in us* to which we can point and say 'there you see the image of God'.

By contrast, many Old Testament specialists would disagree with this approach. They would argue that the image is not a question of a quality in people, but of the fact that God has created people as his counterpart and that human beings can have a history with God. Westermann argues that 'human beings are created in such a way that their very existence is intended to be their relationship to God.'[51] The image, on this view, is not about something we have, or something we can do: it is about a relationship.

First and foremost it is about the particular relationship in which God places himself with human beings, a relationship in which we become God's counterpart, his representative and his glory on the earth.

We will try to explore in what ways this image is seen, from a New Testament perspective. There is only one human being of whom it is specifically said: 'He is the image of the invisible God'.[52] The New Testament makes unmistakably clear that if we wish to see the true 'image of God' in this world, we see it in Jesus Christ. St Paul speaks of 'the glory of Christ, who is the likeness of God',[53] and earlier, writing of our being changed into the likeness of Christ, he uses the analogy of a mirror: 'We all . . . beholding [as in a mirror] the glory of the Lord, are being changed into his likeness'.[54] What does the mirror analogy suggest? We can see an image of a certain object in a mirror if the mirror is at the right angle – or as we may say, in the right relationship – to the object. Jesus Christ

---

[51] Westermann, *Genesis 1 – 11*, p. 158.   [52] Col. 1:15.   [53] 2 Cor. 4:4.
[54] 2 Cor. 3:18.

truly reflects the nature of God because he is in the relationship of Son to his Father: he is God's image and glory on this earth.

To be 'in the image of God', or perhaps better 'as the image of God' then, is not *primarily* a matter of our capacity to be or do anything. It is about the relationship that God has towards us, and – in a derivative way, of our relationship of sonship to the Father. It is not about some characteristic we possess: it is about our whole existence. True humanness is found in personal communion with God – it is in such personal communion that his glory is reflected, his image is seen.

We now need to try to unpack what this means a little more fully, looking back on it, as it were, from the perspectives of our Christian faith.

1. The God we have come to know and worship in Jesus Christ through the Holy Spirit is a Trinity of Persons in whom loving creativity and personal communion belong together. God is 'Being in Communion' (to adapt a phrase from John Zizioulas). This means that personal communion in love between persons is what the image of God is primarily about. Jesus is the image of God in this world because he is in a relationship of loving communion with his Father. And we reflect God's image to the extent that we are growing in personal communion with him and therefore with one another. Some philosophers – John MacMurray, to give one example – say that to speak of 'a person' at all can only have meaning when we speak of 'persons in relation'. I am who I am, as I am in relation to you.[55]

The point is well made in a book which should, I think, be on the shelves of all Christian homes and on the reading lists of all theological colleges: Margery Williams, *The Velveteen Rabbit.*

The Velveteen Rabbit turned to the old wise experienced Skin Horse in the nursery, and asked 'What is Real? Does it mean having things that buzz inside you and a stick-out handle?' The Skin Horse replied: 'Real isn't how you are made. It's a thing that happens to you. When a child loves you for a long, long time, not just to play with, but REALLY loves you, then you become Real.' 'Does it hurt?' asked the Rabbit. 'Sometimes,' said the Skin Horse, for he was always truthful. 'Does it happen all at once, or bit by bit?' 'It doesn't happen all at once,' said the Skin Horse, 'You become. It takes a long time . . . Generally, by the time you are Real most of your hair has been loved off, and your eyes drop out, and you get very shabby . . . but

[55] J. MacMurray, *Persons in Relation* (Faber, 1961).

once you are Real you cannot become unreal again. It lasts for always.[56]

We become Real through relationships of love.

We will come back to this, of course, in Genesis 2 when we hear God say to the man that it is not good to be alone.

It may, incidentally, be worth noting that this 'relational' understanding of the divine image could make some sense of the divine plural in Genesis 1:26, 'Let us make . . . '. While probably a plural of majesty, many Christian commentators have also seen here a glimpse – all unbeknown to the Genesis author – of what was so much later formulated as the doctrine of the Trinity.

St Augustine, for example, says,

When I read that your Spirit moved over the waters, I catch a faint glimpse of the Trinity which you are, my God. For it was you the Father, who created heaven and earth in the Beginning of our Wisdom – which is your Wisdom, born of you, equal to you, and co-eternal with you – that is in your Son. . . . Here, then, is the Trinity, my God, Father, Son and Holy Ghost, the Creator of all creation.[57]

Whether or not Augustine is right, there is certainly a question as to whom God is depicted as talking to when he makes this firm resolve: 'Let us make . . . '. The most likely answer is that he is 'talking to himself' – a communion between the creative Word of God and the creative Spirit of God, in both of whom God's Being is seen in his Creative Acts. Or he may be talking with his heavenly court, who – as the Book of Job suggests – join with the morning stars in shouting for joy![58]

2. The Velveteen Rabbit leads us into the second point: true humanness is about *becoming* not just being. Relationships take place over time. To be in a relationship with God is – as Westermann put it – to 'have a history' with God. In a sense, therefore, while it is proper to speak of Jesus Christ as the true Human Being, we should speak of ourselves as Human Becomings. To understand the image of God primarily in terms of relationship, is to see it as not only a gift from God – as he calls us into relationship with himself – but as a task to be undertaken, a destiny to be followed.

As we said, if we want to see the image of God clearly, we see it in Jesus Christ. What we see in one another is an unclear reflection, because our relationship with God is very far from perfect. The

[56] Margery Williams, *The Velveteen Rabbit* (Heinemann, 1922).
[57] St Augustine, *Confessions*, Book XIII.5.   [58] Jb. 38:4, 7.

story of God's relationship with us is one of forgiveness, regeneration and resurrection. The task of Christian discipleship can be told as the story of God's relationship with us over the time span of our lives when by grace he helps us grow back into the 'measure of the stature of the fullness of Christ'.[59] We are, so to speak, on a journey into personhood. God is the Real Person who loves us into becoming real persons ourselves.

3. To be made as God's image means that human beings represent God on earth. We are God's proxy, so to speak, in the community of creation. Moltmann puts it this way:

> As God's image and appearance on earth, human beings are involved in three fundamental relationships: they rule over other earthly creatures as God's *representatives* and in his name; they are God's *counterpart* on earth, the counterpart to whom he wants to talk, and who is intended to respond to him; and they are the *appearance* of God's splendour, and his glory on earth.[60]

Only human beings are given this status – neither angels nor other animals are made to be God's image. There is, therefore, an affirmation here of the specialness of human beings, which needs to be asserted over against some humanist philosophers, and certain extreme 'Animal Rights' activists, who find this 'specism' (as they call it) as reprehensible as many other '-isms' (like sexism or racism), and who will sometimes even place 'animal rights' above the sanctity of human life. It is human beings, Genesis insists, to whom God gives the task and glory of representing him on earth.

4. There are certain human capacities and abilities which are part of making relationships and learning to love in relationships, and it is not surprising that these have often been identified with one aspect or another of the image of God. Indeed, we may wish to see a healthy, Spirit-filled, strong, rational, moral person, enjoying and growing through relationships with others as someone in whom God's image is becoming clearer. One of those very human capacities – rationality – is, as we said earlier, an important ingredient in the human enterprise we call science. There is a correspondence between our minds and the ordered world outside us which reflects something of the Rationality (Logos) of God. We must beware, however, of suggesting that the infant who is not morally aware (less still the embryo in the womb), the paralysed person, the cancer patient, or the old person in whom rationality is fading, are, because of their incapacity, any less in a relationship with God just because they cannot do certain things. For the image is a task as well as a

---

[59] Eph. 4:13.   [60] Moltmann, *God in Creation*, p. 221.

gift, a history as well as a status. It is a task and a history which moves through many phases from foetal life through infancy to mature adulthood and old age, from health to sickness, from incapacity through capacity to infirmity. What matters is not the presence of certain abilities, so much as the fact that God has set us in a certain relationship to himself.

5. If God's image is something to do with personal communion, we can, perhaps, now see the sense of Barth's linking the divine image to the relationship between the sexes. For as will become clearer in Genesis 2, the complementarity, mutuality and creativity of the relationship between the sexes, male and female in personal communion, symbolized by and deepened through sexual relationship, is one of the most profound aspects of our humanness. If personal communion in love is part of the meaning of male-female relationship, given its most intimate expression in the pilgrimage of marriage, then this, too, is part of the meaning of the image of God.

6. Finally, in Genesis 1:28, the image of God in human beings male and female, is linked to the blessing of fruitfulness: *'Be fruitful and multiply, and fill the earth.'* This stands in marked contrast to the pagan fertility cults, in which human beings tried to persuade the gods to be fruitful. God gives fertility and fruitfulness to human beings. Procreation strictly means creation 'on behalf of another' – in this case him who is Love, God himself. So human creativity, and especially human procreativity, is part of the outworking in our histories of the creative love of God in us as his image. All life is thus seen as God's gift. His blessing, as with all blessings, confers not only a gift, but a task.

Human creativity thus expresses something of the nature of God's creativity, and as Genesis 1:28 makes clear, this is not only found in being fruitful and multiplying, but in subduing the earth and having dominion over it. In the light of all that we have said about God's image, it is even clearer now that 'dominion' cannot be exploitation, but must be seen in the sort of facilitating servanthood which maintains an environment in which persons who reflect something of the nature of God's love and creativity can be at home. Genesis 1 will soon lead us into Genesis 2, where the meaning of humankind's relationship both with God and with the rest of the created order is spelled out in more intimate terms.

7. 'This is good'

a. Blessing

God, we are told, blessed the animals (1:22), he blessed men and women made in his image (1:28). Later he blessed the seventh day (2:3). 'Blessing' in the Bible is a word of vitality, creativity and fulfilment. The whole of the ongoing life of creation is the outworking of God's blessing. The whole of creation is now caught up into the divine blessing – there is an exuberance, a delight, in creation. God's blessing is the music of creation's dance.

b. Food

Part of the divine blessing is seen in God's provision of food for his people (1:29–30). In contrast to the Mesopotamian stories in which human beings have to provide food for the gods, here, God does the providing. And in this provision is another reminder of the interdependence of creation. We are participators in the creation, which we need for life, just as the rest of creation needs us to cultivate and preserve it. The ecosystems in which the life-cycles of all creatures are set; the need each creature has for sustenance from within the rest of the created order; the need, therefore, for a creation in which that mutual need and interdependence is respected: all this needs to be related to the fact that it is God who provides food. 'All look to thee, to give them their food.'[61]

c. Goodness

What a celebration of creation is written in this repeated cry, *God saw that it was good* (1:10, 12, 18, 21, 25) and its crescendo to verse 31: *And God saw everything that he had made, and behold, it was very good*! It really was very good!

Before anything is said about evil, or pain, or sin, or disorder, we need first to hear this note of excited pleasure. What God made is good!

This is the basis for a celebration and enjoyment of God's world, which in some Christian teaching has got lost behind an almost exclusive emphasis on sin. Art and music, drama and dance can all be used to celebrate the goodness of God's world – and indeed, have been. King David, to the embarrassment of his wife, 'danced before the LORD with all his might',[62] in celebration that the ark had been brought to Jerusalem. There is an 'extravagance' of praise and adoration in the celebration of Mary, pouring precious ointment over the feet of Jesus.[63] We need to recover a sense of delight in good things, even though, as we shall see from Genesis 3, there is also a shadow.

Julian of Norwich could see the wonder of God's creative love

---

[61] Ps. 104:27. [62] 2 Sa. 6:14. [63] Jn. 12:3.

in a little hazelnut. 'In this little thing I saw three truths. The first is that God made it; the second that God loves it; and the third that God sustains it . . . .'[64] In the littleness of the hazelnut, in the ordinariness of creation, Julian sees the creative and sustaining love of God.

Blake and Wordsworth celebrated the goodness of what God has made in their poetry. In the seventeenth century, Thomas Traherne wrote:

> You never Enjoy the World aright, till the Sea it self floweth in your Veins, till you are Clothed with the Heavens, and Crowned with the Stars: and Perceiv your self to be the Sole Heir of the whole World: and more then so, becaus Men are in it who are evry one Sole Heirs, as well as you. Till you can Sing and Rejoyce and Delight in God, as Misers do in Gold, and Kings in Scepters, you never Enjoy the World.[65]

Enjoy the world!

The goodness of creation is true of human beings also!

One of the dismaying aspects of our contemporary culture is the loss of personal self-esteem. Underlying much of the depressive illness which is the daily concern of therapists and counsellors, and the difficulties so many of us have in making and sustaining relationships, is a poor view of our self-worth. 'I am nothing', 'I am not worthy' are, of course, true in their proper place in Christian piety. But I am Not Nothing, and I am Not Worthless in the light of this Genesis picture of God's creation. God's image may be tarnished and out of line; there may be much still to be 'made new'; but we may and must say, of ourselves – as of all else God has made – this is really very good.

8. The seventh day (2:1–3)

It is not true to say that Genesis 1 comes to its climax in the creation of human beings. The whole structure of the chapter as a week of days leads to the seventh day as the climactic close of God's creative work. God finished his work. He delighted in it! 'This is good!' He rested. He blessed the seventh day and hallowed it.

The medieval division of chapters at the end of chapter 1 in our Bibles has obscured the true conclusion of this part of the story in chapter 2 verses 1 to 3. There is no concluding formula: 'there was

[64] Julian of Norwich, *Revelations of Divine Love* (Penguin ed.), p. 68.
[65] *The First Century*.29, from H. M. Margoliouth (ed.), *Thomas Traherne* (Oxford, 1958).

evening and there was morning'. The seventh day opens out into the ongoing story of God with his people and with his world. It points us forward. There are two features of this on which we will concentrate: time and the sabbath.

a. Time

One of the striking features of Genesis 1 is its concentration on time. The poem is constructed as a week of days. On Day 4, lights in the firmament are created *to separate the day from the night*, and to be *for signs and for seasons and for days and years* (1:14). The Creator wishes to divide up time, so that it can be ordered. So, as Wolff puts it: 'Ordered time is one of the gifts of God's creation.'[66] This is the picture also in some of the psalms: 'Thine is the day, thine also the night . . . thou hast made summer and winter';[67] 'Thou has made the moon to mark the seasons; the sun knows its time for setting'.[68]

The dividing up of time means that it is possible to invest certain times with particular significance. Genesis 2:1–3 in fact does this by emphasizing the special importance of the seventh day.

When we move further into Genesis chapter 2, 'significant' time comes into more prominence. We have the same idiom in English when we talk about 'the right time' for something to be done. So in Genesis 2, the word 'day' is not used in quite the way it is in chapter 1. In chapter 2 'day' means the event of a divine act: 'In the day that the LORD God made the earth and the heavens' (2:4). The day is invested with significance because of its part in the story of God's relationship with his world.

In later chapters in Genesis, the 'time' for human beings often becomes invested in this way with the significance of their experience of God. Cain is driven away 'this day' (4:14) – for him a day of judgment. After the Flood, Noah is promised that 'seedtime and harvest, cold and heat, summer and winter, day and night, shall not cease' (8:22). And this was a specific promise from God that there would never be another Flood. For Noah, the times of the seasons are invested with the particular significance of God's faithfulness.

To the Hebrew mind, what mattered about time was not so much in what order things happened, as the significance that the moment held.

In Roger Hargreaves' children's book about 'Roundies and Squaries', one of the differences between them is that Roundies

---

[66] H. W. Wolff, 'The Old Testament Concept of Time', in *Anthropology of the Old Testament* (Eng. tr., SCM, 1974), p. 86.   [67] Ps. 74:16–17.
[68] Ps. 104:19.

'get up to catch the sunrise', whereas Squaries 'get up to catch the 8.15'!

The rest of the Old Testament illustrates both these aspects of time. Time is both a chronological sequence of events and it is also, and especially, *significant* times – times of divine action, or of human opportunity. Ecclesiastes, among the later Wisdom writings, gives well-known expression to this second aspect: 'For everything there is a season, and a time for every matter under heaven . . . '.[69]

In the New Testament the same is true. There are several words used to refer to time. To over-simplify what is quite a complicated set of interconnected ideas,[70] we can pick out particularly 'chronos' which is used mostly of the sequence of events (*chronological* time), and 'kairos' used of *significant* time: moments of crisis, or moments of opportunity. So when Jesus opens his preaching ministry in Mark's Gospel with the words 'The time [kairos] is fulfilled', [71] he is not asking his hearers, so to speak, to check their watches – he is proclaiming that God's time has come: this is a moment of significance in God's purposes with his world; this is a moment of decision, a moment of opportunity. Indeed the really important new factor in the Christian understanding of time, beyond that of the Old Testament, is that with the coming of Jesus a new 'kairos' has dawned. All our time now takes its meaning from him whom Barth calls 'The Lord of Time'.

Much of this is foreign to our ways of thinking. We become so used to thinking of time only in terms of chronology. Will we have time? Will we be late? What is the time? How will we fit everything into the time? We waste time, we lose time, we grant time, we make time for things. But the biblical concepts of time require us to see time much more in terms of significance: God's purposes in history, centred and given their meaning by Jesus Christ.

We are not alone in the difficulty we feel in trying to understand time. One of the greatest of the early Fathers of the Christian church, Augustine, struggled with the meaning of time for his Christian faith,[72] though some of his conclusions are not as clear as they might be.

Was there a time, Augustine wonders, before God had created the world? No, he says, 'there was no time, because time itself was of your making.' What then is time? he asks. 'I know well enough what it is, provided that nobody asks me; but if I am asked what it is and try to explain, I am baffled!' Augustine concludes that we

---

[69] See Ec. 3:1–9.

[70] Cf. J. Barr, *Biblical Words for Time* (SCM, 1969); cf. *The New International Dictionary of New Testament Theology*, vol. 3 (Eng. tr., Paternoster, 1978), pp. 826ff.   [71] Mk. 1:15.

[72] St Augustine, *Confessions*, Books XI and XIII.

45

can be aware of time, and measure it only while it is passing. 'You, my Father, are eternal. But I am divided between time gone by and time to come, and its course is a mystery to me . . . You are the eternal Creator of all time.'

While Augustine was right to say that God is the Creator of our earthly time, he is less accurate when he says that the 'eternal' God is outside of time. Barth is more biblical when he speaks of 'God's time' and 'our time'.

The Professor in *The Lion, the Witch and the Wardrobe* makes the same point when he backs up Lucy's story as she tries to persuade her brother and sister that there really was another world through the back of the wardrobe:

'But there was no time,' said Susan. 'Lucy had had no time to have gone anywhere, even if there was such a place. She came running after us the very moment we were out of the room. It was less than a minute, and she pretended to have been away for hours.'

'That is the very thing that makes her story so likely to be true,' said the Professor. 'If there really is a door in this house that leads to some other world . . . I should not be at all surprised to find that the other world had a separate time of its own; so that however long you stayed there it would never take up any of *our* time . . . '

'But do you really mean, sir,' said Peter, 'that there could be other worlds – all over the place, just around the corner – like that?'

'Nothing is more probable,' said the Professor.[73]

Although God, as creator of our time, is beyond our time, he is not timeless. God is in 'his own time', which can impinge on and transform ours. He is the 'lasting' God.[74] When the New Testament tells us of things that are 'eternal', that does not mean timeless. 'Eternal' life is a different *sort* of life – the life which belongs to God, but which we can share both in our time and beyond our time, but which is not limited by our past or present or future. And the 'centre' of God's time, the turning-point of all time, or rather the event around which all the meaning of time ultimately turns, is Jesus Christ, who is, yesterday, today and for ever.[75] In him the unchanging 'now' of God's salvation has arrived.[76]

Although God is always beyond our time, he is always active within our history, though never bound by it.

[73] C. S. Lewis, *The Lion, the Witch and the Wardrobe.*
[74] *Cf.* Ex. 15:18; Ps. 90:1–2; Is. 40:28.   [75] Heb. 13:8.   [76] 2 Cor. 6:2.

Biblical time, then, is not so much a matter of one thing after another, as it is the story of God's interactions with his world; a story in which God gives moments of opportunity, moments of decision, times of repentance, a day of grace.

It is because God invests our time with significance, transforming 'chronos' into 'kairos', that Ephesians tells us to walk in wisdom, 'making the most of the time [kairos]'.[77]

Our times, ordered times, significant times, are gifts of the Creator to be enjoyed and used.

And yet how we panic about time! We find when we are young that we are growing up too fast. Mid-life reminds us how time flies. Are we giving enough time to our children? We get old and wonder where our time has gone. The biblical writers would urge us to rediscover the sense that, as the psalmist put it, 'My times are in thy hand.'[78]

Augustine's strugglings led him eventually to a prayer:

O Lord God, grant us peace, for all that we have is your gift. Grant us the peace of repose, the peace of the Sabbath, the peace which has no evening. For this worldly order in all its beauty will pass away. All these things that are very good will come to an end when the limit of their existence is reached. They have been allotted their morning and their evening.[79]

Michel Quoist put it another way:

You who are beyond time, Lord, you smile to see us fighting it.
And you know what you are doing.
You make no mistakes in your distribution of time to men.
You give each one time to do what you want him to do ...

Lord, I have time,
I have plenty of time,
All the time that you give me,
The years of my life,
The days of my years,
The hours of my days,
They are all mine.
Mine to fill, quietly, calmly,
But to fill completely, up to the brim,
To offer them to you, that of their insipid water
You may make a rich wine such as you made once in Cana of
    Galilee.[80]

[77] Eph. 5:15.   [78] Ps. 31:15.   [79] St Augustine, *Confessions*, Book XIII.
[80] Michel Quoist, *Prayers of Life* (Gill and Son, 1963).

b. Sabbath

One time of particular significance is the sabbath.

'Sabbath observance' has for us a rather negative ring conjuring up pictures of dreary Sunday afternoons, with grandfather dozing in front of a large Victorian Bible, and the children not allowed to do anything that resembled fun. Such negative legalism gets in the way of our understanding what the sabbath is really about.

The sabbath seems to have been an institution which particularly marked out the people of God. It seems to have marked the lives of God's people from as far back as the Exodus from Egypt. Genesis 1, in common with the version of the Ten Commandments given in Exodus 20, links the institution of the sabbath to the creation story itself.[81] It could not be said more clearly that the covenant purposes of God for his people (symbolized by their observance of the sabbath[82]) are rooted in the creative purposes of God for his world. God's creative purposes and God's covenanted love belong together. This is part of what the sabbath tells us.

The writer to the Hebrews interprets God's sabbath rest as something which begins when creation's six days are completed, and which carries on to the present. Through all their history, 'God's rest' has been an invitation to his people to share his fellowship. Through disobedience, as the psalmist makes clear, the fathers in the wilderness did not enjoy God's promised land.[83] However, the invitation to enjoy God's rest still remains – which is why the writer to the Hebrews encourages his readers not to fail to receive it because of disobedience (Heb. 4:11). Instead, with confidence we are to draw near to the throne of God's mercy, to find 'grace to help in time of need' (Heb. 4:16). Through the mercy and grace of God which comes to us in Jesus Christ, we may enjoy fellowship with God, and 'enter his rest'.

In the Ten Commandments recorded in Exodus, the sabbath is linked to creation. 'Remember the sabbath day to keep it holy . . . for in six days the LORD made heaven and earth . . . and rested the seventh day'.[84] And this linking of sabbath to creation indicates a pattern of universal significance. This is not just a special rule for the people of God, linking what they learned in the wilderness[85] back to creation. All people need the rhythm of sabbath rest, for that is the way God has made the world. And in the version of the Ten Commandments in Deuteronomy 5:15, the sabbath command is based on God's rescue of Israel from slavery in Egypt, and the need of toiling man and beast for rest. Perhaps von Rad is

[81] See Ex. 20:11. [82] Cf. Ex. 31:16–17.
[83] Ps. 95:11; cf. Dt. 12:9; cf. Heb. 3:11. [84] Ex. 20:8–11.
[85] Ex. 16:22–30.

right to see the Exodus version as 'thoroughly theological' – rooting the sabbath in the nature of God – and the Deuteronomic version as more 'psychological' – bringing out the benefits of sabbath rest for human and animal life.[86]

In one sense, the whole of Genesis 1 is about the sabbath. The rhythm of six days plus one is the way things are in the world. Our lives are built to reflect that reality. A human being's alternation of work and rest is meant to echo the alternation between work and rest in the creative activity of God. And what is God's rest? Is it not delight in his creation? Is it not looking with joy on his world and saying, 'This is good!'

Our sabbath rest is the opportunity God gives us to share his delight. Human life is meant to include more than labour, more than the struggle for the appropriate stewardship of the world, more than the reforming of society. The six plus one alternation of work and rest is not the rhythm of work plus recovery so as to be able to go back to work. It is a rhythm of engagement with the world in work, and then thankful enjoyment of the world in worship. By 'worship' we do not mean simply – or even primarily – 'church activity'. 'Worship' is our offering back to God, for him to enjoy, our enjoyment of his world. The climax of the creation is Man the Worshipper: Homo Adorans. Here is the one who in fellowship with the Creator *enjoys* the Creator's work.

What is our creation for? That we may be creatures of the seventh day! That we may share God's work of bringing order in his creation; that we may grow in personal communion with him and so reflect his image; and that we may share the delight of his rest. That we may have fellowship with the Creator. That we may be caught up in praise with the sun and moon and stars, the trees and flowers and birds; with all creatures great and small, of fish and of beasts. All these look to God for their life and their sustenance; all these in their silent ways sing the song of their Creator.

In *The Magician's Nephew*, C. S. Lewis, in words of great beauty, tells of the founding of Narnia. 'In the darkness, a voice began to sing. Its low notes were deep enough to be the voice of the earth herself. There were no words. There was hardly even a tune. But it was, beyond comparison, the most beautiful noise [Digory] had ever heard. . . . ' The rich colours, the glorious sounds, the stars, sun, valleys and hills all carry the song of the Lion.

Genesis 1 is such a song. 'All things were made through him,

---

[86] *Cf.* G. von Rad, *Deuteronomy* (Eng. tr., SCM, 1966), p. 58.

and without him was not anything made that was made.'[87] Christ, the Word through whom all creation is called forth, is the Christ who makes the Creator known as our Father.[88] It is through Christ that we can know God, and are therefore bold to say 'I believe in God, the Father Almighty, creator of heaven and earth'. Through him we are given life and breath and all things. All the living universe owes its life to him.

And we human beings have been given something more than life. We are given the gift of understanding something of his majesty and his mysterious freedom. To our species is revealed something of his intimate yet commanding relationship with the world. We, alone among the creatures, are called to reflect his image – to share a history and a destiny with him. We are invited to enjoy the fellowship of the Lord's sabbath. And in the rhythm of our work and our worship we can give a voice to the silent order of the universe, that it too, with us, may sing the Creator's praise.

[87] Jn. 1:3.   [88] Jn. 1:18.

The regimes of concern to fundamental physics, which
are the regimes of the very large (cosmology) and the
very small (elementary particle physics) . . . seem to
display a remarkably beautiful structure. The evolution
of the universe according to the laws of General
Relativity, and the patterns described by particle
physics are sources of considerable intellectual delight to
those privileged to study them.

John Polkinghorne, *Science and Creation*, p. 34.

By an Act of the Understanding therefore be present
now with all the Creatures among which you live: and
hear them in their Beings and Operations Praising GOD
in an Heavenly Maner. Som of them Vocaly, others in
their Ministery, all of them Naturaly and Continualy.
We infinitely wrong our selvs by Laziness and
Confinement. All Creatures in all Nations and Tongues
and People prais God infinitly; and the more, for being
your Sole and Perfect Treasures. You are never what
you ought till you go out of yourself and walk among
them.

Thomas Traherne, *The Second Century*.76.

O God, Creator of light, shine in our darkness,
    Maker of space, give us the freedom to live,
    Source and Sustainer of life, Holder of joy,
        Bearer of pain,
        May we glory in your praise.

51

2:4 – 3:24
2. Expelled from Eden

What ambiguity!

How can human life be so rich and prosperous, and yet so flawed? How can it be that human beings so much long for God, and yet so insistently flee from God? How can human beings create so much that is of excellence and beauty, only to find that our finest achievements are subject to decay? Why are even the most intimate and life-giving aspects of human relationships touched with pain and sorrow? Why is everything and everyone overshadowed by death?

These are universal questions – and they are as much our concern as they were the concern of the author of these chapters. We can point to human achievements of immense magnitude, yet at each point we need to acknowledge human vulnerability and human destructiveness. We can harness nuclear energy for good or for evil. We can intervene in reproductive processes for good or for evil. We have the knowledge and technology available for the elimination of hunger in the world, but not the political will or economic structures or personal motivation to do so. We have developed a standard of living which allows us to concentrate on the quality of our personal relationships in a way earlier generations could not – and yet we find ourselves unable to make personal commitments. Our very lives are threatened by the tiny virus which spreads AIDS.

Genesis chapters 2 and 3 link much of the disorder of the world to the reality of human sin, and show how the 'very good' of God's creation has at point after point been disfigured. We need to be careful, however, not to explain everything that we happen to dislike in these terms. Even Calvin seems to go overboard when he says: 'Many things which are now seen in the world are rather corruptions of it . . . we must come to this conclusion respecting the existence of fleas, caterpillars and other noxious insects'(!).[1] Yet the truth is that the world displays much ambiguity: why is there so much beauty here, and yet so much ugliness?

Pascal writes: 'Man's greatness and wretchedness are so evident that the true religion must necessarily teach us that there is in man some great principle of greatness and some great principle of wretchedness. It must also account for such amazing contradictions.'[2]

In Genesis 2 and 3 we are not offered a logical statement of causes and effcts. We are not merely told what happened so long ago. That we could handle. That would leave us alone. That would distance us sufficiently from the question so that we could blame everything on our past, and excuse ourselves. Rather we are told a story. This is a story in which it is most likely that the writer has 'borrowed various familiar mythological motifs, transformed them, and integrated them into a fresh and original story of his own.'[3] This is a story of primeval history, certainly, yet which is more than a story. It is not history in our usual sense (for cherubim with flaming swords, 3:24, are not the stuff of usual history); nor is it fable in the usual sense (the references to rivers and mineral deposits in 2:10–11 are too factual for that). 'Myth' is a word which suggests that the narrative is only the disguise for unhistorical and timeless truth. But exegesis demands more than this. Karl Barth uses the word 'saga' in the sense of 'an intuitive and poetic picture of a pre-historical reality which is enacted once and for all within the confines of space and time.'[4] It is not altogether clear how much further that takes us – Barth seems to want all the benefits of 'history' without the difficulties.[5] So let us stay with 'story', a story rooted within our space and time, but a story which catches us up into itself, and confronts us with the truth about ourselves.

We see ourselves in the Garden, hearing the Lord call, 'Where are you?' We know what it is to hide through shame. We are skilled at shifting blame on to others. We feel the cost of being expelled from Eden.

This is not to say that what is depicted in these chapters did not happen. To be sure, in the story of humankind's relationship with the Creator, beauty is turned to brokenness, unity to diversity, fellowship to banishment, and life becomes overshadowed by death. But we may not only say that it happened. We must also say that

---

[1] Calvin, *Genesis*, p. 104.   [2] Blaise Pascal, *Pensées* XI.
[3] Wenham, p. 53.   [4] *Church Dogmatics*, III/1, p. 81.
[5] This point is made in connection with Barth's treatment of the resurrection narratives, by Austin van Harvey in *The Historian and the Believer* (SCM, 1967, 1971).

it happens. We are part of the story. We are there in the Garden, and the Word is addressed to us.

A. LIFE IN THE GARDEN (2:4–25)

1. The ongoing story

These are the generations of the heavens and the earth when they were created. (2:4a)

The formula 'these are the generations of' links the narrative of Genesis 1 with what follows. Chapter 2 emerges from and develops what has gone before. That is the force of this connecting formula. It occurs later, for example in 5:1, when the story of Adam continues into the story of Seth. It comes in 10:1 when the story of Noah's sons develops into a genealogy of their descendants. It occurs again throughout Genesis as a title introducing the next section. It means: 'here is a fuller development of the story of . . .'.

So now we read of 'the fuller development of the story of the heavens and the earth'. Here in Genesis 2:4 the formula serves as a link between the panoramic vistas of chapter 1, and the more intimate homely style of the man in the Garden, in chapter 2.

The parallel between the order of events in chapters 1 and 2 is striking. Genesis 1:1 – 2:3 begins with the natural world, and then moves towards the world of animals and finally people. In 2:4b onwards the story is told first in terms of Man's relationship to the natural environment (vv. 4b–17), then also moves to Man's relationships with animals and finally with people (vv. 18–25). Each of these sections ends with a law which relates to Man's life in the environment in question (vv. 16–17 concern life in the Garden and v. 24 concerns marriage).

Despite such similarities of order, however, the change in tone and style between these chapters is immediately obvious to the reader. Even God is given a more intimate name. In chapter 1, he is 'God'. In 2:4b, he is 'the LORD God', the word LORD representing God's covenant name: YAHWEH. Our focus of interest is no longer the cosmic perspective of the One who made the stars. It is the intimacy of fellowship with the One who calls Man by his name.

Genesis 2 and 3 concern the place of human beings in God's world; human creatureliness and human limits; God's requirement of obedience, and the reality of human disobedience; the fragmentation and disorder of a person's relationship to God, to others, to the natural world.

2. Earth and heaven

In the day that the LORD God made the earth and the heavens . . .
(2:4b)

The phrase 'the heavens and the earth' opens and closes Genesis 1 (1:1; 2:1; 2:4a). While it means 'everything', it also, as we saw earlier, carries a distinction. 'Heaven' is God's 'place' and earth is our 'place'. It is on earth that God called forth vegetation and animals and human beings. Earth is separated from heaven. Human beings are not God. We shall find several times in these eleven chapters how human beings graspingly attempt to cross the boundaries between earth and heaven; they try to make themselves as gods. And each time the result is chaos. For heaven is not to be grasped at, not to be owned, not to be controlled. Heaven is received as a gift of love, to be listened to, and welcomed. It is in the One Mediator that heaven comes to earth. In him we can be lifted to the 'heavenly places'. But that is of grace, not of right. Genesis 1 reminded us of the separation of the heavens and the earth. And for human beings to retain their humanity, they need to respect their God-given boundaries, and not grasp at that which belongs to God.

But notice how here in Genesis 2 the sequence is changed. From the 'heavens and earth' of chapter 1 (1:1; 2:1; 2:4a) we are now concerned with *the earth and the heavens* (2:4b).

Chapter 2 is the other side of chapter 1. From the majesty and the grandeur of the Rockies, we are now invited to explore the Garden.

If in chapter 1, as Bonhoeffer says,[6] we see man for God, here we see God for man. There in chapter 1, in other words, human life is depicted as a part of God's purposes for his whole cosmos. Here in chapter 2, God is acting on behalf of man for his welfare. There, the more distant Creator and Lord; here the near, fatherly, covenant God, 'Yahweh Elohim'.

Now the focus of attention is on the human being on God's earth. Where do *we* belong, and how should *we* live in God's world? That is where this chapter takes us now.

3. Earth and life

In the day that the LORD God made the earth and the heavens,
⁵when no plant of the field was yet in the earth and no herb of the
field had yet sprung up – for the LORD God had not caused it to

---

[6] Dietrich Bonhoeffer in *Creation and Fall*.

rain upon the earth, and there was no man to till the ground; [6]*but a mist went up from the earth and watered the whole face of the ground –* [7]*then the LORD God formed man of dust from the ground, and breathed into his nostrils the breath of life; and man became a living being.* (2:4b–7)

The purpose of the Garden is to provide a context for human life.

There is some problem over the grammar of verses 4–7. It is likely that the main clause does not appear until verse 7: *In the day that the LORD God made the earth and the heavens . . . then the LORD God formed man* (2:4b, 7). If this is the case, then all the preliminary subordinate clauses are merely the context for the appearance of human life. In the day that the Lord made the earth and the heaven, while there were no plants, no herbs, no rain, just ground water, *then* the Lord God formed man.

This chapter is primarily about God and human beings. And what are we told about human life? Man is *of the earth*. There is an earthiness to our human nature. Human life is formed 'of the dust'. Human life is of a piece with other animal life. 'Adam' is of a piece with the *'ᵃdāmâ* – the ground. As Anthony Phillips comments: 'Man tills the soil to live, yet in the end is buried in it.'[7] Human life is of the dust. It cannot itself break into immortality.

We then notice that *God formed man*. God shapes the man out of the earth with his own hands. The picture is of the potter moulding the clay,[8] or of the artist.[9] There is a bodily nearness of the Creator to his creature. God, so to speak, gets his hands dirty to bring us to life. This implies God's authority: he shapes me and I am inescapably his creature. It also implies that my body, and what I do to my body, are not unimportant.

There have been times in Christian history when the body was not taken seriously. Sometimes, following more Greek philosophy than Hebraic understanding, Christians have taught that what really matters is the 'soul', and the body is just the prison within which the soul has to live for a while. This can lead to a very negative view of the body – either regarding it as evil, and needing to be punished and subdued by all sorts of ascetic disciplines; or regarding it as unimportant, and believing that it does not matter what we do with it, so opening the way to all sorts of sexual permissiveness. Both seem to have been problems in Corinth, as we can discover from Paul's letters to the church there. There was apparently an ascetic group who wrote to him saying, 'It is well for a man not to touch a woman.'[10] Paul replied to them in terms which

---

[7] Phillips, p. 20.   [8] *Cf.* Je. 18:2.   [9] See Is. 44:9–10.
[10] 1 Cor. 7:1.

affirm our sexuality, and stressing the mutuality and complementarity of the marriage relationship.[11] There were also representatives of the 'sexually liberated' group in Corinth. They quoted the proverb 'Food is meant for the stomach and the stomach for food' to mean 'sex is for the body and the body is for sex'. To these people Paul wrote saying that Christians cannot act as though it is possible to separate out their bodily behaviour from their commitment to Christ. Even consorting with a prostitute in a Corinthian brothel involves a person's whole being, not just the body.[12] The body is a temple of the Holy Spirit.

Human life is embodied life. We need to affirm our bodies as one aspect of the whole of us. We need to be glad of them, look after them, and acknowledge that they are the form that God has given us to live within this physical world. Even at death, the 'soul' does not 'leave the body' in the sense that we become *less* than we were before. No, the whole of us is transformed and reclothed with a 'spiritual body' appropriate for the life of heaven. St Paul gives classic expression to this in 1 Corinthians 15 where, drawing on the analogy of the seed in the earth which dies, and from that death comes the living ear of wheat,[13] he suggests that what is raised is both continuous with what has died, but is also transformed through resurrection into something much more glorious. 'I believe in the resurrection of the body.' What I do with my body matters to God.

4. A living being

I am of the earth, Genesis says. I am near the Creator, and derived from the Creator. And then into his clay model, God breathes life.

Life is God's gift, and the psychophysical unity of the product of clay in God's hands and the breath of God's nostrils – that unity we call a human being – is dependent on God for life and breath and all things. When God takes away his breath, his creatures die and return to dust.[14]

We sometimes get confused by the translation 'living soul', and are led to believe that Genesis 2:7 is speaking of some distinctively human 'soul' which makes us different from other animals. But 'soul' here simply means *living being*. It is the word used elsewhere for 'living creatures' (Gn. 1:20–21). It refers to the principle of life in any living organism.

In his paper 'Life's Irreducible Structure', philosopher Michael Polanyi takes to task those who believe that the whole of life can

---

[11] 1 Cor. 7:2–5.   [12] 1 Cor. 6:12ff.   [13] 1 Cor. 15:36–37.
[14] Ps. 104:29.

be understood in terms of molecular biology.[15] Since the discovery by Crick and Watson of the double helix of DNA, much of the chemistry and physics of life is now understood. Many of the biochemical secrets of genetic replication have been unlocked. Man the scientist can now produce life. This has led some scientists to believe that all of life can be understood in terms of physics and chemistry. Not so, says Polanyi, because DNA acts *as a code* in the production of more DNA. And for us to understand it acting as a code, we need a higher level of explanation than simply that of physics and chemistry.

To give another example, imagine you are at Stratford, watching and listening to a production of Macbeth. The literature is more than sentences; grammar is more than words, and spoken words more than the movement of sound waves. A spoken literary composition needs to be received at several different levels. Similarly, says Polanyi, the phenomena of life need to be explored at a series of levels of understanding, and not in a way which tries to reduce everything to the lowest level of physics and chemistry. The spoken words depend on, though they are not reducible to, the physics of voice production – they are under the control of 'vocabulary' as well as of the physics of sound waves. Similarly, the 'higher levels' of life, and the functioning of the DNA code, are dependent on, but cannot wholly be explained at the lower levels of biochemistry and physics.

Human life is not only 'of the dust of the ground', but has also the higher level of the living organism: 'breath' of life.

There is a different important distinction, this time between living beings and spiritual life, which is made by St Paul in the New Testament, when he says that 'The first man Adam became a living being; the last Adam became a life-giving spirit.'[16] Through Christ, our spirits are given life – or rather, we are made alive to God in the Spirit. At this stage in the Adam story, though, we meet simply a 'living being'.

A further tentative point can be suggested here. Without wishing to read more into this than the text will carry, it does seem appropriate to infer that the man, when he was created, was not complete. Our image of Adam in Paradise is sometimes of a perfect man enjoying the perfection of life. One older Christian tradition going back to Irenaeus suggests rather that Adam was created a child, with a lot of growing up to do. It seems unlikely that this was the picture in the author's mind – particularly in the light of his reference to a man of marriageable age in 2:24. It is more likely to have been a grown-up Adam that is described. But none the less, he is

---

[15] Polanyi, *Knowing and Being*, pp. 225ff.   [16] 1 Cor. 15:45.

an Adam that still needs to learn, to develop and to grow. Whatever age we picture the man to be, he is still not mature. His innocence is intended – so we shall discover – to be transformed into the maturity of holiness by the choices he makes, choices which affect his whole life. The immature dependency of his life on the gift of God's breath is intended to grow into the mature dependency of obedience to God's life-giving Word.

5. Water

A river flowed out of Eden to water the garden, and there it divided and became four rivers. ¹¹The name of the first is Pishon; it is the one which flows around the whole land of Havilah, where there is gold; ¹²and the gold of that land is good; bdellium and onyx stone are there. ¹³The name of the second river is Gihon; it is the one which flows around the whole land of Cush. ¹⁴And the name of the third river is Tigris, which flows east of Assyria. And the fourth river is the Euphrates. (2:10–14)

The author also wants us to learn that God's gift of life in Eden is the source of all life beyond Eden. We can see this by looking at the significance of water for the writer.

At the beginning of chapter 1, water – the earliest stage in God's creation awaiting his purposeful hand – had then to be contained. To that writer – though not to the Creator! – the darkness over the deep seems almost threatening. Then by his creative Word, God separated the waters, and then separated the dry land from the water on the earth.

The water which can carry the destructive power of God, as the story of the Flood will soon show all too graphically, can also be reined in to become a source of life. And here in 2:10–14, water is a principle of life, of growth, of refreshment. Water is needed for life to develop. And in Eden there is plenty of water! There is enough to water the Garden, and to flow out into four huge rivers, one of which flows round the whole land of Havilah, and as it were nourishes civilization and culture – for *the gold of that land is good, bdellium and onyx stone are there.*

The water of the rivers is but the overflow from Eden. The vitality of God's Garden is the source of nourishment for everything else.

Now we look at the Garden itself.

6. The Garden

And the LORD God planted a garden in Eden, in the east; and there he put the man whom he had formed. ⁹And out of the ground the LORD God made to grow every tree that is pleasant to the sight and good for food, the tree of life also in the midst of the garden, and the tree of the knowledge of good and evil. . . .

¹⁵The LORD God took the man and put him in the garden of Eden to till it and keep it. ¹⁶And the Lord God commanded the man, saying, 'You may freely eat of every tree of the garden; ¹⁷but of the tree of the knowledge of good and evil you shall not eat, for in the day that you eat of it you shall die.' (2:8–9, 15–17)

a. The park keeper at work

The Garden is really a park of trees, and the man is the park keeper. He is God's estate manager. His task is 'to till and to guard' (2:15), that is: to cultivate and protect. Work is part of the responsibility laid on human beings here at the beginning, even before things go wrong. May there, though, be just a hint of trouble ahead, in the word 'guard'? Human fulfilment includes the human creativity of work, and the Garden is the place for mankind to find that fulfilment.

Many recent Christian writers have turned to Genesis 1:28 ('have dominion') and to this verse ('to till and to guard') as the basis for a discussion of Christian attitudes to work. Of course such a discussion is vitally important, particularly in an age of such demeaning and depressing high unemployment. But we must not make these verses carry more than they will. If we approach the question of work through New Testament eyes, we find paid employment taking a second place to the concerns of the kingdom of God. We need to seek an answer first to the wider question concerning human action in the world. What should we be doing here?

Karl Barth[17] helpfully describes how our human action is meant to reflect something of God's action – and the action of God is primarily and supremely the establishing of his kingdom under the rule of Christ. This is the centre of God's activity. So, he argues, the centre of our human actions as Christians must be to reflect this focus on the kingdom of God.

But around this centre, there is a periphery. Around and supporting God's action in the kingdom, there is his work of supporting and sustaining his world in being, that the kingdom may be built. We may call this his providence. And we may then speak of human *work* as our human action which corresponds to God's providence. God holds his world in being; we are his estate managers.

---

[17] *Church Dogmatics*, III/4, pp. 470ff.

In this light, human work has a vital, but secondary, significance. And work is not simply to be identified with paid employment. Important as paid work is in our society, both in providing necessary conditions for adequate living standards, and in giving a person a sense of worth in his or her creativity, it is the creative engagement with the world on behalf of God that is the really significant thing.

And in a world in which 'leisure time' is becoming more of a problem; in which high unemployment is increasingly a fact of life; in which technological robotics are thankfully taking the pain and drudgery out of much boring routine, we need to recover a sense of our capacity for creativity, as human beings made in the image of the Creator.

b. Creativity

Let us be clear, though, what this 'creativity' means. In an article in 1986,[18] Philip West illustrates how various recent Christian thinkers have used – he would say misused – the concept of creativity. Some have tried to interpret 'creativity' simply in terms of the production of novelty – creativity just means making something new. Others have used the Genesis texts to justify interpreting creativity solely in the economic sphere – creativity is the production of capital, the creation of wealth. To yet others, creativity is regarded as a matter of self-expression, and human creativity is restricted to the production of works of art. But whatever strands of truth there may be in these approaches, they tend to obscure more than to illuminate. Philip West rightly argues that we need to understand human creativity in terms of the creativity of God. For God is not adequately presented only as the Great Innovator, the Great Economist or the Great Artist. Philip West himself turns to the Psalms and to the Servant Songs in Isaiah, and also to the creative power of the cross of Christ, to fill out his understanding of the creativity of God, but we can also find pointers enough in Genesis. God's creativity is seen (Gn. 1) in bringing form to what is formless, bringing order out of what is chaotic, reining in the storm, and containing the power of the waters so that they may give life. God's creativity is seen (Gn. 2) in his provision of a context in which life can flourish and civilization develop. As we shall see later in Genesis 2, his creativity is seen also in the provision of a human social context for personal love. The story of the Flood (Gn. 6 – 9) will show us the re-creative power of the covenant of grace to make a new world out of a broken one. The Tower of Babel (Gn. 11) will underline the importance of community life

---

[18] *New Blackfriars* (Nov. 1986), p. 478.

being centred on God.

God has put mankind in his Garden, to look after it as his estate manager. If our human creativity is to reflect something of God, it will not be concerned simply with what is new, economically productive or artistically expressive. It will go beyond these to seek to reflect God's concern for a world and a society of which he can say, 'This is *good*'.

Our human creativity should seek to mirror God's, within the freedom of the obedience of faith, to confront the formless and disordered places of our world, and of our lives, and make them places of beauty and goodness. The concerns of town planners for an environment in which the good life can be lived; the work of doctors and therapists in seeking to facilitate that health which is the strength for good living; the personal growth in character which increasingly reflects the beauty and goodness of Christ: these and many others are all aspects of true creativity.

c. Beauty and freedom (2:9, 16–17)

The Garden, we are told, is a place of beauty as well as utility (2:9). God the Artist is part of the story even if, as we have just said, his creativity is so much more than art. The Garden contains trees that are 'pleasant to the sight' as well as 'good for food'. Growth is always enhanced in a good environment, and diminished in a hostile one. Beauty is part of God's good creation. There are some things which are good, just because they are beautiful, even though, no doubt, they could have been sold and the money given to the poor.[19] While our obligation to the poor is not diminished, we do well to remember that Jesus commended the 'beautiful thing'.[20]

In God's pattern for his world, human beings need an environment which is not merely functional but also 'pleasant to the sight'. The answer to inner-city deprivation is not merely the provision of housing and social amenities for those who have suffered in derelict and uninhabitable surroundings. The housing and the amenities need to be provided along with an environment which is enriching, beautiful, and life-enhancing. High-rise flats which provide a roof, but no beauty, meet one need by creating another. The man in the Garden found his environment 'pleasant' (2:9).

And in God's Garden, there is freedom. '*You may freely eat*' (2:16) probably means 'You may eat to the full', and '*of every tree of the garden*'. The man, as we might say, has a free run of the place. It is his to enjoy and to use with no constraint – save one.

---

[19] *Cf.* Mt. 26:6–10.   [20] Mt. 26:10.

The one restrictive command of verse 17 is the only boundary within which there is freedom.

Here is a picture of a place of vitality, freedom and nourishment. Here is a place, too, where God talks to the man. As we saw in the previous chapter, out of the whole range of creatureliness, God called forth this one species, to reflect his image. He addresses the man as a personal 'Thou'. *That* is the distinctively human attribute: to have been commanded forth to a particular task, a particular destiny, a particular life, a particular freedom, by the covenant LORD Yahweh himself, and addressed as a 'Thou'. Man, the living being, is now Man personally addressed by his Creator.

7. At the centre

What is the centre of life in the Garden?

At the centre, in the midst of the Garden, is *the tree of life* and *the tree of the knowledge of good and evil* (2:9). In order for the tree to be at the centre, man himself cannot be at the centre. So here, the freedom of human life is limited by one prohibition (2:17), which reminds the man that the freedom for his life, and therefore the conditions for his life, are given him by God. (In fact, as we shall see on page 65, life is *guaranteed* by this one prohibition. Life and liberty are only found *within* God's gracious law.)

Good and evil probably means 'everything'. The tree is the 'tree of the knowledge of everything', that is, the sort of knowledge which God has. It stands as a symbol of the life that has been given by God. But the man is not God. He cannot have such knowledge. Man must not try to be God; he must keep himself from the centre.

'Good and evil' are also terms which point to moral choices. The knowledge of good and evil would 'make one wise' (Gn. 3:6). And wisdom, as the Wisdom literature makes clear, includes that understanding which belongs only to God.[21] The wise person is one whose fear is in the Lord – and whose faith is obediently dependent on him.

According to Ezekiel 28:6, 15–17, the King of Tyre was thrown out of Eden 'because you consider yourself as wise as a god'. Perhaps Ezekiel had Genesis 2 in mind. The tree of the knowledge of 'good and evil' probably stands for that divine wisdom which human beings cannot and may not grasp. Human beings do not have moral autonomy. Their choices are intended to reflect the goodness which is found in God himself, and which he makes known to us in the revelation of his will. It is the 'will of God' on

[21] Pr. 30:1–4.

which the New Testament bases much of its ethical teaching.[22] It is that will which is summarized here in the Garden in the one divine command 'You shall not eat'.

In our post-Enlightenment world, in which so-called empirical facts are frequently separated off from moral values, and the latter are relegated to the category of personal choice, even of personal taste, we have tended to be persuaded that there are no moral absolutes. Earlier generations understood that moral values were somehow rooted in the ways things are in the world. For them there was an objectivity to morality. Facts were 'laden with value' because they came from the Creator's hands. The decisions to abort the unborn, to deploy nuclear weapons, to exterminate Jews, would in that earlier world have been related to a standard of goodness and an understanding of evil which is more than personal choice, or the statistical morality of 'what the majority of us believe'. But now, though our hearts often tell us otherwise, our minds have too often been conditioned to believe, with Hamlet, that there is nothing either good or bad, but thinking makes it so. Our hearts, however, *know* that some things are evil, and some things are good. Although there are many confused areas of moral borderline where the conflicting claims of different 'goods' make ethical decisions extremely complicated, our hearts know that there is something we can call good which is beyond us and beyond our choices. There is in our nature this moral 'signal of transcendence'. There is an objective moral order. We are not morally autonomous beings, and cannot simply 'invent right and wrong'.[23]

There is a tree in the centre of the Garden which reminds us that moral boundaries are given us for our good: they are part of the way the world is; part of the divine pattern for the Garden. And when we overstep divinely-given boundaries, and seek to trespass into areas which belong to God alone, the word comes to us: *'in the day that you eat of it you shall die'* (2:17). Perhaps we need to write that word clearly over the doors of some establishments which are committed to the escalation of the possibilities of nuclear destruction, or to the violation of human integrity in some experiments in genetic engineering, or research on human subjects. When human beings try to be god, and take to themselves decisions which belong only to God, we succumb to the demonic and the word of God's judgment is heard against us. But it is not only for such extreme cases of flaunted human autonomy that the restrictive divine command is given. It is meant to govern all the life in the Garden in which the centre belongs not to man, but to the Word

[22] *Cf., e.g.,* 1 Thes. 4:3.
[23] *Cf.* the book title *Ethics: Inventing Right and Wrong*, by J. L. Mackie (Penguin, 1977).

of God. We can read back into the significance of this one law the significance also of honesty in our business affairs, faithfulness to our spouse, the respect of the lives of others, our duty of care for the natural environment, and the importance of love for our neighbour.

In these ordinary areas of life, too, God's purposes for human fulfilment cannot be found in the assertion of human autonomy, nor in a quest for knowledge and experience beyond the limits set by God. Human beings find their fulfilment by growing in relationship with God and caring for his Garden, on the basis of obedience to his word. The man is not to touch the tree at the centre.

8. The paradox of freedom

We notice also that this one negative command is set in the context of divine care and provision. It is not a harsh restriction, but rather a symbol of the fact that crossing the God-given limits diminishes rather than enhances human well-being. It gives a boundary within which there is freedom.

Here the author is opening up to us one of the paradoxes of human living. Freedom without bounds can all too quickly become a destructive licence which binds instead of liberates. True liberty is only found within bounds. The goldfish, 'liberated' from its water, will not survive long in its new-found freedom. Its freedom to be a goldfish depends on respect for the appropriate context for its life. So with humans. This apparently restrictive command, 'Live only within the bounds of the divine word,' is in fact the only basis on which personal freedom can be found. 'His service is perfect freedom.' It is God's law which guarantees our freedom.

The point can be made another way by noticing that God is not in the Garden. He comes round for an evening (or possibly early morning?[24]) stroll in the cool of the day (3:8), but for most of the time all that man has to go on is God's word. This is what faith is about: living by God's word, when God is absent from the Garden. Learning to trust even when we do not see and do not fully understand. Keeping away from the tree just because that is the way God wants it, even though we can find many good reasons for not doing so. Accepting that there are boundaries set for us which though unclear are, we believe, not arbitrary. Growth comes by learning to live in commitment, obedience and trust, on the basis of the word God has spoken.

[24] Cf. Song 2:17.

9. Knowledge by participation

Interestingly, 'commitment' is a word which has come back into some recent work in the philosophy of science. Writers like Michael Polanyi argue cogently that there is no such thing as a wholly 'objective' detached scientific knowledge. All knowledge includes an inescapably personal commitment. Even in the least 'personal' of the sciences – physics – the processes of discovery, the formulation of theories, and the procedures for testing hypotheses all involve a personal commitment on the part of the scientist. Evaluation of results, for example, is often a matter of statistical correlations and of weighing probabilities. But weighing probabilities is not a scientific concept – it involves personal judgment based on experience and skill. Equally, the use of apparatus, the way results are recorded, even the choice of the topic of research in the first place, involve personal evaluations based on a commitment to the subject matter under investigation. Discovery is rooted in the conviction that there is something there to be found, and that my theory will then open up knowledge of hitherto undreamed possibilities about the subject matter. It is a 'faith seeking understanding' (to borrow the classic expression initially used to describe the task of theology!).

True knowledge, Polanyi then goes on to argue, arises through participation, or as he says, 'indwelling'. To give one example: I cannot tell you how to ride a bicycle: I know how only through doing – through participating. My feet 'indwell' the pedals which thus become an extension of myself for the purpose of riding. I am, however, only tacitly aware of the pedals. In fact if I concentrate on the pedals, I will fall off. But I use this tacit knowledge as part of my total knowledge of bicycle-riding which is a knowledge attained not by detachment, but by participation. The knowledge arrived at by scientific discovery is also, according to Polanyi, a knowledge by participation. His whole approach to the philosophy of science goes against what for several generations has been the 'paradigm' of scientific knowledge – namely 'knowledge by detachment'. This heritage from Descartes and the Enlightenment has actually been a blind alley which has resulted in the unfortunate dualistic splits in our culture between 'facts' and 'values', 'mind and body', 'reason and emotion', 'spirit and matter' and so on.

But 'scientific detachment' is a phoney ideal. All knowledge is personal knowledge, involving the personal participation of the person who knows. There is a 'community' between the person and his world. We are not gods, standing over the world with our superior rationality, nor are we at the mercy of something utterly incomprehensible. We are both part of the world, indwelling it, and also able to transcend it through our God-given powers of perception, imagination and reason.[25] We are of the dust and yet open to the word of God; part of the created order, and yet given the freedom of the Garden to explore, to enjoy, to use and to know.

Christian thinkers should well understand what Polanyi means by 'knowledge by participation'. This is the way the New Testament speaks of our knowing God. 'I know whom I have believed', writes St Paul.[26] It also speaks of our 'indwelling' – our being 'in Christ' and he 'in us'. True knowledge of God comes through commitment, trust and participation in him.

Indeed, the knowledge of God to which this little paragraph about the Man in the Garden points forward, becomes in the light of the New Testament gospel the characteristic form of Christian obedience – the obedience of faith in Christ, the Word of God. Once again Karl Barth expresses it well, in his discussion of the 'God whom we must fear above all things because we may love him above all things':

> Knowledge of God is in obedience to God. This obedience is not that of a slave, but of a child. It is not blind, but seeing. It is not coerced but free. For that very reason it is real obedience . . . God stands before man as the One who awakens, creates and sustains his faith . . . the knowledge that springs from this love will continually be real because it is itself from God.[27]

That faith is given and received in Jesus Christ. God is 'the source of your life in Christ Jesus,' writes St Paul, 'whom God made our wisdom'.[28]

It was a knowledge of God by participation, by mutual indwelling, the knowledge which comes through the obedience of faith, which Adam was to enjoy in the Garden. In fact, as we shall see, and know all too well, he sought rather a knowledge by detachment, a knowledge based on supposed human autonomy, a knowledge grasped through disobedience – and the results were disorder and death.

10. Tenancy, authority and fellowship

If the true relationship of human beings towards God is portrayed in terms of trusting obedience to his word, their true relationships towards the natural order are portrayed in terms of tenancy,

[25] Cf. C. Gunton, *Enlightenment and Alienation* (Marshall, Morgan and Scott, 1985), p. 48.   [26] 2 Tim. 1:12.
[27] *Church Dogmatics*, II/1, pp. 3f., 26ff.   [28] 1 Cor. 1:30.

67

towards other animals in terms of authority, and towards one another in terms of fellowship.

The tenancy we have already noted: man is the keeper of God's park. Now we need to look at his authority.

a. Not good alone

Then the LORD said, 'It is not good that the man should be alone; I will make him a helper fit for him.' ¹⁹So out of the ground the LORD God formed every beast of the field and every bird of the air, and brought them to the man to see what he would call them; and whatever the man called every living creature, that was its name. ²⁰The man gave names to all cattle, and to the birds of the air, and to every beast of the field; but for the man there was not found a helper fit for him. (2:18–20)

It is not good that the man should be alone (2:18). We have already mentioned the Velveteen Rabbit. That story is only one way of expressing the foundational truth about what it is to be human: that we are made for fellowship. One of the disastrous consequences of Enlightenment philosophy – despite all the good light that it shone on many questions – was its concentration on the individual as a centre of rational self-consciousness. The end of that road is the misery of the 'Me-generation'. Deep cracks open up in our culture, as we have seen, between facts and values, mind and body, reason and emotion, subject and object – and words like meaning, purpose, fellowship and community so easily fall through. Yet personal communion is what the image of God is about – and not only communion between Man and God, but between Man and the rest of his environment, especially his fellow human beings. The sense of isolation and of alienation of so much of contemporary society, where even families are often defined only by their sharing the same roof and the same television set while each pursues his or her detached and separate life, serve to underline this Genesis text: it is not good to be alone.

So the Lord God proposes to make *a helper fit for him* (2:18).

As we know, this comes to its fulfilment in the creation of the woman described in 2:21–22. But we need to pause here and ask what it means, for this phrase has sometimes been grossly misused, and treated as a charter for male domination over women.

The Hebrew phrase includes two words *ēzer kᵉnegdô*. The first of these, translated 'helper', implies someone who assists and encourages. 'Help' provides support for what is lacking in the one who needs help. It is a word that is used several times in the Old

Testament for the help which comes from God.[29] The 'helper' is then qualified by *keͤnegdô*, which seems to be related to the verb meaning 'to be plain or visible'. A related noun refers to an 'eminent' person. So perhaps 'helper fit for him' means 'a helper matching his eminence' or perhaps 'his distinctiveness'. It certainly points to one who is fit to stand before the man, opposite him, as his counterpart, companion and complement. There is no sense of inferiority, subordination or servitude implied here – rather it is one who is 'like him', but 'like opposite him' (to give a literal rendering). Advocates of male superiority and authority will have to find support somewhere other than Genesis 2.

However, before the 'helper to match his eminence' is found, there is a delay. Instead of one like the man, we are reminded that the Lord made cattle, birds and beasts, and they are brought before the man on a grand zoological parade.

b. Authority and naming

By giving names to the animals, Adam is doing two things. He is first recognizing the categories in which things come, bringing together what belongs together, discriminating between things that differ. He is thus beginning to order his world. Man the scientist is not too far away. He is also recognizing that this animal environment has been given to him by God – these too are God's creatures – and by bringing some order out of the confusion by allocating names, Adam is reflecting something of the image of God, which was described in chapter 1 as 'having dominion' over the rest of creation. But secondly, in the ancient world name-giving was an exercise in sovereignty. Adam is taking authority over the rest of the created order. The responsibility for stewardship in the natural order now extends to the animal world, and the man takes it on.

So this little episode causes the reader to pause, and ask what is happening. Were we not told that it was not good for man to be alone? Were we not expecting a helper to be provided? We know what is in the Lord's mind for the man. And now the man has to wait and come to terms first with his animal companions. Perhaps this is the way he realizes for himself that it is not good to be alone. Perhaps he himself is here learning to think about himself as God thinks about him. Gradually the animals pair off and move off, and Adam is left by himself. Now he, too, knows what God has known all along, that in the goodness of his creation, there is still a 'not good' to be remedied. The man now realizes that surely

[29] Cf. Ps. 33:20.

more is to come! Surely God must have something better even than the animals in mind?

So we are ready for the further action of God in verse 21: 'So the Lord . . .'.

c. Ishshah

So the LORD God caused a deep sleep to fall upon the man, and while he slept took one of his ribs and closed up its place with flesh; ²²*and the rib which the LORD God had taken from the man he made into a woman and brought her to the man.* ²³*Then the man said,*

> *'This at last is bone of my bones*
> *and flesh of my flesh;*
> *she shall be called Woman,*
> *because she was taken out of Man.'*

²⁴*Therefore a man leaves his father and his mother and cleaves to his wife, and they become one flesh.* ²⁵*And the man and his wife were both naked, and were not ashamed.*   (2:21–25)

Adam is put to sleep. 'God's miraculous creating permits no watching', as von Rad puts it. 'Man cannot perceive God "in the act", cannot observe his miracles in their genesis; he can revere God's creativity only as an actually accomplished fact.'

And so we are led to the climax of this chapter. God's word: 'It is not good that the man should be alone' is met by the provision of woman. God provides the man with one like him, but yet not like him, to be his counterpart. The incompleteness of the man without the woman is now satisfied by the gift of one from his side, to be at his side.

This is of course a crucial verse for understanding how the Bible thinks of marriage. It is quoted several times in the New Testament. We will explore a theology of marriage in a little while. But before we do, we must notice that it is personal intercommunion between the sexes which is what life in the Garden now seems to be all about. Men and women are personal beings who can delight in the presence of other persons.

Let us unpack this in a little more detail.

First, we notice how Adam greets the woman whom God brings to him as a father brings forward the bride: *'This at last is bone of my bones and flesh of my flesh'* (2:23). 'Bone of my bones' is the Hebrew expression which corresponds to our idiom 'blood relations'. Here is the closest human kinship, which 'sets man and woman on an equal footing as regards their humanity, yet sets them apart from the animals'.[30] There is also here a sense of satisfied relief that the waiting is over. God's provisions exactly fitted his need. The two were 'made for each other'. The ecstatic response is expressed poetically. There is a sense of delight and joyful embrace about the welcome. No wonder Barth was tempted to see the union of the sexes as a central part of the meaning of the image of God!

Secondly, as Matthew Henry has delightfully put it: 'Not made out of his head to top him, not out of his feet to be trampled upon by him, but out of his side to be equal with him, under his arm to be protected, and near his heart to be beloved.'[31]

Whatever the story of the Fall in Genesis 3 implies for the relationship between the sexes, Genesis 1 and 2 make the equality of men and women, women and men, as the image of God, unmistakably clear. The removal of a piece of the man in order to create the woman implies that from now on neither is complete without the other. The man needs the woman for his wholeness, and the woman needs the man for hers. Each is equal in need in relation to the other. Nothing could make clearer the complementarity and equality of the sexes.

How much this needs to be reasserted today, in contrast to asserted male supremacy in some quarters on the one hand, radical feminist insistence that there is no need for men at all on the other, and a refusal by some, especially in the gay liberation movements, even to take seriously at all the complementarity and mutuality of the sexes as part of a God-given order.

Thirdly, there is no basis for the assertion of female inferiority that some seek to find in the fact that Adam says, *'She shall be called Woman'* (2:23). Adam does not 'name' his wife Eve until Genesis 3:20. Here, he does not use the standard naming formula which he used for the animals. That formula includes the verb 'to call' and the noun 'name' – as in 2:19. It is used in 4:25: 'she bore a son and called his name Seth'. So Adam is not here pictured as exercising authority over his wife: this rather is a cry of delight and welcome. 'She shall be called *Ishshah*, because she was taken out of *Ish*.' These Hebrew words are the male and female counterparts of each other: another statement if any were needed of male-female complementarity and equality.

11. Creation and sexuality

We can now attempt to summarize what Genesis has so far told

---

[30] Wenham, p. 70.

[31] Matthew Henry, *Commentary on the Whole Bible* (Marshall, Morgan and Scott, 1961).

us concerning our sexuality. As we survey some themes from this ancient text, we will have in mind also the questions raised for us as Christians by the changing sexual patterns of our culture – partly in the rejection of marriage as a norm, and partly in the affirmation by increasing numbers of people of the homosexual life-style as an acceptable option for Christians. Our response to these will become clearer as we proceed.

First, all human beings have a value and preciousness as persons. The basic assumption of all our approaches to one another must be the fact that God has created us all to reflect his image. This must rebuke all condemning and judgmental discrimination against others, whether of race, creed, colour, or sexual orientation. The first thing we need to affirm about one another is our value as persons before God. Too often the single person in the church, or the person of homosexual orientation, the divorcee or the widow, have felt themselves to be pushed to the margins of the Christian fellowship, and at times simply excluded. In the light of the teaching of Genesis on the image of God, homophobia, rejection, ridicule and stereotyping must have no place in Christian relationships. Even where we may evaluate another's life-style to be incompatible with the Christian gospel, as some Christians do concerning remarriage after divorce, and some do concerning homosexual relationships, we need first to remember our Lord's words about logs and specks,[32] and that the divine image is not seen without distortion in any of us.

Secondly, Genesis 2 affirms body-life. We are embodied persons; our sexuality, which is indelibly related to our anatomy, is an integral part of who we are. We need therefore to remind ourselves that human beings come in two sorts. There is no category of 'person' which is separate from our embodiedness: we are either male persons or female persons. The distinction Jung draws between *animus* and *anima* (the masculine in the female and the feminine in the male) does not diminish the fundamental distinction within humanity between male and female. Humanity is, so to speak, bipolar – and we diminish something of the rich variety of God's creation, and we fail to acknowledge the importance of body-life, if we seek to minimize the importance of sexual complementarity. There are those who advocate what they call a 'personalist ethic', which attempts to concentrate on the person, without reference to gender. This is nearer to a gnostic separation of the 'soul' from the 'body', than to a Hebraic understanding of our nature as embodied souls and ensouled bodies.

Thirdly, these chapters affirm the importance of personal

32 Mt. 7:1–5.

72

relationships. It is not good that we should be alone. To a large degree we realize our personhood in mutual relationships. Just as the Being of God himself is personal communion within the Trinity, so to be in the image of God is to be in personal communion with other persons. Aloneness is not part of God's creation intention. Marriage, as we shall see, is one way in which personal communion with another person may be enjoyed, but as the life of our Lord himself illustrates, it is not the only way. The single life is not without the need or possibility of personal communion. In the Christian church we have not, however, made it easy for those who are not married, or who are no longer married, or indeed for those whose marriages are more struggle than joy, to find the richness of fellowship for which all of us are made, and which all of us need. One of the problems of those who find themselves unwillingly single is the failure of the church to be a community of friendship. One of the things we need to recover within the Christian community is the beauty and value of friendships both between the sexes and between members of the same sex. Our churches should be communities of friendship – to stand against all the ways in which our modern patterns of life and thinking push us into individualism and loneliness. We are made for fellowship, and whether in marriage and family, or in a life of celibacy, or community, we need to find ways of dealing with the fact that it is not good to be alone.

Fourthly, sexual complementarity is very far from being the same thing as male dominance and female subservience. The picture of Eden as we have illustrated repeatedly, is of equality, yet difference. For too long, Christian people have given way to a concept of patriarchal dominance in sexual relationships which is far from the divine intention. As we shall see, Genesis 3 gives us a picture of the ruling male and the struggling female – but that is a description of the distortions caused by sin. Genesis 1 and Genesis 2 speak of sexual equality, mutuality and joy in 'la différence'.

Fifthly, Genesis 2 describes the human person at many levels of life: physical, emotional, relational, spiritual. Our sexuality covers all of these. If it is true, as we shall see, that what we may call 'genitality' belongs within marriage, it is also true that people who are not married are not for that reason non-sexual persons. There is a sexual dimension to our affectionate relationships with men and women of the same and the opposite sex, which needs to find appropriate and creative expression, even when 'eroticization' is inappropriate.

Sixthly, Genesis 2 paints us a picture of sexual celebration, and the pleasure and fun of sexual love. 'This at last . . . ' in 2:23 gives a very strong hint of the joy of sex, picked up later in the Old

Testament by the delight of the bridegroom for his bride in the free eroticism of the Song of Songs, and the positive words about sexual delight in Proverbs 5:18–19. Although the Christian church often seems to have had trouble with sex, the Old Testament tells us that sexual relationships are good, to be rejoiced in and affirmed.

Finally, sex finds its meaning in the context of loving commitment. Over against, on the one hand the view of sex which robs it of all mystery, and sees it only as a technique for individual fulfilment and satisfaction, and on the other hand an over-romanticized view of sex which links it only to the realm of erotic feelings and fails to recognize the importance of the will in sexual love, the Bible places sexual relationships in the context of commitment. The delight of Genesis 2:23 is followed immediately by the narrator's comment in 2:24. It could not be said more clearly that marriage is the context of committed love in which the fully physical expression of sexual relationships is meant to belong.

12. Marriage

Therefore a man leaves his father and his mother and cleaves to his wife, and they become one flesh. (2:24)

The characteristic biblical understanding of marriage is 'covenant'. The interchange of analogies by which God's covenant with his people is expressed in marriage terms (*cf.* Hosea), and by which the relationship of husband and wife is to be patterned on God's relationship with his people[33] can be traced throughout the Old Testament – and underlies much of the marriage teaching in the New Testament.[34]

A covenant begins with a promise from one partner to another; it involves the acceptance of that promise by the other; the giving and receiving of promises is publicly known and publicly acknowledged in some covenant sign; and then this external legal covenant framework becomes the context in which a relationship based on these promises begins to grow. The covenant thus has an external social and legal framework, and an internal heart centred on personal relationship.

The marriage covenant, likewise, has a social, external, legal dimension: marriage is not simply a private arrangement between two people – a marriage begins a new social arrangement in which they accept some accountability as a couple to their wider society. But the centre of the marriage covenant is the personal relationship

---

[33] Mal. 2:14.   [34] *Cf.* Eph 5:21ff.

of committed love: 'Either was the other's Mine'.[35] It is a relationship which ideally grows and changes and matures in time. Marriage can thus become the context in which many of the words which are true of God's relationship with his covenant people (steadfast love, faithfulness, forgiveness, sacrifice, patience, blessing, healing) can become true in the covenant between a husband and wife. As Jack Dominian helpfully shows in *Marriage, Faith and Love*, a good marriage is to be the context in which each can be to the other a means by which each receives sustenance, healing and growth in maturity.[36]

Our Genesis text illustrates three of the legs on which the marriage covenant stands – and like a milk-maid's three-legged stool, each leg is important: leaving, cleaving and 'one flesh'.

'Leaving' points to the establishment of a new family unit. Not only must the emotional and psychological security within a marriage require an emotional as well as a physical separation from father and mother, but the new marriage is established in a publicly known way. There is to be no question but that this particular man who has left father and mother is now married to this particular woman and not another. The marriage covenant relationship is set in a social institution. This is why the ceremony is important – why we should 'bother with the piece of paper'. Such social constraints can act as supports for the personal relationships which, in the harder times, may be difficult to sustain without such social accountability.

'Cleaving' is the covenant-faithfulness word. This is the central concept of covenant fidelity. It points to the committed faithfulness that one promises to the other; that whatever the future holds, the couple intend to face it as a pair. This is the sense behind the old word 'troth'. Troth, as Olthuis comments,[37] is 'the moral expression of love'. 'Fidelity' seems these days to have a rather negative ring to it. It too often amounts merely to 'putting a leash on lust'. But the concept is very positive, creative and dynamic. It covers at least the following levels (to follow the exposition of this in Lewis Smedes' splendid book, *Sex in the Real World*).[38]

1. *Faithfulness to a vow.* Married life is sustained by willing choice. It is an intention that for better or worse, the partners will not let circumstances or fate determine the future of their relationship. Marriage is built on more than romantic feelings. Faithfulness to a vow can mean that, even in the troubled times when eros

[35] Shakespeare, *The Phoenix and the Turtle*. Cf. Song 2:16; 6:3.
[36] J. Dominian, *Marriage, Faith and Love* (Darton, Longman and Todd, 1981).
[37] James Olthuis, *I Pledge You My Troth* (Harper and Row, 1975).
[38] L. Smedes, *Sex in the Real World* (Lion Publishing, 1982).

75

has apparently burned out, it can, with the right will, be revived.

2. *Faithfulness to a calling.* Against the romantic view which sees marriage only as an intimate relationship chosen for personal fulfilment, and against the institutional view which sees marriage as merely a social status, we need to revive the sense that marriage is a calling to be lived before God, open to the resources of his grace, and a means by which his covenant love can be displayed.

3. *Faithfulness to a person.* Faithfulness is not to be based just on function: a staying together for the sake of appearances. 'Cleaving' is essentially a person-directed word, and faithfulness involves a positive commitment to the freedom and maturity and growth of the other person.

4. *Faithfulness to a relationship.* As Lewis Smedes puts it: 'At the beating heart of any marriage is the delicate, fragile, often painful but potentially joyful relationship of two persons face to face in personal encounter.' It is a commitment to allow the grace of God, through all the changes and chances, through all the joys and sorrows, to create in the relationship of these two people an image of his covenant of love. As we have said before, God himself is Being in Communion. The marriage relationship is intended to reflect something of him.

One flesh is the third leg on which the marriage covenant stands. It refers to the personal union of man with woman, woman with man, at all levels of their lives, which is expressed in and deepened through the sexual relationship. 'One flesh' does not only mean sexual intercourse, though it includes it. But it refers to that oneness which – initially in intention, and gradually more and more a reality through time – marks a good marriage relationship. Sexual intercourse is thus given a meaning: it is meant to express, consolidate and deepen the 'one flesh' union of man and wife, as they grow more and more together in a relationship which expresses something of God.

More than that, 'one flesh' may also point to the link between sexuality and creativity which brings marriage and family life together. For the 'one flesh' relationship of husband and wife can issue in the one flesh of their child. By linking the marriage covenant to the family in this way, we can see the divine intention that the family is the context in which children are to be brought up by, and not just begotten by, their parents. In other words, the marriage and family interrelationship of Genesis 2:24 is the divinely intended pattern in which the creation command of Genesis 1:27–28 ('Be fruitful and multiply') is intended to be fulfilled.

While, therefore, a primary purpose of human sexual relationship is the *unitive* purpose of expressing and deepening personal communion between the marriage partners, a further purpose is the *procreative* one of building a family. Husband and wife are to be *procreative* – 'creative on behalf of' God, in whom love and creativity belong together. The unitive and the procreative aspects of human sexual relationship thus also belong together.

There are several implications we can draw from all this:

First, if the 'unitive' and 'procreative' aspects to human sexual relationships belong in principle together, we need to be careful of practices which separate them. Some Christians, particularly in the Roman Catholic tradition, believe that this rules out all contraception. This does not seem to follow. It seems perfectly possible that a marriage is intended to be a context in which love and creativity belong together, that a marriage indeed is open to parenthood, without requiring that every sexual act must be 'open to the transmission of life'. Indeed, by far the more important focus in Genesis 2 is the unitive aspect of the marriage relationship. It is only when this is right that the couple can decide on the way their particular responsibility for the continuance of the species (which was indicated in Genesis 1:28) should be exercised. Responsible parents can surely be grateful for the benefits of contraception, without separating procreativity from love. However, there are other practices, such as Artificial Insemination by a Donor, or Embryo Transfer, not to mention surrogate motherhood, which separate procreative activity completely from the love-relationship of husband and wife. These do not seem possible to justify on the basis of the theology of sexuality we have outlined.

Secondly, in the light of the above, we can now see more clearly why the Christian tradition has reserved sexual intercourse for the one context of heterosexual marriage. For sex to symbolize a covenant commitment, and to deepen a relationship of faithful love, it needs a context of consistency and reliability – that is permanence. Sex without relationship, as in pornography, or sex in transient relationships, falls short of the meaning which the sexual union is meant to carry. Indeed, St Paul goes further and says that even consorting with a prostitute is to engage in an action which is meant to express a permanent 'one flesh' relationship.[39]

Thirdly, in the light of this, we can now see why the Christian tradition has never felt able to affirm homosexual relationships. The not-good of the Creator that man should be alone is met by the provision of the woman to complete and complement him.

God's mind regarding human sexuality is most clearly seen in what he did. He provided the isolated Adam with a helper like-opposite him in the person not of another man, nor a child, nor a beast, but of *Ishshah*, the Woman. Heterosexuality is part of the

[39] 1 Cor. 6:12f.

givenness of God's creation. It celebrates the 'otherness' of the opposite sex. Male and female complementarity – however hard it is to find ways of expressing this – is part of the way things are. That, at least, is the understanding of Genesis 2. Add to this the link that is forged between heterosexuality and procreation, and it is hard to see how sexual homosexual relationships can be affirmed as anything other than a falling short of the divine pattern.

The consistent biblical witness is that all sexual relationships outside the context of heterosexual marriage fall short of God's intention. We cannot, therefore, endorse the view that homosexuality is simply something 'natural'. Indeed, it is to the 'naturalness' of the *creation* pattern that St Paul appeals in Romans 1 where he gives the example of homosexual relationships as one among several illustrations of a society which has abandoned the ways of God. We must, however, recognize the extreme difficulty in which this often places the Christian who finds that his or her sexual preferences are directed to members of the same sex. We must make a distinction between a homosexual orientation (for which a person must be helped to refuse to carry any burden of guilt), and homosexual intercourse which comes within the arena of responsible choice. We must reject the homophobia which has too often tended to label everything homosexual as a self-chosen perversion, and repent of the pain which this has caused to countless homosexual people. We need to recover a sense of common human justice in which issues of civil rights for homosexual people can be addressed on the basis of their humanity in the image of God, and not on the basis of sexual morality. (If sexual morality were the criterion for granting civil rights, where would many heterosexual people be?) We need to find ways of celebrating friendships between people of the same and of the opposite sex. Some would also wish to regard a committed loving homosexual relationship at a certain stage in a person's life journey as a 'least detrimental alternative' – and surely preferable to a life of sexual chaos, and in practical terms, certainly in the face of AIDS, that may well be so. But from Genesis 2 we are not at liberty simply to affirm homosexual relationships as an alternative to heterosexuality. To do so is to fly in the face of the consistent witness of biblical theology and Christian tradition.

The Bible offers us two life-styles in which, as sexual beings, we may hold together something of the love and creativity of God: celibacy and heterosexual marriage. Celibacy, as the life of our Lord illustrates, sets a person free to develop creative friendships of love within the community, in which the affective dimensions of our sexuality can find full and appropriate expression. Heterosexual marriage provides a context of loving intimacy in which the genital dimensions of a person's sexuality can also be given appropriate expression, in commitment to one other person, enhanced in many cases by parenthood.

13. Naked and unashamed

The story in Genesis 2 closes by telling us that the man and the woman in the Garden were naked and not ashamed. There was between them an openness and a unity, not masked by guilt, not disordered by lust, not hampered by shame. We must assume that our author wished to stress this fact here to throw into sharp relief the reality of shame in human relationships of which we are soon to read in chapter 3.

The sad truth is, of course, that all our sexuality in its heterosexual and homosexual forms is now disordered. Sexual relationships are sometimes marked more by fear than fellowship or fun; our sexual fantasies and temptations get out of hand; sexuality becomes a context for guilt. Increasingly often sexuality can be the vehicle not for love but for human destructiveness and degradation. And now, for perhaps the first time, since the advent of AIDS, we have to face the frightening paradox, and the new questions that are posed by it, that the life-giving power of sex can also be the bearer of death.

And not our sexuality only: every aspect of what it means to be a person made in the divine image is now fractured and out of line. The glory, beauty and freedom of the Garden is not a reality of the world we know. We have eaten of the Tree, and all our senses are awry. The authority of the man over the rest of the created order is now tainted with exploitative selfishness. His relationship to the rest of the animal kingdom is as much that of cruelty as of companionship. His human relationships are all askew; his aloneness is still part of the story and it is still 'not good'. The picture of sexual freedom and joy can now only be held out as an ideal towards which we tremblingly aspire. For the tragedy of the story is that God's risk in creating human beings in freedom was that their freedom would be expressed in disobedience. The alienation between people and their God, their environment and each other, is a fact of the world as we know and experience it. Or, to use Tillich's phrase, the 'universal tragic estrangement' between God and his creation is part of the risk God took when he created the world with the possibility of man's Fall. Why he did it this way is a question we ultimately have to leave within the mystery of God. What is inescapably clear, however, is that Genesis 2 can only ever now be read from our side of Genesis 3.

B. ADAM, WHERE ARE YOU? (3:1-24)

If the picture of the Garden given us in Genesis 2 comes to us reflected, as it were, in a clear and unspoiled mirror, in Genesis 3 that mirror is shattered into a thousand pieces. Each little piece still reflects something of the earlier beauty, but now the picture is fragmented, the perspectives are distorted, it is hard to see things whole. The world seen through the broken glass of chapter 3 is no longer a normal world. Everything is ambiguous; nothing is any more 'very good'.

By showing us how Genesis 2 and 3 belong inseparably together, the author is exposing and exploring this ambiguity: the wonder of human life, and yet its tragedy; the richness of its life, and yet its death; the joy of human fellowship but always covered by shame; and the word of the Creator God now heard as cursing instead of blessing. This chapter probes these questions to their roots in the very mystery of God himself.

1. The snake

Now the serpent was more subtle than any other wild creature that the Lord *God had made. He said to the woman, 'Did God say, "You shall not eat of any tree of the garden"?' ²And the woman said to the serpent, 'We may eat of the fruit of the trees of the garden; ³but God said, "You shall not eat of the fruit of the tree which is in the midst of the garden, neither shall you touch it, lest you die." ' ⁴But the serpent said to the woman, 'You will not die. ⁵For God knows that when you eat of it your eyes will be opened, and you will be like God, knowing good and evil.'*   (3:1-5)

Genesis 3 begins with the temptation experienced by the woman and the man not to trust God.

By some inscrutable providence, the voice of temptation comes to the human person from outside himself, yet from within the created order. It is in God's Garden that evil is to be found! Within the structures of the created world, within the fabric of a universe which in terms of physical science is described by some scientists as the weaving together of chance and necessity, within a Garden in which God himself was prepared to take the risk of human freedom, we now read of something evil. And human beings are faced with the question of their responsible choice. Part of the freedom of the Garden is the freedom not to trust God. Once that course is taken, as the story of chapter 3 will make clear, it is a choice against every other freedom which is ours in fellowship with

God. The freedom not to trust God becomes the doorway to the loss of freedom itself. And the human being is faced with that choice by the tempting voice of the snake.

The snake has often been taken as a symbol for the devil – the Book of Revelation speaks of the devil as that 'ancient serpent'[40] and it well may be that in Genesis some supernatural evil stands behind the voice of the tempting snake. An author who is at home in the world of cherubim with flaming swords would not have difficulty with the belief expressed much more clearly elsewhere in the Bible that there is a power of evil within the world which is at war with God. It is not only in animistic cultures where devil-worship maintains its stranglehold over people's lives. There are witches' covens in London and Birmingham, Satan-worshippers in suburbia, tarot cards on many a middle-class mantelpiece, and ouija boards in the toy shops. And for every one for whom such activities are seemingly harmless fun, there is another whose mental health has been disturbed, whose relationships have been disrupted, and whose way into the peace and joy of Christ has been strewn with demonic garbage.

Many churches find that their pastors at some time or another are called on to minister to those oppressed by occult powers, and the Christian ministry of deliverance proclaims the power and victory of Christ over 'the principalities and powers' in the heavenly places.[41]

The demonic is found not only in the weird and the occult – but also in the paralysing systems of destructive power in society, in the slanderous world of lies,[42] deceit and doing the other down which is so prevalent in our decaying culture, in the blame-shifting, the aggressiveness and the law of retaliation and revenge which so disfigures much of our international life. It is seen also, according to St Paul, in dissension and falsehood in the Christian church.[43] Satan, as the book title says, is 'alive and well' on planet earth.[44]

But the snake does not appear as the devil to the woman. The voice of temptation does not come as the voice of evil. If Satan is present in the story of Genesis 3, he is wearing a careful mask. He is hidden in the ordinariness and the everydayness of a creature in the Garden.

The snake does not feature in this story as the cause of human failure, but as that which faces human beings with the reality of their trust in God.

From other parts of the biblical witness we may wish to identify

---

[40] Rev. 20:2.   [41] Col. 2:15.
[42] Cf. M. Scott Peck, People of the Lie (Harper and Row, 1986).
[43] 2 Cor. 11:12–13.
[44] Hal Lindsay and C. C. Carlson, Satan is Alive and Well (Zondervan, 1983).

the Tempter's voice with that of God's satanic adversary, and indeed in the imagery of the Garden in Genesis 3, the picture is of a voice from outside the human pair: there is an objective evil world. Yet this chapter also quickly cautions us against shifting responsibility for human failure away from ourselves. In fact, our constant tendency to find causes for our sin from elsewhere than in our own heart is a tendency first seen in the woman's reply to the snake.

So we need to be clear what this story is saying, and avoid asking it questions which it does not address. It refuses to ask the question: How did evil come into the world?

When we are faced with suffering and disappointment, when we hear of wars and rumours of wars, when hundreds die in a tidal wave, thousands in a famine, millions in a gas chamber; when bad things happen to good people, and the wicked seem to flourish; when God seems to allow us to develop the wonders of technology to put people in space, but does not prevent a frozen rubber ring on the rocket boosters from exploding the whole enterprise to pieces; when we fail an exam, or lose our job, or are unjustly trapped in 'the system'; then our hearts cry out to God: Why? why? Why has God forsaken us? Why does God let it happen? Why such evil in the world? Where does it come from?

Christians always know that such questions pose the greatest threats to our belief in the goodness of God. And we look for reasons to explain why things are as they are. We blame human free will – and the wrong choices people make, or perhaps try to shift the blame on to our background, or our genes, or our grandparents. Or we put the responsibility out on to Satan and his demonic hosts of evil. Or perhaps we blame God himself: if he is all goodness, he could not have wanted this disorder; if he is all powerful, surely he could have prevented it.

But Genesis 3 will not help us with our searching for causes. It does not tell us where evil comes from. It will not allow us to pin everything on some external cause. The snake simply faces us with the question of our own responsibility, and the response we make to the word of God. The origin of evil is left within the mystery of God.

2. The anatomy of temptation

Temptation begins to take root in the woman's heart. The serpent began the conversation in the seemingly harmless terms of a discussion about God. The serpent does not deny the goodness of God, he simply sows small seeds of mistrust. The serpent is not paraded as embodied evil: that we should recognize and turn from.

It simply moves from the woman's knowledge of God's goodness to cause doubt about the one prohibition God has given for human freedom. It does so by twisting, ever so slightly, the word which embodied a gift of freedom (2:16) to tinge it with a sense of God's meanness: 'Did God say you shall not eat of *any* of the trees?' If God is really as bountiful as we have come to believe, if God really cares for our welfare, surely he would not deny us this small thing which looks good for food and which is a delight for the eyes. God knows we need food. God wants us to delight in his world. Surely he cannot have meant to forbid this one thing?

When we have started down that road, we have already gone too far. God had forbidden man to eat of this fruit – he had as it were set a fence around this one area of life as a boundary for human obedience and therefore human welfare, and freedom. Once we have opened a discussion with the Tempter as to what God really meant, we have placed ourselves in a situation where escape is very difficult. As Helmut Thielicke writes:

> Significantly, the Lord's Prayer teaches us the petition: 'Lead us not into temptation; do not even allow us to get into the critical situation in the first place.' Significantly, the petition does not read: 'Lead us *out of* temptation' (once we are in it): but rather, 'Lead us *not into* temptation.' Once we are near the tree, our pulse begins to stir, curiosity flares up, and passions are aroused. In such a situation, our ability to make decisions is paralyzed.[45]

Temptation begins with trivia. How can it be that so great a fall can begin with so small an incident? One piece of forbidden fruit! – surely the whole world will not fall apart for such a trivial thing? And yet so often our spiritual health and destiny does depend on the one thing in our lives which blocks our way to God. For each of us, the God who gives us all things richly to enjoy, also asks of us that we trust him. The serpent touches the woman at the one small, trivial point in her life where she was not ready to give everything over to God. The serpent touches us at the one thing in our lives where we would rather God did not trouble us. We will give him everything else, but we will hold this one part of life to ourselves.

Thielicke puts it so well:

> But that's the way it is; that's the way it really is – in your life and in mine. The fact is that all of us have sectors in the territory of our life which we are quite content to leave to God. But each

---

[45] Thielicke, p. 130.

83

of us also has a point which we will by no means let God approach. This point may be my ambition whereby I am determined to beat my way to success in my career at any price. It may be my sexuality to which I am determined to give rein no matter what happens and no matter what it costs. It may be a bottomless hatred toward one of my fellow men which I literally nurse and which gives me a kind of sensual pleasure which then comes between me and God and robs me of my peace. God can have everything, *but not this one thing!*[46]

Some habit, some possession, some secret sin, some bitter resentment – in the context of our whole life, it seems so small, and yet it is at that one point that our trust in God is tested. If we will not let God be God at this one small, trivial, yet so crucial a point, then we really do not trust him where it matters at all. 'No, there is no escape,' writes George MacDonald. 'There is no heaven with a little of hell in it – no plan to retain this or that of the devil in our hearts or our pockets. Out Satan must go, every hair and feather.'[47]

The serpent's temptation to the woman was that she should doubt God's word. It seemed in the context so unreasonable that God should have made this one small prohibition. The serpent sets her faith and trust over against her common sense, and forces a gap between them through which he will soon drive a coach and horses. In the Garden of chapter 2, there is of course no gap between faith and reason – for reasoning faith holds on to God in obedience to his word, even when that word is mysterious. Reasoning faith acknowledges that in the space between heaven and earth, there are secret things which belong to the Lord. Reasoning faith looks up in gratitude to the Creator, knowing that as the heavens are higher than the earth, so are the Lord's ways higher than ours, his thoughts than our thoughts. Reasoning faith knows God by committed trust in him, by participation in his life, by sharing his fellowship, by experiencing his love. But the serpent puts all this in question. By enticing Eve with the prospect of knowing as God knows – knowing good and evil – the serpent creates a doubt about the boundaries of her creaturely knowledge.

And the woman, dropping the intimate divine name, 'Yahweh', and referring simply to the perhaps more distant 'God', catches something of the serpent's suggestion. She herself then adds to what God had said (often as sinfully dangerous as taking away![48]) in 2:16, in words that make God seem just a little bit harsh: '*You*

---

[46] Thielicke, p. 134.
[47] Quoted by C. S. Lewis on the title page of *The Great Divorce*.
[48] *Cf.* Rev. 22:18–19.

shall not eat of the fruit of the tree . . . neither shall you touch it, *lest you die'* (3:3).

The snake now pushes her just a little further by questioning even the certainty of death: 'Not *certainly* die?' (3:4; *cf.* Wenham). With her emotions stimulated (*a delight to the eyes*), and her intellect appealed to (*desired to make one wise*) in 3:6, she wonders whether, perhaps, after all, there is not a way to satisfying knowledge which can be had by way of detachment from God and his word; a knowledge by which I can assess God's claim on my life; a knowledge which marks out some neutral grounds to stand on where I can judge God and assess his usefulness to me.

But once I have moved there, I have in fact already abandoned trust. I have begun to separate myself from the possibility of true knowledge by participation. I have detached myself from the source of truth and life.

In Erik Erikson's model of the growth of personal identity in a child, the most basic and most critical phase of childhood development is that in which the child experiences or fails to experience 'basic trust'.[49] Is the infantile environment of parental care sufficiently good for the child to be able to develop the capacity to trust? Basic mistrust is the tap root of disorders through all the other critical phases of emotional and relational development. That certainly is the picture here. The Tempter moves from casting doubt on God's trustworthiness (*'Did God say . . . ?'*) to casting doubt on the truth of his word (*'You will not die'*). This disparagement of the character of God is the tap root of all the disorders which follow in the story. From then on temptation gave way to disobedient action. Then Adam and Eve experienced the power of wrong in their lives. Their eyes were opened. Then they knew something of good and evil. Knowledge of good, as Milton said 'bought dear by knowing ill'.[50] They were going to have to face God in a different light. Then they knew their nakedness.

3. The anatomy of sin

So when the woman saw that the tree was good for food, and that it was a delight to the eyes, and that the tree was to be desired to make one wise, she took of its fruit and ate; and she also gave some to her husband, and he ate. [7]Then the eyes of both were opened, and they knew that they were naked; and they sewed fig leaves together and made themselves aprons.

[8]And they heard the sound of the LORD God walking in the garden in the cool of the day, and the man and his wife hid

[49] E. Erikson, *Childhood and Society* (Triad, 1977).   [50] *Paradise Lost*, II.

themselves from the presence of the LORD *God among the trees of the garden.* [9]*But the* LORD *God called to the man, and said to him, 'Where are you?'* [10]*And he said, 'I heard the sound of thee in the garden, and I was afraid, because I was naked; and I hid myself.'* [11]*He said, 'Who told you that you were naked? Have you eaten of the tree of which I commanded you not to eat?'* [12]*The man said, 'The woman whom thou gavest to be with me, she gave me fruit of the tree, and I ate.'* [13]*Then the* LORD *God said to the woman, 'What is this that you have done?' The woman said, 'The serpent beguiled me, and I ate.'* (3:6–13)

a. Obedience gives way to rebellion

Whereas God's intention was that his human partners should grow up in their knowledge of him on the basis of trusting obedience, they chose to grow on the basis of rebellion and protest.

The artist draws us a picture of the woman standing, pensive before the tree, wondering what to decide. Verse 6 comes at the centre point of this whole narrative (2:4 – 3:24) – it marks the crucial moment in the story.

Then, as von Rad comments, with it 'we rush through an entire scale of emotions'.[51] The coarse sensuality of 'good for food', the aesthetic pleasure in 'a delight to the eyes', the intellectual enticement 'was to be desired to make one wise' find a New Testament parallel in 1 John 2:16: 'the lust of the flesh and the lust of the eyes and the pride of life'. So she saw, she took, she ate, she gave. Perhaps, as Wenham indicates, there are even suggestions here in the choice of verbs that the woman is usurping the prerogative of God, for the last time we read 'He saw that it *was good*', the subject was God. Here it is the woman, who 'saw that the tree *was good*'. It was God who 'took' the man and the rib in chapter 2 (vv. 15, 21–23): here the woman does the 'taking'.[52]

She who has been led astray now becomes the source of temptation to her partner. He becomes associated with her in wrong, and indeed his is the 'last and decisive act of disobedience'.[53]

One of the easiest paths from temptation to sin is the path of instant gratification. 'She saw . . . she took . . . ' The path of obedience tells us to make space in the light of God's truth to reflect on what we 'see' so temptingly; to bring our wishes into line with what we know of the love and beauty of God; and to delay gratification until we are clear what it is that God is asking of us. The way of rebellion puts immediate pleasure in front of possible consequences, and sets our own perceptions of what is

[51] Von Rad, p. 87.   [52] *Cf.* Wenham, p. 75.   [53] Wenham, p. 76.

good for us against what God has told us about ourselves and his world. Sin is the name given to that separation from God which begins with the abandonment of trust in God's goodness and God's love.

b. Openness gives way to shame

In 2:25 we read that the man and his wife were naked and unashamed. By 3:7 there is shame – that sense of unease with yourself at the heart of your being. Not being able to be comfortable with yourself as you are, and therefore not being comfortable in the presence of another: that is shame.

In verse 8 we read of the Lord God taking an early evening stroll around the Garden. 'Maybe a daily chat between the Almighty and his creatures was customary.'[54] Here again is an intimacy between God and his world – this is the communion of creation. Yet, instead of being there to enjoy God's fellowship in openness and comfort, the man and the woman are hiding with shame.

Bonhoeffer writes:

When the one accepts the other as the companion given to him by God, where he is content with understanding himself as beginning from and ending in the other and in belonging to him, man is not unashamed. In the unity of unbroken obedience man is naked in the presence of man, uncovered, revealing both body and soul, and yet he is not ashamed. Shame only comes into existence in the world of division.[55]

And yet our world has become a world of division. Not only are we divided from one another, but we are divided from ourselves. One of the key underlying features of much of the anxiety and depression which keeps the world of psychotherapy and counselling so fully occupied is the loss of a sense of self-esteem. People feel worthless and thus hopeless; they do not hear the strong word of loving affirmation: 'Made as the Image of God!' They write firmly on their videos and stereos as a mark of quality and a statement of approval, 'Made in England'. But they cannot bear the mark of the much greater affirmation 'Made as the Image of God'! They dislike themselves, and perceive that others dislike them too. They want to make aprons to cover themselves, and hide behind the trees of the garden to escape. They are not comfortable just being them. They are ashamed.

Now we must be careful not to link all personal shame to

[54] Wenham, p. 76.   [55] Bonhoeffer, p. 63.

particular personal sin. The Book of Job tells of depression in one who was righteous. Several times in the New Testament we are warned not to link a person's suffering with their own sins.[56] Sometimes, of course, personal wrongdoing is the cause of a person's shame, but often the lack of self-worth stems rather from other people's sins. As the anatomy of sin is unfolded through the pages of the Bible, we see how the sins of the fathers are visited on the children – how broken relationships in families and societies can contribute to personal disorder and a low sense of personal worth. But shame is an all too common part of personal life: it is a symptom of the fact that it is no longer 'very good' in the Garden.

c. Responsible living gives way to guilt

Now the Lord God is depicted as the Judge calling, as it were in court, for an explanation: *The LORD God called to the man* (3:9).

We have to accept responsibility for our choices. Of course the person who chooses is constrained by all sorts of determinants, personal and social. There are things we cannot choose to do at all. We cannot choose to fly, for example, because we are limited by our body structure. Our choices may also be limited by our genetic make-up, by our early learning experiences, by our social environment and so on. I am who I am to some degree because of who my parents were, and what I learned of life from them. And my choices may therefore be limited. But I still have the freedom to choose at what points I will accept their teaching, collude with it, confront it, or modify it for my own. I am responsible within limits for the choices I make. I cannot shift blame for my mistakes off on to my genes or my parents. I cannot evade my responsibilities, as did Adam, by blaming Eve – as did Eve, by blaming the serpent. Blame-shifting is one of the most common mechanisms for avoiding responsibility – and its constant travelling companion is guilt.

We use the word 'guilt' in a number of different ways. The Jewish philosopher Martin Buber identifies three, which he calls 'civic' guilt, 'subjective' guilt and 'existential' guilt. By civic guilt, he means our status as a wrongdoer before the civic law. If I travel at 71 m.p.h. down a motorway I am a wrongdoer in the eyes of the law, and am guilty, whether I feel so or not. By subjective guilt, Buber means the guilty feeling of which we are all too well aware. When I believe myself to be in the wrong relationship to someone or something to whom or to which I am under some obligation, then I may be aware of feelings of unease, of anxiety

---

[56] Jn. 9:1–3; Lk. 13:2ff.

or of pain which weight me down, cloud my judgment and blacken my mind.

It is, of course, possible to be guilty without feeling guilty – we can so blunt our consciences that the pains of true guilt are soothed away.

It is also possible to feel guilty when we are not guilty. Much of the neurotic guilt of people seeking therapeutic help is at the level of wrong guilty feelings deriving from a false view of themselves or of their situation. Even some Christian churches seem quite skilled at times at evoking inappropriate feelings of guilt! Sometimes preachers motivate their congregations by trading on their capacity to feel guilty. Sadly, all too often, such practices engage with people whose emotional state is predisposed to wrong subjective guilt-feelings, when what such people need to hear first are words of acceptance, grace and love. The New Testament does not support a 'guilt-motivation' which focuses on the self, dwells on the feelings, and is ultimately destructive. While recognizing that 'sin . . . dwells within me',[57] it speaks more of a 'godly sorrow' for sin, which focuses on God and our neighbour,[58] and is directed towards constructive change and positive growth. We need to beware of exploiting the guilty feelings of others.

Thirdly, Buber talks about existential guilt, by which he means the true moral guilt, whether we acknowledge it or not, of our estranged relationship with God. We are no longer in fellowship with our Creator in the unspoiled beauty of the Garden. We have abandoned responsible sonship by failing to choose the way of obedience. Now the sound of the Lord God walking in the Garden in the cool of the day is no longer received with joy that the Lord is seeking our fellowship, but as threat. We evade our responsibilities by shifting blame. We take refuge behind the trees from the presence of the Lord God. We tremble with fear when we hear his call: *'Where are you?'*

Acknowledgment of our true moral guilt before God, and acceptance of our personal responsibilities, is part of the journey towards the 'godly sorrow' which leads to forgiveness, restoration and growth. From Freud onwards, too much of the world of psychotherapy has refused to take moral guilt seriously. It has operated with a view of human nature based either on the determinism of biological instincts, or the social control of behavioural stimuli. More recently this deterministic, or 'medical', model of human disorder has been challenged within the world of psychiatry and psychotherapy. Many authors, notably Karl Menninger in *What-*

[57] Ro. 7:17–20.
[58] *Cf.* S. B. Narramore, *No Condemnation* (Zondervan, 1984).

89

ever Became of Sin?, and O. Hobart Mowrer in *The Crisis in Psychiatry and Religion*[59] have opened the way for a challenge to the medical model, and the acceptance of a more fully personal (and that includes moral) model instead. For we are not machines; we are persons with all the ambiguity that involves. We are made to be the image of God, with a task and a destiny before us, with the capacity for choice and for responsibility. We are also naked, ashamed and guilty before God and before our neighbours. There is a moral flaw in our nature for which we can be held to account.

d. Freedom gives way to bondage

The man and the woman now have nowhere to move. God has not come round the Garden to spy out their nakedness, but to enjoy his creation. He wants their fellowship. He wants to enjoy their freedom. But they are in hiding, with no way out. The trees which were meant as the context for their freedom ('You may freely eat of every tree', 2:16) are now the context of a cover-up. The park becomes a prison. They are trapped in their shame and their guilt.

Sin sometimes traps us so that there are no ways open to us which are good. The sins of the fathers are sometimes visited on the children, who then become trapped in patterns of behaviour or emotional response or even in physical conditions which dog them through their lives. The family tree becomes a tree of disorder, passed from one generation to another. What Pincus and Dare call 'Secrets in the Family' can be destructive and imprisoning secrets, habits and attitudes which powerfully dominate our lives.[60]

How different the Garden seems now from the picture drawn in chapter 2. Where is the man, God's estate manager, his park keeper? Where is the man with authority to name the animals? Where is the delight in the sexual embrace as woman is introduced to man? Where is the human being made to be the image of God? Where is the human person made to share the joy and rest of the seventh day in the worship and adoration of his Creator?

'Adam, where are you?' – Naked, rebellious, ashamed, guilty, shifting blame, afraid and hiding behind the trees.

'What sort of freak, then, is man!' says Pascal. 'How novel, how monstrous, how chaotic, how paradoxical, how prodigious! Judge of all things, feeble earthworm, repository of truth, sink of doubt and error, glory and refuse of the universe!'[61] – He needs clothing, peace, affirmation, forgiveness, love and a welcome back home.

[59] K. Menninger, *Whatever Became of Sin?* (Bantam, New York, 1978), and O. H. Mowrer, *The Crisis in Psychiatry and Religion* (Van Nostrand, New York, 1961).   [60] L. Pincus and C. Dare, *Secrets in the Family* (London, 1978).
[61] Blaise Pascal, *Pensées* VII: 'Contradictions'.

How good (in every sense of that word) that we are able to read Genesis 3 through the eyes of the New Testament. For there, as shown most clearly by St Paul, we learn that although being 'in Adam', the representative head of humanity under the power of sin, keeps us in the thraldom of death, much more does being 'in Christ', the representative Head of a new humanity born from the gift of grace, give us the freedom once more to *live*.[62]

How good that we are told of someone who stands in the breach as a Mediator with a word of Good News. The clothing of his righteousness, the acceptance, forgiveness, love and peace of his gospel, and the power of his resurrection, bring life back to the dead. Through Christ, the second Adam, life can begin again. Through him, the way can be opened again to the tree of life. Through him we can know our Creator once more as our Father, and in the fellowship of his Body can begin again to be made whole. For the word 'Where are you?' is not only a word of judgment; it is primarily a word of love. The Father looks out for his son and welcomes him back to the feast.

But that is to move ahead. Genesis 3 has yet harsher things to say first.

4. The anatomy of estrangement

The LORD God said to the serpent,

> 'Because you have done this,
>   cursed you are above all cattle,
>   and above all wild animals;
> upon your belly you shall go,
>   and dust you shall eat
>   all the days of your life.
> [15] I will put enmity between you and the woman,
>   and between your seed and her seed;
> he shall bruise your head,
>   and you shall bruise his heel.'

[16]*To the woman he said,*

> 'I will greatly multiply your pain in childbearing;
>   in pain you shall bring forth children,
> yet your desire shall be for your husband,
>   and he shall rule over you.'

[17]*And to Adam he said,*

---

[62] Rom. 5:12ff.; 1 Cor. 15:21–22, 45–49.

91

> 'Because you have listened to the voice of your wife,
>   and have eaten of the tree
> of which I commanded you,
>   "You shall not eat of it,"
> cursed is the ground because of you;
>   in the toil you shall eat of it all the days of your life;
> ¹⁸ thorns and thistles it shall bring forth to you;
>   and you shall eat the plants of the field.
> ¹⁹ In the sweat of your face
>   you shall eat bread
> till you return to the ground,
>   for out of it you were taken;
> you are dust,
>   and to dust you shall return.'

²⁰The man called his wife's name Eve, because she was the mother of all living. ²¹And the LORD God made for Adam and for his wife garments of skins, and clothed them.

²²Then the LORD God said, 'Behold, the man has become like one of us, knowing good and evil; and now, lest he put forth his hand and take also of the tree of life, and eat, and live for ever' – ²³therefore the LORD God sent him forth from the garden of Eden, to till the ground from which he was taken. ²⁴He drove out the man; and at the east of the garden of Eden he placed the cherubim, and a flaming sword which turned every way, to guard the way to the tree of life.   (3:14–24)

Genesis 3 illustrates the disruption which results from the human pair's fatal choice. They were told in 2:17 that in the day that they ate of the fruit of the tree, they would die. We can see the outworking of that threat in the disruptions which then become part of life. The evil power which used part of God's creation as a voice of temptation is seen in the amazing fact that human beings can, by an act of the will, stand against the authority of God. The result of that rebellion is described in the catalogue of disorders to which the rest of this chapter points.

We must not see these verses as merely pointing to disorders which affect human beings and their relationships, true though that is. The first, most serious, and most mysterious thing of all, is that these verses also point to something which has affected God.

For just as it was God's word which defined the moral framework for life in the Garden (2:16), it is God who now pronounces judgment on the snake, on the earth, and on the man and the woman. And it is the estrangement which is now enacted between human beings and their Creator which is at the basis of the other estrangements of which we read. The people who hide behind the trees for cover from God's searching and questioning voice, experience disruption within their own personal selves. There is a disruption in their relationships with one another. There is a disruption, too, in their relationship to the rest of the natural order. There is no place to turn which is not now tainted by sin, which is not now in some way estranged from God, which does not need to hear the word of rescue and regeneration and the chance to begin again. But behind, and beneath, all our experience of alienation is the deeper truth of God's alienation from what he has made. It is this which is worked out in the cursings, the toil, the banishment and the death to which these sombre verses now turn our attention.

a. Blessing becomes curse

To the serpent, and to the ground, God says, 'You are cursed' (3:14, 17). The curse is the converse of the blessing. God, we are told, blessed the creatures and human beings with fruitful life (1:22, 28), indicating that blessing is the gift of vitality and creativity. The whole of the ongoing life of creation is the outworking of God's blessing. God also blessed the seventh day and hallowed it (2:3), showing that the whole of creation is now caught up in the rhythm of creativity and praise. There is an exuberance in divine blessing, and abundance of life in all its fullness, a joy and a delight. But the word here in chapter 3 is 'curse'. This is an expression of God's judgment, an indication of coming misfortune. The blessings are reversed. The joyous dance of creation becomes a dirge, as a shadow falls over all things.

Later in the Old Testament, God's curse is linked to actions of disobedience to his covenant law. To be under God's curse is to have to bear his judgment. It does not, however, put us beyond his reach. And as we are able to read this chapter from the vantage-point of the cross of Christ, we can see something of the beginnings of creation restored when Christ 'redeemed us from the curse of the law, having become a curse for us'.[63]

b. Complementarity becomes subordination

Another of the symptoms of the broken world is the dislocation between the sexes. Whereas in chapter 2 the man and the woman were equals, with a mutuality of need and gift, each the complement of the other, here in chapter 3 we read of male dominance and female subservience. The woman is told that her sexual desire will

[63] Gal. 3:13.

93

become a grasping urge, perhaps to manipulate her husband for her own satisfaction. But then we read of the man that *'he shall rule over you'*. This is not a divine prescription of what should be, but a description in the fallen world of what will be.

It is only now, after the Fall, that the man gives his wife a name, as earlier he had taken authority over the animals by naming them (3:20). The complementarity of *Ish* and *Ishshah* (2:23; see pp. 70–71) has now become a relationship of male authoritarian domination. The woman is further depersonalized by the fact that she is only referred to in functional terms, as a bearer of children – no longer the one 'like opposite' the man; perhaps merely a 'baby-machine'.

It is hard to see how discussions of 'male headship' as an 'ordinance of creation' can be sustained by an appeal to this chapter. This chapter describes how things should not be; this is the broken world.

The gospel of Christ shows its revolutionary perspectives nowhere more clearly than in Jesus' treatment of women. In his relationships with his mother, Mary Magdalene, with the sisters at Bethany, and with others, there is a tenderness and an acceptance which upholds the dignity, equality and respect which sin all too often discards.

And it is with the gospel perspective in mind that we should now read Ephesians 5, with its teaching on the mutual submission of the man and the wife to each other in marriage, reflecting their mutual submission to Christ[64] as a commentary on Genesis 3:16. The husband is described as 'head', but in the sense that Christ is earlier described as 'the head',[65] namely the one who is responsible for the life of the body. Christ does not 'lord it over us' in a domineering way, but through the 'headship' of service,[66] loves, cherishes and cares for the welfare of his body, the church.[67] Husbands, likewise, should love their wives – they do not own them like property (as so often the ancient world believed). The revolutionary gospel pattern – reversing the judgment of Eden – is that they should *love* their wives, just as they take care of their own bodies. That is the husband's submission of himself into the calling of marriage. And the wife's submission of herself is that she should not 'graspingly desire to manipulate' her husband, as the word in Eden perhaps indicates, but should willingly submit herself also into the pattern of marriage which reflects the reordering grace of the gospel: not with selfish desire but with respect.[68] There is a complementarity and an equality to be found again in a marriage

---

[64] Eph. 5:21. [65] Eph. 4:15. [66] *Cf.* Mk. 10:42–45.
[67] Eph. 5:29. [68] Eph. 5:33.

which reflects the pattern of Christ. In the gospel of Christ the relationships between the sexes can be brought back once more into line.

c. Work becomes toil

Instead of the freedom of man's authority over the natural order and the animals, the estate manager now finds that the blessing of work becomes a toil. The vibrancy and vitality of the natural order is now marked by thorns and thistles (Gn. 3:17–19). And mankind's relationship with the natural world now takes on the features of a struggle.

There is a significant reference to 'eating'. The sin of verse 6 was that they 'ate' (cf. 3.17a). Now in everything they eat, they will have this reminder of the result of their sin (3:17b); for the ground which will give them their food will only yield its fruit through toil (3:17) and sweat (3:19).

What more poignant description of the struggle for life could be given than that of the pain associated with bringing life into the world. For the woman, the pain is that of childbirth. The bringing of a new life is now a task, marked by travail and hardship. For the man, it is the toil and sweat of the cultivation of fertile ground. The two earlier divine commands, to be fruitful and to till the ground, are now both occasions for misery.

The giving of life and the processes of life are now marred by struggle and pain. The man taken from the dust of the ground, one with the created order, now finds himself at odds with it. It is as if the creation itself, degraded and defiled by human sin, is fighting back, enraged that its beauty has been marred, for it remains God's creation and on his side. There is, as it were, a 'moral vitality' to the natural order, still filled with the life of the Holy God, and yet struggling against its defiling inhabitants.[69] Here is the basis for our environmental theology, and, indeed, for a theology of the economic order. The earth is the Lord's and the fullness thereof. Our task is to recover again a sense of respect towards God's creation, and our role as facilitating servants in cultivating and protecting it for him.

The groaning of creation, complaining, as it were, against human sin, is also the groaning of the birth pangs of a new age. God will not leave his broken world unredeemed. For the whole creation is groaning, and 'standing on tiptoe' eagerly waiting for the redemption of God's new humanity. With us, the whole created order will

---

[69] Cf. Lv. 18:25. Cf. J. A. Motyer, Law and Life (Lawyers' Christian Fellowship, 1978), p. 7.

be brought into the kingdom of God's glory, and all will one day once again sing the Creator's praise.[70]

d. Fellowship becomes banishment

'Where are you?' was, in part, a call to fellowship. God was missing Adam's company. But now that moment is passed. In 3:23, the Lord sent him forth: man is no longer welcome in the Garden, having grasped at that which can never belong to him. The word is one of divine anger (God 'drove him forth'), and placed cherubim and flaming swords to guard the way back into the Garden.

Now the people are not only 'alienated' from one another, but are 'without God in the world'.[71]

It is to the gospel we must turn once more – a gospel story which begins, to be sure, here in Genesis, but which comes to its fullness in Christ – if we would read of the Christ who makes peace once more between human beings and their creator,[72] reconciling us to God,[73] and reconciling God to us. It is in the gospel that we read of a Father who waits longingly for the prodigal to come back home.

e. Life becomes death

The curse, the disruption, the toil, the banishment, are all outworkings of the divine word from 2:17: 'in the day that you eat of it you shall die.' Its outworkings through the generations in time we will explore further when we come to Genesis 5. But we need to pause here to see in what sense the man 'died' through eating the forbidden fruit. For physically, he clearly kept going, according to our narrator, for quite a time yet. Seth was born when Adam was 130, and there were still another 800 years left to him then! (Gn. 5:3–5). Yet the straightforward reading of Genesis 2:17 and 3:3 is that the result of taking of the tree of the knowledge of good and evil would be death. Death thus means more than the physical cessation of life. Maybe, our narrator might be suggesting, the processes of physical decay began in Genesis 3, and gradually worked themselves out over the years of Adam's remaining life. But he is surely suggesting more. His view of death is not 'the end' – death for him is a change. Adam's death is a change of place (from within the Garden to outside the Garden) and a change of situation before God (in fellowship with God, to alienated from God). And all death can be so understood: the person continues,

[70] Cf. Rom. 8:18ff.   [71] Cf. Eph. 2:12.   [72] Eph. 2:11–18.
[73] 2 Cor. 5:18.

but in a different 'place' and in a different situation before God. So although 'death', from our perspective, faces us with the edge of our existence, from the theological perspective of our text, death speaks of change: from the blessing, freedom, vitality and fellowship of the Garden, to curse, bondage, toil and alienation outside the gate on the East of the Garden, with our way back barred by cherubim and a flaming sword. In the later biblical traditions, Death also puts on the clothing of a powerful ruler, who holds us in his thrall.

Once more we can look to Christ as the one who took our human nature 'that through death he might destroy him who has the power of death, that is, the devil, and deliver all those who through fear of death were subject to lifelong bondage'.[74] It is in his death that Death itself is swallowed up in victory.[75]

5. The promise of life again

In Christ we are no longer banished, but accepted. In him there is freedom from the bondage of sin, from the condemnation and guilt of the law, from the shame of self-reproach, and from the overpowering rule of death. In him life does begin again. The gospel tells us that in the new Heaven and the new Earth, there is no more separation, no more condemnation, no more pain, no more tears, no more death.[76] In Christ nothing can any more separate us from the love of God, a love which casts out fear, overcomes evil, and rebuilds life and relationships.

Though the Genesis narrative has to wait until chapter 12, with the history of Abraham, before the story of that redeeming grace can begin to be told as the history of God's covenant people leading to Christ, there are hints and pointers even here in chapter 3.

The serpent is cursed by God, and there is a promise that though the woman will die, her seed will live to bruise the serpent's head (3:15). The picture is that through a man, the serpent who has been instrumental in the downfall of a man will itself be crushed. No doubt the author could not look on the day of which the New Testament speaks, nor of the 'Proper Man' (Luther) in whom a new humanity is born. But we can now stand within Genesis 3 and look forward in the knowledge that the power of evil, hidden behind the all-too-subtle mask of the serpent, will one day be exposed, and overcome, on a cross outside a city wall. On that day, Christus Victor will 'disarm the principalities and powers', making 'a public example of them'.[77] On that day the sting of Death itself will be drawn, and the Last Enemy defeated.[78]

[74] Heb. 2:14–15.   [75] 1 Cor. 15:54.   [76] See, e.g., Rev. 21:3–4; 22:1ff.
[77] Col. 2:15.   [78] 1 Cor. 15.

But Genesis does not only point forward to a Day when the serpent will be crushed. It tells us that even now, God meets his ashamed and guilty people in their need, and provides a covering for them. As Calvin put it so vividly: 'Truly it was a sad and horrid spectacle: that he in whom recently the glory of the Divine image was shining, should lie hidden under fetid skins to cover his own disgrace, and that there should be more comeliness in a dead animal than in a living man!'[79] Yet, though Calvin leaves us there, contemplating these animal skins as a sign of man's disgrace, can we not see in them also a covering and a provision? One has died, that Adam may be covered. In that sacrifice, is there not a hint of God's way with his world: that new life is given through life laid down?

God's action in sending his man out of the Garden is also in a sense to preserve him. The perplexing unfinished sentence in 3:22 conveys the sense that God is not only banishing man from the Garden as a judgment, but also for his good. Is it a way of saying that God does not want man to eat of the tree of eternity in his present broken state – indeed that there are fearful and eternal consequences, known to God, unknown to us, should he do so? God is providing an opportunity for grace. Adam, though in a sense overshadowed by death, for some years yet has his life preserved.

God offers his gracious provision and protection to the person broken and sinful and in such need. And in counterpoint to this, is there just a glimmer of faith in the man himself as he calls his wife Eve, 'Life'? – for as the narrator says, she is the mother of all living. Is there a hint here that God will not abandon his precious creation, but that even out of death, God will bring life again? This is surely implied in 3:15 where those under the edict of death are promised a 'seed' – life will be prolonged into coming generations. Some have taken this further to refer to a prediction of one particular 'seed'[80] and have linked it to the one 'offspring' referred to in Galatians 3:16ff. – namely Christ our Lord.

We will find those hints strengthened in later chapters in Genesis 1 – 11. But side by side with the promises of grace, we will discover that the power of sin itself spreads and darkens. Genesis 2 and 3 together paint us a picture of an ambiguous, wonderful but broken world. That is the world we know, and in which we share. But we have more than even the author of these chapters could have dreamed. We have a gospel embodied in a Person who, in the power of his resurrection life, is making all things new.

---

[79] Calvin, p. 183.
[80] *I.e.*, rather as the prediction of David's line in 2 Sam. 7 issued in one very particular King (*cf.* Lk. 1:69; 2:4–7).

In evil long I took delight,
  Unawed by shame or fear,
Till a new object struck my sight,
  And stopped my wild career:
I saw One hanging on a Tree
  In agonies and blood,
Who fix'd His languid eyes on me,
  As near His Cross I stood.

Sure never till my latest breath
  Can I forget that look:
It seem'd to charge me with His death,
  Though not a word He spoke:
My conscience felt and owned the guilt,
  And plunged me in despair;
I saw my sins His Blood had spilt,
  And help'd to nail Him there.

Alas! I knew not what I did!
  But now my tears are vain:
Where shall my trembling soul be hid?
  For I the Lord have slain!
– A second look He gave, which said,
  'I freely all forgive;
This Blood is for thy ransom paid;
  I die, that thou may'st live.'

Thus, while His death my sin displays
  In all its blackest hue,
Such is the mystery of grace,
  It seals my pardon too.
With pleasing grief, and mournful joy,
  My spirit now is fill'd,
That I should such a life destroy, –
  Yet live by Him I kill'd!

John Newton (1725–1807)

4:1–26
3. Envy and gratitude

1. Life goes on

Now Adam knew Eve his wife, and she conceived and bore Cain, saying, 'I have gotten a man with the help of the LORD.' ²And again, she bore his brother Abel. (4:1–2a)

Genesis 4 opens with a new life. Even as the door is shut on the way back to the Garden, and the cherubim are placed to guard the way to the tree of life, our author is looking forwards.

God allows *life* to continue even in the fallen world outside the Garden.

Furthermore, *faith* continues outside the Garden: the life is a life of faith. Here in the world disordered by the entrance of sin, it is still possible – it is essential – to live by faith. Eve opens the chapter with a statement of faith: *'I have gotten a man with the help of the LORD'* (4:1). Hers, though, may be a faith that is discoloured with a measure of pride, for this difficult text might possibly mean 'I, too, like Yahweh, am a creator'. The author concludes the chapter with a pointer to faith: 'At that time men began to call upon the name of the LORD' (4:26), noting the beginnings of patterns of regular worship. And Abel, one of the main actors in this drama in Genesis 4, tops the bill of the heroes of faith recorded in Hebrews 11: 'By faith Abel offered to God a more acceptable sacrifice than Cain.'[1]

This chapter tells us, then, about life and about faith; it also tells us that community is beginning, worship is beginning and technology is becoming possible. But it tells us too about conflict and murder, about punishment and vengeance, about alienation and anxiety, about the corruption of marriage into polygamy. The predicament of human beings banished from Eden at the end of

[1] Heb. 11:4.

chapter 3 is now elaborated further in chapter 4. Once again Genesis is opening up the *ambiguity* of our human predicament. *In this world* there is Abel, and there is Cain. In *ourselves* also, perhaps, there is Abel and there is Cain.

This primeval history once again catches us up into its story. As Wenham's commentary indicates, there are parallels in this story found in aspects of the Sumerian flood story from Babylon: man's nomadic plight, the building of the first city, the establishment of worship. However, whereas the Mesopotamian story rests on an overall optimism of human nature which believes in human progress, the theme of Genesis 4 is precisely the reverse. This chapter shows us both how the sins and disorders of Genesis 3 extend outwards in history to subsequent generations, and also that sin which is expressed in *personal* terms in the story of Adam and Eve also has a *social* dimension. Sin has now become a fact of human nature. Now we find wrongdoing arising within the depths of the human heart – there is no reference here to an external serpentine tempter. Sinfulness has infected the human condition to the next generation. Murder, vengeance, the corruption of marriage: these are the negative themes of Genesis 4, and they each have a personal and a social dimension. And in both personal and social aspects, we are involved.

For here we are introduced not only to two brothers and the personal envy which divides them – which rings true to much of our experience. We are faced also with a primitive but major social division of humankind. Abel was a keeper of sheep and Cain a tiller of the ground. Throughout human history there have been social divisions marked by various occupations – and in this chapter we have a pointer towards the positive and the negative aspects of social life. The division of labour – some to sheep farming, some to agriculture – is presented without comment, and we can presume that it was thought to be beneficial. But there is also a social division depicted here which can, as we know all too well, lead to conflicts based on envy.

The author now assumes the presence of communities. We read later of a group who might take vengeance on Cain (4:15); then of a community from which Cain can take a wife (4:17), and in which he can find refuge. As well, therefore, as what we can learn about brotherliness from Cain and Abel, we can also see here a theological evaluation of social sin, social division, and the destructive competitiveness which marks the human community outside the Garden. The roots of such social divisions are found in the fragmentation of a society which has lost its touch with God.

The life of faith outside the Garden has to be lived in relationship to our neighbour, and is not immune from the destructive forces embedded in the social context of our human situation. If 'the devil' is active in the voice of the snake in chapter 3, here we are in 'the world' (human society organized over against God), and struggling with 'the flesh' (human nature that has gone astray).

2. Life seems unfair

Now Abel was a keeper of sheep, and Cain a tiller of the ground. *[3]In the course of time Cain brought to the Lord an offering of the fruit of the ground, [4]and Abel brought of the firstlings of his flock and of their fat portions. And the Lord had regard for Abel and his offering, [5]but for Cain and his offering he had no regard. So Cain was very angry, and his countenance fell.* (4:2b–5)

At first sight, the paragraph of verses 1–5 is very perplexing. We tend, of course, to read this through New Testament eyes. The writer to the Hebrews tells us of Abel's faith by which he offered a more acceptable sacrifice than Cain,[2] and refers to the blood of Abel alongside reference to the blood of Jesus.[3] Matthew speaks of the 'blood of innocent Abel',[4] and in the First Letter of John, we are exhorted to love one another, and 'not be like Cain who was of the evil one and murdered his brother. And why did he murder him? Because his own deeds were evil, and his brother's righteous'[5] (1 Jn. 3:12). It all suggests that Abel is the good man and Cain is the bad man.

But if we did not come to Genesis 4 through a New Testament perspective, what would we make of it? Where do the New Testament writers get the idea that Abel is a man of faith, and Cain is of the evil one? What we are told in Genesis 4 is that both brought a sacrifice and the Lord had regard for Abel's sacrifice, but not for Cain's.

On the face of it, and without probing further, it all seems rather unfair. It may even be this unfairness that the author wants to highlight. Life is unfair! Some people prosper and others do not. Some become the people of God and others do not. Why were the Hebrews chosen and others rejected? From our partial human perspective it all seems rather arbitrary, if not capricious. But – and perhaps this is the question which Genesis is wanting to pose – is not God free to act as he wills without asking our permission? Cain has no rights over God. No-one has rights over God. Only God is in a position to know what is fair – or rather, to say why things are as they are, fair or unfair.[6] In his sovereign wisdom, he

---

[2] Heb. 11:4.   [3] Heb. 12:2.   [4] Mt. 23:35.   [5] 1 Jn. 3:12.
[6] *Cf.* Phillips, p. 31.

chose Abel's sacrifice, just as in his sovereign wisdom he chose the Hebrews to be his people, *not* because of anything they had done, but simply because he loves.

Deuteronomy 7:7 gives this thought its classic expression: 'It was not because you were more in number than any other people that the LORD set his love upon you and chose you, for you were the fewest of all peoples; but it is because the LORD loves you . . . '.

Is this what the author is wanting to magnify here – the grace of God? The people of God are who they are not because of works, but only because of God's grace. Faith has to live with what seems to us unfairnesses, and leave some uncertainties unresolved, within the mystery of God's gracious providence.

The psalmist, too, struggled with this question. Why did the wicked triumph and the people of God suffer? Why was life so unfair? Psalm 73 asks these questions. The turning-point came in the psalmist's mind when he was able to see things from a different perspective. He stopped seeing each unfair detail of the lives of others, but rather saw their whole life story – from the perspective of eternity. 'When I thought how to understand this, it seemed to me a wearisome task, *until* I went into the sanctuary of God; then I perceived their end.'[7]

The same questions come to our minds when we read the parable Jesus told about the labourers in the vineyard. Some having agreed to work for a denarius a day did a day's labour. Others were also paid a denarius after having only worked an hour. When the householder was challenged he replied: 'Friend, I am doing you no wrong; did you not agree with me for a denarius? Take what belongs to you and go; I choose to give to this last as I give to you.' He continues with these telling words: 'Am I not allowed to do what I choose with what belongs to me? Or do you begrudge my generosity?'[8]

The kingdom of heaven, we are told, is like that householder.[9] And the parable is told in answer to a question from Peter. 'We have left everything and followed you,' said Peter. 'What then shall we have?'[10] Jesus' reply in the form of this story shows Peter that the kingdom of heaven is not at all about 'what we shall get'. Our world operates on the basis of 'you owe so you must pay'; the law of apparent fairness which so quickly becomes the law of retaliation and retribution. The kingdom of heaven, by contrast, operates on the basis of grace: the generosity of the householder. This is not to charge God with arbitrariness, but simply to acknowledge that here, once again, we meet an edge to our understanding. The secret things belong to the Lord. Part of his secret is the mystery of grace

---

[7] Ps. 73:16–17.   [8] Mt. 20:13–15.   [9] Mt. 20:1ff.   [10] Mt. 19:27.

– a mystery which can look to us like unfairness, but which, from the perspective of the kingdom, and the character of the King, we can trust is part of his generosity.

To be sure it does not always feel like that! The labourers who had borne the heat of the day felt aggrieved. But from the perspective of a different vantage-point than the sweat of the vineyard, the truth is clear. What governs the life of the vineyard is ultimately the grace and generosity of its lord. All the seeming unfairnesses of the ways in which we think God should have dealt with us differently need to be seen in that light.

3. Brotherly love?

Seeming unfairness may be part of the story of Genesis 4, but there are two hints that enable us to probe a little further, and perhaps help us to see more clearly why Abel's offering was accepted and Cain's was not.

1. There may be a hint in their names. 'Cain' is related to the word 'get'. We saw this in 4:1: 'I have gotten a man with the help of the LORD.' The name points, perhaps, to self-sufficiency, to strength, to the first-born with first rights to everything, to the will for power and self-assertion. By contrast, 'Abel' means something like 'nothingness; frailty'. As Helmut Thielicke puts it in his sermon on 'The Cain within us',[11] 'He [Abel] is the representative of those who get the short end of the stick.'

So perhaps in their names, we are meant to discern a picture of two brothers in this fundamental inequality of roles and attitudes – rather like the Pharisee and the publican in another story, told much later on.[12]

To follow Thielicke's lead, we can say that Cain perhaps speaks of cynicism towards the neighbour: an urge to make myself the centre and to relate to others only in so far as they are useful to me; whereas Abel is the wet, the weakling, the 'also-ran', who in this world's terms counts for nothing but foolishness.

Are we meant to find this distinction in their names? It would help explain some of Cain's anger when his offering is not accepted while the gift from this nonentity brother of his seems to be more highly regarded. And if *that* is the evil-heartedness of Cain, that total disregard for any semblance of neighbourly respect – which eventually becomes murderous – we see why it is appropriate for the First Letter of John to refer to this story in the discussion of brotherly love.

2. Perhaps there is another hint too. Although von Rad says that

---

[11] Thielicke, pp. 187f.   [12] *Cf.* Lk. 18:9–14.

'the only clue one can find in the narrative is that the sacrifice of blood was more pleasing to Yahweh',[13] there may be another clue also. Abel brought *the firstlings of his flock and of their fat portions* (4:4). As Wenham notes, the very positive connotations of 'firstling' and 'fat' in the Old Testament support the view of a good number of Old Testament and rabbinic commentators that Abel offered the pick of his flock to the Lord. So this may be a pointer that Abel was offering his best – and the best of his best. His was an offering of consecration, a sacrifice that was costly to him. Cain, however, just brought what was nearest to hand.

Most of all, even if Abel and Cain both approach God's altar with a clean heart, there is something neither of them yet knows: what sort of sacrifice does God want? How can they know? Presumably only by offering what they have in faith, and seeing if it is acceptable. They may, who knows, have learned from the covering of Adam and Eve with skins something of the approach to God by way of sacrifice. This may, indeed, have been part of their knowledge of God – part of the revelation by which they lived. But maybe they were not sure. The man of faith offers what he has, sometimes in the dark, and is willing to hear God's reply. Sometimes that reply is a word of acceptance. But sometimes God says, 'No: that is not what I want you to do.' And the man of faith accepts the 'no' as a learning time. This is how his faculties become 'trained by practice to distinguish good from evil'.[14] This is part of how a person learns God's will for him – by taking the risk of trying God out.

If Cain had been trusting God with that sort of faith, he would have accepted that God's way was other than he had supposed. But such a faith is not there. Rather, he gets angry. Notice that he is not blamed for bringing his offering. Nor is he blamed for getting it wrong! Often we are cautious about taking risks in faith, for fear that we will get it wrong. The truth is we will *always* – at least to some extent – get it wrong. But that is not the issue. If God only accepted us if we got it right, where would any of us be? The issue is the willingness to bring in faith and gratitude what little bits and pieces we have to offer so that – like the boy with the loaves and fishes – they can be taken and made into something more. And that faith and gratitude includes the willingness to learn when we have got it wrong, so that we may change. But that, alas, is where Cain fell down. He was not blamed for his mistake. What is blameworthy is his angry reaction to the Lord's response. The law of life outside the Garden is the same as the law inside: trusting obedience to God. But Cain is not willing for that, and he gets

[13] Von Rad, pp. 99ff.   [14] Heb. 5:14.

angry. And his anger towards God is then transferred into jealousy toward Abel. How easily a failure to trust God leads to a failure to respect our brother!

Brotherly love involves recognizing that what our weak, non-entity brother has to offer is sometimes more important to God than what we choose to bring.

Love is sometimes seen most clearly in gratitude that God has gifted another person. 'Love', says St Paul, 'is the fulfilling of the law', and the last of the Ten Commandments is a law against covetousness. True love of neighbour is seen when I love my brother enough not to be envious.

There was a certain famous preacher in the United States last century, who pulled the crowds, and was generally regarded as one of the greats. The day came when another preacher was invited to his town. He, too, pulled the crowds, so much so that some started to leave the first and go rather to hear the second. Envy began to grow, and of course the first preacher's ministry was affected. The more envious he grew, the less effective was his work for God. The circle, which all too quickly became vicious, was broken when he began to pray for his rival, and thank God for the gifts that his fellow preacher had been given. Love broke through again when envy was overwhelmed by gratitude.

Love, as Scott Peck puts it, is 'the will to extend oneself for the purpose of nurturing one's own or another's spiritual growth'.[15] In other words, love is about willingly giving oneself. Love for brother is especially clearly seen in gratitude to God for his gifts. But Cain's attitude is the antithesis of brotherly love. 'The Cain within us' is seen in our jealousy of others' gifts. Cain is seen in our resentment of others' service to God, in our hatred of the fact that others seem more 'spiritually successful' than we are, and in our anger that God apparently delights to accept the offerings of others, when we surely know better. How hard it is sometimes to rejoice in others' gifts, when we wish they were our own.

So Cain was very angry, and his countenance fell.

4. The system

This chapter, as we noted before, opens up questions about the 'flesh' and the 'world'. Nowhere is that combination more powerful than in the operation of 'the system'. The psychology of inter-personal relationships, of group dynamics and of systems theory, has introduced us to ways of understanding the power of human groups. In the interaction of human communities, the pains of

[15] M. Scott Peck, *The Road Less Travelled* (Simon and Schuster, 1978), p. 81.

personal psychological needs can be magnified. Very deep-seated fears, jealousies and aggression can surface in groups, and, by what Melanie Klein calls the mechanisms of 'splitting' and 'projection', can be focused from one person on to another.

When a group is also tied to a hierarchy of authority, the issue of who exercises power over whom can become exceedingly complex and painful. For when power becomes inflamed by personal jealousies and fears, aggressions can become murderous.

Let us imagine a superior in a place of work who falls out with a subordinate. The former describes the dispute in terms of the subordinate's professional incompetence. The latter thinks the boss is swayed by professional jealousy. Eventually the superior's constant criticism leads to those in authority invoking a disciplinary procedure. The superior does not really want this – it casts a bad light on his ability to deal with his staff. The junior does not want it either, but is left in the position of playing their game or merely resigning. The boss then has to keep looking for things to complain about to justify the disciplinary procedure. The subordinate finds the constant surveillance so threatening that his standard of work does actually fall and begins to provide real grounds for complaint. No-one comes out of this well. The 'system' has taken over, and no one feels in a position to stop the flow of events.

Jealousy and fear can serve as the fuel for a most destructive 'system' in which personal value gets lost, any chance of re-establishing friendly relationships is rapidly reduced, and human sensitivities get trodden on. This is the destructive power of 'the world' – human relationships organized without reference to God.

The story of Cain illustrates this destructive power by focusing on the relationship between two brothers. But it serves as a paradigm of the destructiveness of the system in which Cain's fears and jealousies can lead to murderous aggressiveness between people.

5. Responsibility

The LORD said to Cain, 'Why are you angry, and why has your countenance fallen? *'If you do well, will you not be accepted? And if you do not do well, sin is couching at the door; its desire is for you, but you must master it.* (4:6–7)

These verses remind us that Cain is still responsible for his actions. They open up the interplay between belief, behaviour and emotion. Sometimes emotional changes in us lead to changes in attitude and behaviour. Here the pattern is the reverse: wrong beliefs lead to wrong behaviour, and a bad behavioural response leads to depression.

107

It is, of course, very unwise to derive general principles from isolated texts. In his book *Competent to Counsel*, Jay Adams tends to do this when he uses this text to justify his behaviourist model of counselling. Referring to Genesis 4:5ff., he says: 'Here God sets forth the important principle that behaviour determines feelings.'[16] He goes on to argue that Cain's sin led to God's rejection; Cain's subsequent anger at God led to depression; God's warning ('Do right and you will feel right, but if you misbehave you will fall into deeper sin', 4:6–7), went unheeded, and Cain's grudge, self-pity and anger, leading to guilt and depression, led on to further sin and further pain in a deepening cycle of behavioural mistakes.

True as this picture may be in some situations, Jay Adams' use of Scripture here needs to be treated with some caution, and this story not made into an all-embracing principle of counselling. For it is equally clear that in other scriptural stories, the cycle goes the other way: changes in feelings lead to changes in behaviour. Ruth's sadness at her bereavement contributed to her commitment to Naomi, for example. The interconnection of belief, behaviour and feelings is complex.

Within that wider and more complex model, however, there is a time in the counselling process when an emphasis on personal responsibility may well be appropriate, and this the experience of Cain helpfully illustrates. Pastoral counsellors need the wisdom to know the extent to which a person's depression may be directly related to wrong choices that person has made, and the wisdom also to know at what points a depressed person can be encouraged towards responsibility for their actions. It is at the point of Cain's responsibility for his behaviour, with consequences of guilt, depression and the cycle of wrong-doing, that God here confronts him. Within all the interplay of belief and emotion, there is none the less a fixed point of personal responsibility. Standing, as it were, at the altar, God points to Cain's sadness of countenance, and offers the hope of change: You do not have to stay like this. You can choose to make that change of attitude, belief system or behaviour pattern that will result in your knowing yourself to be accepted. Or you can choose not to.

Genesis 4:7 is complicated, but possibly means: if you set your face against God and his ways you are placing yourself in the service of sin which, like a wild beast lying in wait for its prey, will dominate you. But however tempting the wild beast becomes, however powerful its control, none the less the imperative indicating your own responsibility still remains: *you must master it.* Despite all the extenuating circumstances which we rightly call in

[16] J. Adams, *Competent to Counsel* (Baker Book House, 1977), p. 93.

108

to establish 'diminished responsibility' in certain situations, there is a point at which each of us, within our limits, can choose.

6. My brother's keeper

Cain said to Abel his brother, 'Let us go out to the field.' And when they were in the field, Cain rose up against his brother Abel, and killed him. ⁹Then the LORD said to Cain, 'Where is Abel your brother?' He said, 'I do not know; am I my brother's keeper?' ¹⁰And the LORD said, 'What have you done? The voice of your brother's blood is crying to me from the ground. ¹¹And now you are cursed from the ground, which has opened its mouth to receive your brother's blood from your hand. ¹²When you till the ground, it shall no longer yield to you its strength; you shall be a fugitive and a wanderer on the earth.' (4:8–12)

Cain did not master the wild beast. It began to devour him. Resentment and jealousy turn to deceit: 'Let us go out where no one can see us.' Deceit leads on to murder.

And now the Lord speaks to Cain: *Where is Abel your brother?*

Before (4:6), God was by the altar, offering a way out, a way to renewed acceptance. Here God is with Cain out in the field, and the word is one of straight confrontation.

How powerfully God's question parallels the question to Adam in chapter 3:

> Adam, where are you? (3:9)

> Cain, where is your brother? (4:9)

The individual question to Adam becomes the social question to Cain.

And to Cain's impertinent 'Shall I shepherd the shepherd?' (as we might paraphrase v. 9), the implication Genesis wants to convey can only be 'yes': responsibility before God *is* responsibility for our brother. And that word is addressed to Cain not at the altar, but out in the field – out in his world – out in his work place – out in his everyday environment. It is there that God calls us to exercise responsibility towards our brothers.

Cain's resistance to change even at this point of direct divine confrontation perhaps illustrates how deadened the conscience can become through persistent refusal to listen to God. The result is that we judge ourselves as set over against God; we place ourselves in confrontation with the will of God – and that is itself the judgment of God against us. As Calvin comments,

The force of divine judgment is clearly perceived; for it so pierces into the iron hearts of the wicked, that they are inwardly compelled to be their own judges; nor does it suffer them so to obliterate the sense of guilt which it has extorted, as not to leave the trace or scar of searing.[17]

In other words, the way God's judgment works in our lives, is very often to leave us to the judgment we have made of ourselves. If you will live without God, you will live without God.

There is something even more subtle here, hidden in God's reference to Abel's blood in verses 10 and 11.

Blood and life belong to God. To shed another's life is to take from that person something which belongs to God. One of the keystones of Israel's faith – seen in some of its criminal law, as well as its cultic practices, is the conviction that life is in the blood.[18] Shed blood is the most polluting of all things. After Abel's death, the 'voice of his blood, more eloquent than the voice of any orator' cries out with complaint. Wenham compares the cry to that of 'the desperate cry of men without food (Gn. 41:55) expecting to die (Ex. 14:10), or oppressed by their enemies (Jdg. 4:3). It is also the scream for help of a woman being raped (Dt. 22:24, 27).'[19] And here the blood of Abel 'cries out' to be avenged. To say this is to emphasize that Abel's blood was God's property – that God is the guardian and protector of all life. Cain should not have taken it. Yet, by taking possession of Abel's blood, Cain *has* in a twisted sense become his brother's keeper.

There is a way of 'keeping our brother' which expresses care, concern for his life, acceptance of his gifts, a cherishing of his different contribution, a respect for his offering. And there is a way of 'keeping our brother' which is for our own benefit. It is an expression of jealousy, of destructive mastery – of taking from him what is not even his to give, because it belongs to God. The first is the way of brotherly love. The second is the way of Cain.

One of the most pointed examples of Cainite behaviour in our modern world is the appalling exploitation of the poor periphery of powerless and hungry nations by the small core of the rich and powerful. The social injustice of third-world deprivation, and the refusal of those who have plenty to work for a more equitable distribution of earth's resources, in favour of those who have so little, means that our brothers and sisters are dying through lack of love. Their blood, like Abel's, cries to God from the ground. No-one can injure his brother without wounding God himself.

---

[17] Calvin, p. 206.　　[18] *Cf.* Lv. 17:11.　　[19] Wenham, p. 107.

7. The land of Nod

Cain said to the LORD, 'My punishment is greater than I can bear.
[14]Behold, thou hast driven me this day away from the ground; and
from thy face I shall be hidden; and I shall be a fugitive and
a wanderer on the earth, and whoever finds me will slay me.'
(4:13-14)

The way of Cain leads to the land of 'restlessness' (4:16). There is
no peace for human beings unless they can discover the freedom
of living within the providence of God, can see their lives as the
focus of his care, and believe that their highest good is found in
living under his will. For God's will expresses both God's own
nature of goodness, and also what is an appropriate pattern of life
for the welfare of his people. God's will is his goodness; God's
goodness is expressed in his will.

One of the classic dilemmas of moral philosophy is that first
described by Plato in his Dialogue called *Euthyphro*. In its simplest
terms, the question is this: Is something good because God wills
it, or does God will things because they are good? Put like that,
both questions impale us on the horns of a dilemma. If we say that
something is good because God wills it, this suggests a very arbitrary notion of goodness. What God wills would then by definition
be good – and if God willed something that we would call evil, it
would still none the less be good. We are rightly unhappy with
this, because we want what God says is good to fit in with our
own basic sense of what is good. But the other horn of the dilemma
may be even worse: it seems to suggest that there is some standard
of goodness outside God to which his will can be conformed. And
thus God would cease to be God because even he would have to
bow to some higher authority.

The way that biblical faith undercuts the *Euthyphro* dilemma is
by saying that God is the sort of God whose will is identical with
what makes for the best for human life. This is one of the distinctive
features of the religion of Israel as contrasted with the pagan gods
of the religions around; for while they were always bound by some
higher, and unknown fate, Yahweh the God of Israel is subordinate
to none. He is the One who is God, the LORD, and in whom all
things have their being. To live within the will of God is the way
of peace.

But when, as with Cain, we are separated from God, our world
is one of constantly searching anxiety. For in him is our satisfaction.
Anywhere else, as Augustine said, our hearts are restless until they
rest in God.

Once again, Calvin's comment hits the nail on the head:

111

There is no peace for men, unless they acquiesce in the providence of God, and are persuaded that their lives are the objects of his care . . . they can only quietly enjoy any of God's benefits so long as they regard themselves as placed in the world, on this condition, that they pass their lives under his government.[20]

But Cain, instead, hears God's curse. 'You are cursed away from the land' – that is, you are banished. Perhaps, as Cassuto suggests, the phrase also means that just as Abel's blood cried from the ground, so now the ground itself curses Cain. Just as Genesis 4, following Genesis 3, indicates the spreading and development of sin, so also it indicates the deepening of the judgment of God. For in chapter 3 it was the serpent and the ground which were cursed. Now the curse is spoken to a man. Cain regards himself as being *driven* away (4:14) – driven from God, driven from his home.

So Cain went away from the presence of the Lord, and became 'a fugitive and a wanderer' (4:12). His life was now marked by searching, wandering, visions of dread (*'whoever finds me will slay me'*, 4:14), haunted by the crying blood, hunted by fear, dominated, in other words, by all pervasive anxiety.

Helmut Thielicke comments on these verses:

When the world becomes fatherless, it becomes a weird and homeless place, and I am driven into unending flight. Every tree, every milestone becomes a threat. So I try to charm away the weirdness with a talisman that dangles in my car. Or I consult the stars for some dodge by which to escape being caught in my run of bad luck. Or I procure lucky numbers to increase my chances and find out the dates and the times when I must be careful because they are unlucky times. This is the law of life in the land of Nod – when the security of home is gone.[21]

This is the anxiety which Kierkegaard calls 'the sickness unto death'.

For anxious Cain has lost not only God, he has also lost the earth. The land which was his sustenance has now drunk Abel's blood. *It shall no longer yield to you its strength* (4:12). Cain's whole existence is out of line.

That is his anxiety – that is the land of restlessness – the desperate homesickness which pervades the land of Nod. Is not this all around us? Does not the restlessness of Cain picture vividly a life that is lived outside the presence of God?

[20] Calvin, p. 212.   [21] Thielicke, pp. 218ff.

8. The mark of Cain

Then the LORD *said to him, 'Not so! If any one slays Cain, vengeance shall be taken on him sevenfold.' And the* LORD *put a mark on Cain, lest any who came upon him should kill him.* ¹⁶*Then Cain went away from the presence of the* LORD, *and dwelt in the land of Nod, east of Eden.*

¹⁷*Cain knew his wife, and she conceived and bore Enoch; and he built a city, and called the name of the city after the name of his son, Enoch.* ¹⁸ *To Enoch was born Irad; and Irad was the father of Mehujael, and Mehujael the father of Methushael, and Methushael the father of Lamech.* ¹⁹*And Lamech took two wives; the name of the one was Adah, and the name of the other Zillah.* ²⁰*Adah bore Jabal; he was the father of those who dwell in tents and have cattle.* ²¹*His brother's name was Jubal; he was the father of all those who play the lyre and pipe.* ²²*Zillah bore Tubal-cain; he was the forger of all instruments of bronze and iron. The sister of Tubal-cain was Naamah.*

²³*Lamech said to his wives:*

> *'Adah and Zillah, hear my voice;*
> *you wives of Lamech, hearken to what I say:*
> *I have slain a man for wounding me,*
> *a young man for striking me.*
> ²⁴ *If Cain is avenged sevenfold,*
> *truly Lamech seventy-sevenfold.'*   (4:15–24)

To speak of Cain's restlessness is by no means to say that all Cain's life is valueless. Not at all. In his restlessness he is active and creative. He builds a city (4:17); he fathers a family (4:18); his descendants develop farming (4:20); some play the lyre and the pipe (4:21); others forge instruments of bronze and iron (4:22). Civilization begins to grow outside the Garden. Even in the land of restlessness, there is culture, there is art. Surprisingly, it is through Cain the homeless, the fugitive, the prodigal, that God's commission to his people to work and to subdue creation begins to be established.

And perhaps this is part of the meaning of the mark God put upon Cain (4:15). This is a mark not of divine judgment but of divine protection, divine restraint. It is given lest vengeance should get out of hand. God does not abandon Cain, but places him under a protective shield. The law of retaliation will not have the last word. Cain's fear is that others, perhaps seeing the divine protection as some sort of precedent, will themselves follow Cain's example and murder him. But no, the mark of protection is also a mark of warning. No-one may imitate Cain! No-one can plead custom as

113

an excuse for sinning! God's purposes are not achieved through the law of retaliation. The mark on Cain is not a protection that removes all homesickness, but it does prevent the full force of evil power from exercising its destructiveness. Even in the far country, the prodigal Cain bears God's mark.

And maybe some of the ordering processes of what we call civilization function as protective shields in God's mercy for his people. God restrains the full force of evil's power, by the ordering of societies, by the provision of governments, and by the refreshment of culture. God is concerned with the growth of art, of society, of technology even in a world which is homesick for him: even for people who are out of touch with his love. The sons of Cain, too, have gifts from God (4:17–22).

It is worth quoting Calvin once more. Often perceived as a theologian of divine judgment, Calvin is also the clearest exponent of 'common grace':

> It is truly wonderful that this race, which had most deeply fallen from integrity, should have excelled the rest of the posterity of Adam in rare endowments. . . . Let us know then, that the sons of Cain, though deprived of the Spirit of regeneration, were yet endued with gifts of no despicable kind; just as the experience of all ages teaches us how widely the rays of divine light have shone on unbelieving nations, for the benefit of the present life; and we see at the present time, that the excellent gifts of the Spirit are diffused through the whole human race.[22]

There is much in the world of the arts and the sciences which bears witness to the common grace and enriching gifts of the Creator, even among those who do not acknowledge him, and would not attribute their skills to his enabling. Let us thank God that every expression of creativity and beauty, every advance of science, every new composition in music and every line of poetry, speaks in some measure of the creative grace of God.

But, sadly, that is not the whole story. All this positive good has to be set in the context of decay. For, though Cain is protected by God, he still seeks a security outside God. Another aspect to his building a city is seen in the symbol of the city as a man-made security in the land of restlessness. It was, we are told, 'east of Eden', as if to point up Cain's glance back towards the Garden. But instead of returning to the place of divine pleasure, Cain substitutes his own security for that which comes from God.

As Ellul notes, he called the city 'Enoch', the same name as his

---

[22] Calvin, p. 218.

son. Is Cain seeking here to 'make a name' for himself and his family? If so, that is a theme which later chapters of Genesis 1 – 11 will also explore. 'Enoch' is a name which may mean 'dedication' or 'initiation'. So Cain is beginning again. But:

> In Cain's eyes it is not a beginning again, but a beginning. God's creation is seen as nothing. God did nothing and in no case did he finish anything. Now a start is made, and it is no longer God beginning but man. And thus Cain, with everything he does, digs a little deeper the abyss between himself and God.[23]

While not endorsing all Ellul's despair at the meaning of the city as a symbol of the work of man set over against God, he is surely right to remind us again of the ambiguity of life outside the Garden.

In this chapter, the ambiguity of it all is unambiguously stressed. Technical achievement is set over against moral perversity. Polygamy (4:19), violence, brutality and self-assertion (4:23–24) still, despite God's restraining hand, mark the life in the land of restlessness.

Humanist psychiatrist R. D. Laing makes a similar diagnosis:

> We are born into a world where alienation awaits us. We are potentially men, but are in an alienated state, and this state is not simply a natural system. Alienation as our present destiny is achieved only by outrageous violence perpetrated by human beings on human beings.[24]

In Genesis 4 Lamech is singled out for comment. As Kidner remarks on verse 24, 'Lamech's taunt-song reveals the swift progress of sin. Where Cain had succumbed to it (7), Lamech exults in it.'[25] Lamech's boast is that he has killed a young child 'for wounding me', and he proclaims a seventy-sevenfold vengeance. Lamech is going far beyond the divinely given boundary which applied to Cain (see 4:15). Lamech stands for one among many in these chapters who tries to break the bounds which God has laid down. In him the law of retaliation reigns supreme. It is also much more severe than the *lex talionis* which formed the basis for ancient Israel's law. In that law,[26] justice required only an eye for an eye, only a tooth for a tooth. Without that protecting law (as Wenham points out), 'even the able-bodied, let alone the weak, will be at the mercy of men like Lamech'. Surely Jesus must have had Genesis 4:24 in mind when he urged not retaliation but forgiveness to

---

[23] J. Ellul, *The Meaning of the City* (Eerdmans, 1970), p. 6.
[24] R. D. Laing, *The Politics of Experience* (Penguin, 1967), p. 12.
[25] Kidner, p. 78.   [26] Ex. 21:22–25.

115

'seventy-times seven'.[27] The steward who, having been forgiven a fortune by his lord, then demanded from a fellow servant that he pay his trifling debt of a few pence, was severely judged. He showed by his behaviour to his fellow that he had never really appreciated what forgiveness from his lord had meant. The way of the kingdom of heaven is the absolute converse of the law of retaliation.

Everywhere there is Cain: jealousy, hatred, brutality, fear of retaliation, restlessness, anxiety. Cain had not come to God in humble dependence on grace, but in arrogant self-sufficiency.

But Abel had brought a lamb, and the sacrifice of the lamb brought in faith was accepted by God. As Hebrews 11:4 tells us, Abel illustrates here a theme which is expanded time and again through the Bible: that approach to God from within the fallen world is on the basis of sacrifice; on the basis of life laid down in death; on the basis of the shed blood of a lamb. What Abel did not know was that in God's economy there would be another Lamb whose shed blood cried out to God on behalf of all men. And it is in this other Lamb that God provides his ultimate answer to Cain. In Christ, the law of retaliation is for ever set aside. As a lamb before its shearers is dumb, so when unjustly accused, he did not open his mouth.[28] 'When he was reviled, he did not revile in return; when he suffered, he did not threaten; but he trusted to him who judges justly.'[29] He himself bore our sins in his body on the tree. In him the sin is covered. In him we are given a new name: a share in his Name. In him the fear can be cast out, the anxiety removed. In him the homesick prodigal can hear a welcome back home, and begin again to learn how to love his brother.

9. Seth

And Adam knew his wife again, and she bore a son and called his name Seth, for she said, 'God has appointed for me another child instead of Abel, for Cain slew him.' [26]*To Seth also a son was born, and he called his name Enosh. At that time men began to call upon the name of the LORD.* (4:25–26)

We return now to Adam and his family. The story of primeval history continues. *Adam knew his wife* (4:25) – and from their intimate relationship Seth is born. The name 'Seth' means 'appointing', and Eve's faith here that God has appointed Seth is in marked contrast to her claim at the start of the chapter (4:1). Several commentators suggest that Eve is less proud and triumphant now. As

[27] Cf. Mt. 18:22.   [28] Cf. Is. 53:7.   [29] 1 Pet. 2:23.

she mourns the loss of her two sons, it is God, she says, who has appointed another child in place of Abel. She does not use the personal name Yahweh – which was used in verse 1. Now God, perhaps, is seen more as the majestic Creator; less the intimate LORD. There is, perhaps, an allusion back to 3:15 in the word 'offspring' ('God has sent me other offspring') – and perhaps the looking forward also to a new line of children from this new son.

At that time, says verse 26, *men began to call upon the name of the LORD* – referring now to the worship of Yahweh, the one whose personal Name belongs to the covenant community.

Christian writers have sometimes contrasted the family of Cain, marked by alienation from God, with this new family, born of faith in Yahweh. Here, some say, is a prefiguring of the church. Seth is seen as a godly and faithful man, and after he had begotten a son like himself, 'the face of the church began to appear'.

Whether glimmerings after such thoughts were in this author's mind is hard to tell. One of the purposes in including this short genealogy is to lead us on into the story of Noah and the Flood. For it is from this line, from Adam through Seth, that Noah, the 'herald of righteousness'[30] is born. What is clear, though, is that the author's own faith shines through. Despite all the ravages of sin, its spreading through the generations, its violence, vengeance and murderous rage, the isolation, alienation and anxiety to which it leads, and the disorders and ambiguities of life in this broken world, God can still be known. Eve said so in her cry of faith (4:25). The story-teller says so too: *At that time men began to call upon the name of the LORD* (4:26).

[30] 2 Pet. 2:5.

117

5:1 – 8:22
4. The eye of the storm

The story of the Flood faces us not only with the faith of Noah, and the patience of God, but it sets these in an apocalyptic context of world history and sovereign grace. The Flood tells us of the end of a world order, and of a new beginning. It is the story of salvation woven into a backcloth of creation, providence and judgment. It is salvation, not only for a man and his family, but for the human race and for every living creature. It is about survival when the fabric of all things is under threat of extinction. It is a story especially appropriate for a world facing global catastrophe. It tells us that God remains committed to his world.

We have commented before on the crises which face life on this earth. We are rapidly using up our raw materials and fossil fuels. We are polluting the air and the seas. We are destroying, on a vast scale, irreplaceable forests. We are creating a global greenhouse with possibly horrendous consequences. Species of animals are fast becoming extinct. Man-made radiation hazards are making parts of the globe uninhabitable. The 'developed' nations are squandering billions of pounds on ever more sophisticated weapons of mass destruction; their deterrence theory deliberately trades on threat and deceit. The possibilities of a nuclear holocaust, and of a subsequent nuclear winter are ever alive. Violent crime is on the increase, and our societies are more and more engulfed in fear – and in the apathy and depression which fear can breed. Death by AIDS may become a pandemic. There are wars and rumours of wars, nation rises against nation, kingdom against kingdom. There are famines and earthquakes in various places. Many fall away from their faith, betrayal and hatred are all around. False prophets keep appearing, promising hopes which they cannot ever fulfil. All around us are features of the End-Time.

It was in such a context that Jesus made his only reference to the story of Noah. 'As it was in the days of Noah, so will it be in

119

the days of the Son of man.'¹ There Jesus' concern is about the
End-Time. His use of the Noah story illustrates the fact that divine
judgment is coming to the world and yet men and women carry
on regardless. It is as though they were saying, 'It won't happen
to me.' 'They did not know until the flood came and swept them
all away.'² 'Watch, therefore,' Jesus says: 'your Lord is coming.'³
Let the story of the Flood be a warning to take God seriously.

The story of Noah is no Sunday School fantasy of a Worzel
Gummidge figure. This is about world history, world judgment,
world destiny and world salvation.

As Richard Bauckham has made clear, however,⁴ the apocalyptic
questions facing our world are of a different order from those in
the Noah story. There the threat to survival was from without –
from the forces of nature. And God's promise was that there would
never be another flood. Now the questions of human destiny,
whether of ecological pollution or nuclear holocaust, are issues we
have brought upon ourselves. We hold the power to destroy the
world. And God does not necessarily promise to stop us. We must
be prepared to read this story, therefore, not simply as a divine
reassurance of security, but to take God's commitment to the well-
being of the world as a rebuke to our vaunted human pride and
recklessness. If God is committed to his world, how dare we take
to ourselves decisions of world destiny which belong only to
him?

The narrative takes up Genesis 6 – 9. In much of it there are
parallels with flood stories in other ancient Near Eastern texts.
There is a Babylonian story in the famous *Epic of Gilgamesh* in
which the hero gains immortality by passing through the waters of
a flood. After being warned by God in a dream, Utnapishtim, with
all kinds of animals, is rescued from the deluge in a huge ship. The
ship grounds on a mountain, and Utnapishtim sends out a dove, a
swallow and a raven. The hero offers a sacrifice to the gods, who
grant immortality to Utnapishtim and his wife. A necklace of lapis
lazuli is given as a sign of remembrance.

There is a Sumerian flood story also, illustrating many of the
same themes. Certainly, there seem to have been floods at very
early dates from the evidence of excavations in Ur of the Chaldees,
and in other Mesopotamian cities. The dates do not all correspond,
however. There is no flood story, though, in the ancient literature
of, for example, Egypt, and certainly no widely agreed archeological
evidence for a universal global flood.

What does seem certain is that between the Tigris and the

---

¹ Lk. 17:26; see also Mt. 24:37.   ² Mt. 24:39.   ³ Mt. 24:42.
⁴ 'The Genesis Flood and the Nuclear Holocaust: A Hermeneutical Reflection',
Churchman, 1985, no. 2, pp. 146ff.

Euphrates there was a history of severe flooding, and that these
traumatic events were taken into the self-understanding of the
peoples, and interpreted as having particular religious significance.
The simplicity of the biblical story in comparison with the Babylonian one suggests that the people of Yahweh had kept their
account free from some of the embellishments found in the Gilgamesh Epic.[5] In the biblical version, the people's self-understanding comes from their knowledge that they were the people of
Yahweh. Their interpretation of their flood stressed the significance
that God himself attached to this experience.

God's revelation of his truth is always through event plus
interpretation. Who could have guessed the significance of the
snake, the rainbow, of circumcision, of baptism, or of the death of
a carpenter on a Judean hill? These events are given their significance by God's word about them. Revelation is rooted in objective
fact – there is an objectivity to divine truth. But the facts become
revelatory through the light of the significance given them by the
divine word. The Flood story as told in Genesis is about God: his
judgments, his blessing, his covenant.

1. From Adam to Noah

*This is the book of the generations of Adam. When God created
man, he made him in the likeness of God. ²Male and female he
created them, and he blessed them and named them Man when
they were created. ³When Adam had lived a hundred and thirty
years, he became the father of a son in his own likeness, after his
image, and named him Seth. ⁴The days of Adam after he became
the father of Seth were eight hundred years; and he had other sons
and daughters. ⁵Thus all the days that Adam lived were nine hundred and thirty years; and he died.*

*⁶When Seth had lived a hundred and five years, he became the
father of Enosh. ⁷Seth lived after the birth of Enosh eight hundred
and seven years, and had other sons and daughters. ⁸Thus all the
days of Seth were nine hundred and twelve years; and he died.*

*⁹When Enosh had lived ninety years, he became the father of
Kenan. ¹⁰Enosh lived after the birth of Kenan eight hundred and
fifteen years, and had other sons and daughters. ¹¹Thus all the days
of Enosh were nine hundred and five years; and he died.*

*¹²When Kenan had lived seventy years, he became the father of
Mahalalel. ¹³Kenan lived after the birth of Mahalalel eight hundred
and forty years, and had other sons and daughters. ¹⁴Thus all the
days of Kenan were nine hundred and ten years; and he died.*

[5] *Cf.* Wenham, p. 164.

[15]*When Mahalalel had lived sixty-five years, he became the father of Jared.* [16]*Mahalalel lived after the birth of Jared eight hundred and thirty years, and had other sons and daughters.* [17]*Thus all the days of Mahalalel were eight hundred and ninety-five years; and he died.*

[18]*When Jared had lived a hundred and sixty-two years he became the father of Enoch.* [19]*Jared lived after the birth of Enoch eight hundred years, and had other sons and daughters.* [20]*Thus all the days of Jared were nine hundred and sixty-two years; and he died.*

[21]*When Enoch had lived sixty-five years, he became the father of Methuselah.* [22]*Enoch walked with God after the birth of Methuselah three hundred years, and had other sons and daughters.* [23]*Thus all the days of Enoch were three hundred and sixty-five years.* [24]*Enoch walked with God; and he was not, for God took him.*

[25]*When Methuselah had lived a hundred and eighty-seven years, he became the father of Lamech.* [26]*Methuselah lived after the birth of Lamech seven hundred and eighty-two years, and had other sons and daughters.* [27]*Thus all the days of Methuselah were nine hundred and sixty-nine years; and he died.*

[28]*When Lamech had lived a hundred and eighty-two years, he became the father of a son,* [29]*and called his name Noah, saying, 'Out of the ground which the LORD has cursed this one shall bring us relief from our work and from the toil of our hands.'* [30]*Lamech lived after the birth of Noah five hundred and ninety-five years, and had other sons and daughters.* [31]*Thus all the days of Lamech were seven hundred and seventy-seven years; and he died.*

[32]*After Noah was five hundred years old, Noah became the father of Shem, Ham, and Japheth.*

(5:1–32)

The Flood story as we have it in our Bibles is prefaced with a genealogy. Genealogies 'set the scene' historically. We find the same pattern in the Gospels in the New Testament. At the beginning of the stories of salvation through Jesus Christ given by Matthew and by Luke, we find lists of ancestors,[6] and the line of God's dealings with his people traced from generation to generation. They remind us of our inter-connectedness as human beings with one another. They point us to a God who acts in history. As in the Gospels, so here in Genesis 1 – 11, the story of salvation is prefaced with such a historical survey – and a history that is portrayed theologically. Interestingly, as Wenham notes, in the Sumerian flood story (parallels with which we noted in the story of Cain and Abel, with references to nomads, city-building and the beginnings of public

[6] Mk. 1:1–17; Lk. 3:23–38.

worship), the description of the flood is preceded there also by reference to the kings who reigned before the Flood – some of them for an exceptionally long time. The resemblances between the Sumerian king lists and the lists of generations in Genesis 5 have been noted by many commentators. None the less, as Wenham argues, there are significant differences in the names, the times, and the purposes of these different accounts.[7] For as before, the editors of Genesis have a particular theological theme in mind.

So what is going on in this strange chapter?

Here we find in particular three threads woven together: creative blessing; judgment; and fellowship with God.

a. Blessing

After the formula indicating the 'developing story' (*the book of the generations of* . . . ; see p. 54), Genesis 5 opens with a summary of creation, the co-humanity of male and female in the divine likeness, and the birth of Seth in the likeness of his father.

In the Eastern Church, this picture of the Adam family, all in the image and likeness of God, was often used as a symbol of the Trinity. And this led to an understanding of what we might call a 'social' doctrine of the divine image. It is not the human individual who fully represents God, nor even the first pair, Adam and Eve, but the first family. Although this interpretation did not find favour in the Western Church, and is clearly going beyond the text, it does serve to remind us of the *community* of creation: that God is Being-in-Communion and that human beings are intended to reflect the life of the Trinity – personal relationships of communion and love.

The author now launches forth into a long description of the generations. God's creative blessing on humankind is expressed partly in the significance which God attaches to individual people. Ten patriarchs are mentioned in this chapter, their ages recorded, and their sons' names also. But God's blessing is also, and perhaps much more fully, expressed in their inter-connectedness with each other. To be a human person is to be in a given set of relationships, to be a creature in time, with a past and a future. As we noted when we were discussing the meaning of the 'divine image' (see pp. 36–37), to be in God's image primarily means to be in a certain relationship with him. It is our relationship with God which then gives meaning to our relationships with one another. This genealogy reminds us of such relationships, and of the divine blessing which can come through them. God's creative blessing extends through

[7] Wenham, p. 125.

123

time. God works by families. The story of salvation which we will read in the following chapters of Genesis is of a piece with world history – the history of families – to which Genesis 5 points, which stretches from Adam to Noah.

b. The time-line

The faith of this writer, in common with the Old Testament authors generally, is distinctive in many ways from the religions of neighbouring cultures. Nowhere is this clearer than in their understanding of time.

Whereas some other cultures worked with a cyclical view in which all things are merely part of an endless turning of the wheel of nature, with no start, no end, no significance, the Old Testament views time as linear. There was a beginning – the author refers to that once more (5:1). There will be an end; much of this chapter is about endings (*and he died*, e.g. vv. 5, 8, 11, 14, *etc.*). In between, unique and unrepeatable events happen. People live their lives, make their choices, marry and are given in marriage, have their children, celebrate their joys, reap the result of their failures. Each event has *significance*.

We noted in chapter 1 how the mind of the writer there was not far from the concerns of science. We saw the same in chapter 2, in the ordering of the animal world. Here is another pointer in the same direction. For, as Stanley Jaki[8] and others have asked, why was it that science did not become viable in any of the great civilizations of antiquity? Why not in ancient China with its highly developed technology? Why not in Persia or Egypt, Mexico or Peru? Why did the flame of science which began to burn in Greece all too soon flicker and die? Why did science have to wait till seventeenth-century Europe for it to begin to grow? Jaki argues that for science to live, two things have to come together: sufficient conditions of a material sort (a limited technology and a capacity for notation, for example) *and* also a shared approach to truth. There are, indeed, many aspects of Christian Europe of the seventeenth century which contributed to the viability of science, but among them was its biblical understanding of time. If we look at how many of the other civilizations (China, India, Babylon, Egypt, Greece, the Incas, the Mayas, the Aztecs) conceive of time, we often find in them the idea that the universe is eternally oscillating in such a way that all events are repeated an infinite number of times. This basic belief produces a fatalism about the cosmos, and there can be no science when such a Fate is in control. For fatalism

---

[8] In *Science and Creation* (Scottish Academic Press, 1974).

saps the confidence of people in the significance of their lives. Nothing *matters* any more. So the curiosity needed for discovery is simply not developed. Occasionally isolated individuals break from this pattern and achieve remarkable discoveries, but there is no supportive intellectual world within which science can grow.

Biblical faith, however, gives a view of history and of time, which has a beginning and an end. Within such a time-line, the activities of individual people do have purpose, direction, achievement. What we do *matters* and makes a difference to the world. For each individual is an unrepeatable event, and each action unique: neither has precisely happened before, nor will again. That is part of the reason why the Bible bothers with genealogies: we are people who belong within a significant history. There is no cosmic fatalism here. Our actions of creativity express the blessing of God. Our wrongdoings – as we shall see more clearly in chapter 6 – bring us under divine judgment.

The genealogies also remind us that there is a limit to the time we are allotted on earth. Our individual lives had a beginning, and will have an end. There was a time before which we were not. As far as each individual is concerned, there is a void of non-being before our birth, as we trace our own time-line back. And though, as we get older, we move further from that void – and think more of the other end of life, none the less the question presses: What was there before I was? Where am I from? What is it that has made me me?

The fascination with genealogy is a fascination with that question – a deep searching for a meaning to my life before I was. And the answer of biblical faith is that though I was not there, God was there. The limit to my life at its beginning is part of God's gift to me. The God who is Creator of the heavens and the earth has given me my allotted life-time. And as his character is made known as Yahweh, the gracious covenant Lord, I can receive that gift of life as one of loving blessing. The genealogy tells me that I, too, belong. And the New Testament fills out the picture for me that Jesus Christ, the one to whom I belong, is the Lord of time, the King of the Ages.[9]

c. Judgment

But Genesis 5 is also about judgment. Or, rather, it is about the outworking of that word to Adam: 'You will surely die.' For the striking mark of chapter 5 is the universality of the rule of death. Of each of these characters we are told that he lived for a while –

---

[9] 1 Tim. 1:7.

125

and for some of them, apparently, for quite a while!! – 'and he died', 'and he died', 'and he died'. Quite what we are to make of the enormously long life-spans is not clear. Many authors of the ancient world recorded similar longevity for distant ancestors. It may be a way of marking the distance between primeval history and the contemporary world. Or perhaps the numbers have symbolic meanings of one sort or another. The puzzle is still unsolved. But what is clear is the author's insistence that despite the creative vitality of these ancestors, even their long lives ended in death.

Even the descendants of Seth are subject to the power of death.

Just as our allotted time-span has a beginning before which we were not, it will have an end, after which we are faced with the very edge of our existence. Our life in time will end. There will come a moment, as Barth puts it, when, still alive, we shall not be able to live any further. 'For the time we shall then have will be a time with a present (and with our whole past behind us), but with no more future.'[10] And now we are faced – if we are willing to face it – with the threat of non-being again. Death overshadows us. Whatever our existence in death means – and for the Christian, there is a glorious hope in resurrection – it cannot consist in the continuation of life in time. Our life in time will end.

While we can rejoice in the blessing of God in the gift of life – for he is the giver of life – what are we to say of the end of life? Is that, too, part of the divine blessing? Ernest Becker's book *The Denial of Death* indicates how the deepest human emotions, the most powerful human motivations, often derive from a refusal to accept death as a reality.[11] Death is a denial of life. Genesis 5 tells us again and again what Genesis 3 had already taught, that death is a sign of God's judgment on sinful people.

However much, therefore, we may thank God for the opening up of terminal care for dying people, for the discovery of means by which we can help one another to die without physical pain, for the psychological insights into the processes of 'letting go' of life, and – at a biological level – of seeing death as 'natural' and 'normal', from a biblical perspective we must say more. We cannot avoid the theological judgment that far from being 'natural', death is the most unnatural of events. Far from being our 'friend', death is the Last Enemy. Death is not part of the creation which was 'very good'.

Barth seems nearer to the truth when he writes:

The man who fears death, even though he contrives to put a

[10] *Church Dogmatics*, III/2, p. 587.
[11] E. Becker, *The Denial of Death* (New York: The Free Press, 1973).

somewhat better face on it, is at least nearer to the truth than the man who does not fear it, or rather pretends that there is no reason why he should do so. Since it is the sign of the divine judgement on human sin and guilt, it is very much to be feared.[12]

It is only when all this has been said, and the awful persistence of the theme of death in Genesis 5 has been appreciated, that the New Testament picture of Jesus' confrontation with death can fill us with hope. For we may be spared the pain and fear of death only because Another has suffered it in his death for us. In him, the Last Enemy is overcome, and the power of resurrection life is displayed.

It is the enemy, the 'last enemy' of man whom God, in the death of Jesus, declares to be His enemy as well, and treats as such by placing Himself at the side of man in the verdict there pronounced, and snatching man from its jaws by the death of Jesus for him. It remains for us as a sign of the divine judgement. We no longer have to suffer the judgement itself.[13]

It is because Christ has suffered death for us – facing for us in the Garden of Gethsemane and on the Cross of Calvary, the pain of the abyss of non-being, of being cut off from the source of life, of bearing the judgment of God for human sin, of 'descending to the place of the dead' (as the Creed puts it), that we can be welcomed back into fellowship with the Father. Only in him do we find the love that casts out fear. Only in him do we know that when we reach the edge of our life in time, he stands beside us. Only in him do we hear the Father's voice welcoming us home, and telling us that our death is no longer our Enemy, but is 'falling asleep in Christ'. It is the power of Christ's resurrection which forces back into our fears, and back too into the fears of generations past, the message of hope for the people of God. Without that we would merely be left with Genesis 5's mournful litany of despair: 'and he died.'

d. Fellowship

Human history is the story of the creative blessing of God; it is the story also of the universal rule of death.

But one man breaks the pattern. As a glittering jewel in a pile of otherwise rather dull stones, we are told of Enoch. *Enoch walked with God; and he was not, for God took him* (5:24). There is a

[12] *Church Dogmatics*, III/4, p. 598.   [13] *Ibid.*, p. 600.

small remnant of faith; there can be true fellowship with God which breaks the thraldom of death, even though change and decay in all around I see.

Enoch's faith was his life. After the birth of his son – was that a particularly significant moment in his life of faith? – we read that he *walked with God*, or, as Hebrews 11:5 has it, he 'pleased God'. Here is another of Hebrews' men of faith – his walking with God, we may judge, was the walking of faithful obedience. Noah, too, 'walked with God' (Gn. 6:9). Abraham walked before God (Gn. 17:1), and the high point of eighth-century prophecy is summed up in Micah 6:8, which includes the requirement that all people should 'walk humbly with your God'. Enoch is singled out among these representatives of the godly line of Seth; of him it is twice said that he walked with God. The writer wants to underline the significance of the obedience of faith which Enoch illustrates. And by faith, we learn, Enoch was 'taken up so that he should not see death'.[14] Here is a vivid portrayal of the power of God over death, and the faith that in God death is ultimately conquered by life. In Enoch, the 'heavens' break into the normal pattern of things on 'earth'; Enoch is caught up, like Elijah, into the heavens.[15] There are elaborate apocalyptic traditions in Jewish writings about Enoch (in the apocryphal Book of Enoch, for example). By contrast, Genesis 5 gives us this restrained reference to the mystery and power of God: *he was not, for God took him.*

So even back here in the primeval history, there are glimpses of hope. Fellowship with God means the restoration of life, and life which is no longer bounded by the limits of time. As we have seen, Genesis refers several times to the separation of heaven and earth. God's 'place' and man's 'place' are not to be confused. When human beings try to put themselves in the place of God, the result is confusion, disorder and death. But as we have said before, heaven and earth can meet. The New Testament tells us that they meet in Christ our Lord, the one Mediator between man and God. The divine word is made flesh in the incarnation. Humanity is taken into God in the resurrection and ascension. The meeting-place of heaven and earth is Jesus Christ: and the two 'places' meet in us who are 'in Christ'. In him we are brought into 'God's place'. In him we are 'raised . . . up with him, and made [to] sit with him in the heavenly places in Christ Jesus'.[16] But this, we need to remind ourselves, is 'by grace'.[17] By God's grace, the boundary between heaven and earth is breached, and we are welcomed into fellowship with the Father, through Christ in the Spirit, and can walk in his

[14] Heb. 11:5.   [15] *Cf.* 2 Ki. 2:9ff.   [16] Eph. 2:6.   [17] Eph. 2:8.

love, his light and his wisdom.[18]

And in all this, Enoch is our forerunner: he *walked with God.*

Genesis 5 acts as a trailer for chapters 6 – 9. It provides the link between Adam and Noah: God's beginning and God's beginning again. And in these chapters, the threads woven together in chapter 5 are elaborated into a much fuller tapestry. For in the story of Noah, on much broader canvas and in much more vivid colours, we will also find depicted the universality of divine judgment, and the power of death, and yet also the gift of grace, and the remnant of faith. Noah, too, walked with God (Gn. 6:9).

2. Angel marriages: crossing the boundaries

When men began to multiply on the face of the ground, and daughters were born to them, ²the sons of God saw that the daughters of men were fair; and they took to wife such of them as they chose. ³Then the LORD said, 'My spirit shall not abide in man for ever, for he is flesh, but his days shall be a hundred and twenty years.' ⁴The Nephilim were on the earth in those days, and also afterward, when the sons of God came in to the daughters of men, and they bore children to them. These were the mighty men that were of old, the men of renown. (6:1–4)

What function does this bizarre little paragraph serve? There have been a number of Christian commentators who believe that this describes the intermarriage of the sons of the godly line of Seth with the daughters of other ungodly families. The spread of the evil which provoked the judgment of the Flood – for as we shall see, that is how it is described – was this dilution of the purity of the people of God, this loss of their distinctiveness, a failure to remain true to their God? There are, of course, many passages in the Bible which illustrate this theme. The holiness code of Leviticus 19 indicates the way in which the character of God, 'I am the LORD', is to find expression in many of the varied aspects of life, including marriage, of the people – and all are ways of obeying the word 'You shall be holy; for I, the LORD your God am holy'.[19] After the Exile, both Ezra and Nehemiah condemn mixed marriages between the people of God and other nations.[20] And in the New Testament St Paul urges his readers in Corinth not to be 'mismated with unbelievers. For what partnership have righteousness and iniquity? Or what fellowship has light with darkness?'[21]

[18] Eph. 5:2, 8, 15.   [19] Lv. 19:2.   [20] Ezr. 9:1–2; 10:1–44; Ne. 13:23ff.
[21] 2 Cor. 6:14.

If this is what the opening paragraph of Genesis 6 is about, there are other biblical writers to support the case.

It seems likely, however, to mean something else. Most commentators reject this view, not least because the phrase 'sons of God' is not usually used to speak of God's people. Usually the phrase means 'angels',[22] and the difficult passages in 1 Peter 3:19–20 and 2 Peter 2:4–6 would seem to support this interpretation. Some angelic beings have 'left their proper dwelling',[23] and these *sons of God* are taking to wife *the daughters of men*. There are many stories of the marriage between men and the gods in the literature of the ancient world, yet in comparison with many other traditions, the Genesis text is remarkably free from mythological features. We are told that the sons of God saw that the daughters of men were *fair* (literally 'good'), and they took to wife such of them as they chose. The same sequence of words as described the downfall of the woman in the Garden (Gn. 3:6) is repeated here: 'saw . . . good . . . took'.[24] Here is a pointer to the underlying theology of this paragraph. Here again we are reminded of the spread of wickedness in the world. It might be, as David Clines indicates, that the phrase 'sons of God' includes the sense both of divine beings and of human rulers – ancient rulers of the pre-Flood world who were regarded as divine or semi-divine.[25] Whoever they were, there is something passionate about their embrace (6:2), and something monstrous about its outcome (6:4). *The Nephilim* refer, apparently, to giants,[26] the origin of some of whom at least, if not all, is traced to these angel marriages.

So what is all this about?

In the first place, as we have seen before in Genesis, the boundaries between 'heaven and earth' are being blurred: once again the boundary between the divine and the human is breached in a crossing of God-given limits. And once again, there is disaster. Some commentators see here a description of the proud tyranny of power, in which might is right. Whatever else these giants stand for, they illustrate a monstrous pushing out beyond the ways of God. In these few vivid sentences, the author is calling the people of God back to their limits. It is *God* who sets the boundaries for human life. There are certain things human beings may not do if they are to retain their humanity. This story of the intercourse between the earthly and the heavenly beings indicates a refusal to accept those bounds. Here is another extension and deepening of the meaning of sin. There are overpowering forces within the world which drive us to overstep God's bounds. And when we try to

[22] *E.g.* Jb. 1:6; Ps. 29:1. [23] *Cf.* Jude 6. [24] *Cf.* Wenham, p. 141.
[25] D. Clines, 'The significance of the "Sons of God" episode in the context of primeval history', *JSOT* 13 (1979), pp. 33ff. [26] *Cf.* Nu. 13:33.

take to ourselves that which belongs only within the providence of God, we are likely to succumb to the demonic. The 'demonization of the world': is that the author's concern here? The evil within humankind can, if not restrained, overstep God-given limits, and when it does, it produces giants that human beings can no longer handle. It sets free powers which should have no place in this world.

Secondly, there is another breaking of the boundaries in the 'violent and polygamous lust of the "sons of God" ' (Clines). The order established by God in the Garden was monogamous. Lamech, we are told, broke the boundaries by taking two wives. Here the 'sons of God' take as many as they choose (6:2).

Thirdly, whereas in the Garden, the man who bears the divine image represents God on the earth, exercising benign dominion over the rest of creation, here 'we now have the presence of the divine on earth in a form that utterly misrepresents God through its exercise of royal violence and despotic authority over other humans' (Clines). Here is a 'satanic parody of the idea of the image of God'.

Fourthly, the Nephilim were *the men of renown* – literally 'men of name'. We noted how striving for a name was seen in Cain's naming his city after his son (*cf*. Gn. 4:17). We shall see it again in the builders of Babel who sought to make a name for themselves (11:4). But this is more than arrogance. It is an attack on the prerogative of God. For it is God who gives his people a name and makes them renowned.[27] It is God who will say to Abraham, 'I will . . . make your name great' (12:3).

The sons of God saw that the daughters of men were fair, and they took them as wives, breaking through the bounds of God's created order.

But God speaks his Word! God sets the limits. God decrees at what point the judgment shall come. Even the giant, as with the Satan in the book of Job, is an adversary on a chain. God is still in control. And in his word of judgment, God first contrasts his *spirit* with human *flesh* (6:3). God's spirit is his life-giving power. 'Flesh' describes the human person from the perspective of mortality. Isaiah contrasts 'men' and 'flesh' with 'God' and 'spirit'.[28] Without the breath of God's Spirit, human life decays. If this incident points to yet another attempt by human beings to grasp at immortality, God reminds men and women that they are 'flesh'. Verse 3 is complicated, but probably means that God's life-giving breath will not remain in humankind for ever. It will be withdrawn. There is no through route to immortality this way. 'You are dust,'

---

[27] *Cf*. Zp. 3:19–20.   [28] Is. 31:3.

God said to Adam, 'and to dust you shall return' (Gn. 3:19). There is no immortality which is ours by nature: our span of life is inevitably bounded by death. Life beyond death is of God's gracious gift; it does not come through human activity – even intercourse with angels! 'Flesh' can also stand for human nature out of line with God. God's image has become merely 'flesh'. As the margin of the Revised Version has it: 'In their going astray they are flesh'.

So God sets a boundary to human life: *his days shall be a hundred and twenty years.* This stands as a sign of man's mortality; a reminder that God allots the span of life; a pointer perhaps, also, to the withdrawal of the divine breath from (practically) all living things in the forthcoming Flood. The problem of relating the number 120 to the figures actually given for the ages of the primeval patriarchs has not been satisfactorily explained. Perhaps the life-spans gradually tail off until in the history of Abraham they are around 120 years. But whatever '120 years' means, its main function in this paragraph is to remind us that the boundaries of life are set by God.

And so from this sombre introduction, we are led into the judgment of the Flood.

3. God and Noah

The LORD saw that the wickedness of man was great in the earth, and that every imagination of the thoughts of his heart was only evil continually. ⁶*And the LORD was sorry that he had made man on the earth, and it grieved him to his heart.* ⁷*So the LORD said, 'I will blot out man whom I have created from the face of the ground, man and beast and creeping things and birds of the air, for I am sorry that I have made them.'* ⁸*But Noah found favour in the eyes of the LORD.*

⁹*These are the generations of Noah. Noah was a righteous man, blameless in his generation; Noah walked with God.* ¹⁰*And Noah had three sons, Shem, Ham, and Japheth.*

¹¹*Now the earth was corrupt in God's sight, and the earth was filled with violence.* ¹²*And God saw the earth, and behold, it was corrupt; for all flesh had corrupted their way upon the earth.* ¹³*And God said to Noah, 'I have determined to make an end of all flesh; for the earth is filled with violence through them; behold, I will destroy them with the earth.* ¹⁴*Make yourself an ark of gopher wood; make rooms in the ark, and cover it inside and out with pitch.* ¹⁵*This is how you are to make it: the length of the ark three hundred cubits, its breadth fifty cubits, and its height thirty cubits.* ¹⁶*Make a roof for the ark, and finish it to a cubit above; and set*

the door of the ark in its side; make it with lower, second, and third decks. ¹⁷For behold, I will bring a flood of waters upon the earth, to destroy all flesh in which is the breath of life from under heaven; everything that is on the earth shall die. ¹⁸But I will establish my covenant with you; and you shall come into the ark, you, your sons, your wife, and your sons' wives with you. ¹⁹And of every living thing of all flesh, you shall bring two of every sort into the ark, to keep them alive with you; they shall be male and female. ²⁰Of the birds according to their kinds, and of the animals according to their kinds, of every creeping thing of the ground according to its kind, two of every sort shall come in to you, to keep them alive. ²¹Also take with you every sort of food that is eaten, and store it up; and it shall serve as food for you and for them.' ²²Noah did this; he did all that God commanded him.

⁷:¹Then the LORD said to Noah, 'Go into the ark, you and all your household, for I have seen that you are righteous before me in this generation. ²Take with you seven pairs of all clean animals, the male and his mate; and a pair of the animals that are not clean, the male and his mate; ³and seven pairs of the birds of the air also, male and female, to keep their kind alive upon the face of all the earth. ⁴For in seven days I will send rain upon the earth forty days and forty nights; and every living thing that I have made I will blot out from the face of the ground.' ⁵And Noah did all that the LORD had commanded him.

⁶Noah was six hundred years old when the flood of waters came upon the earth. ⁷And Noah and his sons and his wife and his sons' wives with him went into the ark, to escape the waters of the flood. ⁸Of clean animals, and of animals that are not clean, and of birds, and of everything that creeps on the ground, ⁹two and two, male and female, went into the ark with Noah, as God had commanded Noah. ¹⁰And after seven days the waters of the flood came upon the earth.

¹¹In the six hundredth year of Noah's life, in the second month, on the seventeenth day of the month, on that day all the fountains of the great deep burst forth, and the windows of the heavens were opened. ¹²And rain fell upon the earth forty days and forty nights. ¹³On the very same day Noah and his sons, Shem and Ham and Japheth, and Noah's wife and the three wives of his sons with them entered the ark, ¹⁴they and every beast according to its kind, and all the cattle according to their kind, and every creeping thing that creeps on the earth according to its kind, and every bird according to its kind, every bird of every sort. ¹⁵They went in the ark with Noah, two and two of all flesh in which there was the breath of life. ¹⁶And they that entered, male and female of all flesh, went in as God had commanded him; and the LORD shut him in.

133

[17]The flood continued forty days upon the earth; and the waters increased, and bore up the ark, and it rose high above the earth. [18]The waters prevailed and increased greatly upon the earth; and the ark floated on the face of the waters. [19]And the waters prevailed so mightily upon the earth that all the high mountains under the whole heaven were covered; [20]the waters prevailed above the mountains, covering them fifteen cubits deep. [21]And all flesh died that moved upon the earth, birds, cattle, beasts, all swarming creatures that swarm upon the earth, and every man; [22]everything on the dry land in whose nostrils was the breath of life died. [23]He blotted out every living thing that was upon the face of the ground, man and animals and creeping things and birds of the air; they were blotted out from the earth. Only Noah was left, and those that were with him in the ark. [24]And the waters prevailed upon the earth a hundred and fifty days.

[8:1]But God remembered Noah and all the beasts and all the cattle that were with him in the ark. And God made a wind blow over the earth, and the waters subsided; [2]the fountains of the deep and the windows of the heavens were closed, the rain from the heavens was restrained, [3]and the waters receded from the earth continually. At the end of a hundred and fifty days the waters had abated; [4]and in the seventh month, on the seventeenth day of the month, the ark came to rest upon the mountains of Ararat. [5]And the waters continued to abate until the tenth month; in the tenth month, on the first day of the month, the tops of the mountains were seen.

[6]At the end of forty days Noah opened the window of the ark which he had made, [7]and sent forth a raven; and it went to and fro until the waters were dried up from the earth. [8]Then he sent forth a dove from him, to see if the waters had subsided from the face of the ground; [9]but the dove found no place to set her foot, and she returned to him to the ark, for the waters were still on the face of the whole earth. So he put forth his hand and took her and brought her into the ark with him. [10]He waited another seven days, and again he sent forth the dove out of the ark; [11]and the dove came back to him in the evening, and lo, in her mouth a freshly plucked olive leaf; so Noah knew that the waters had subsided from the earth. [12]Then he waited another seven days, and sent forth the dove; and she did not return to him any more.

[13]In the six hundred and first year, in the first month, the first day of the month, the waters were dried from off the earth; and Noah removed the covering of the ark, and looked, and behold, the face of the ground was dry. [14]In the second month, on the twenty-seventh day of the month, the earth was dry. [15]Then God said to Noah, [16]'Go forth from the ark, you and your wife, and your sons and your sons' wives with you. [17]Bring forth with you

every living thing that is with you of all flesh – birds and animals and every creeping thing that creeps on the earth – that they may breed abundantly on the earth, and be fruitful and multiply upon the earth.' ¹⁸*So Noah went forth, and his sons and his wife and his sons' wives with him.* ¹⁹*And every beast, every creeping thing, and every bird, everything that moves upon the earth, went forth by families out of the ark.*

²⁰*Then Noah built an altar to the* LORD, *and took of every clean animal and of every clean bird, and offered burnt offerings on the altar.* ²¹*And when the* LORD *smelled the pleasing odour, the* LORD *said in his heart, 'I will never again curse the ground because of man, for the imagination of man's heart is evil from his youth; neither will I ever again destroy every living creature as I have done.* ²²*While the earth remains, seedtime and harvest, cold and heat, summer and winter, day and night, shall not cease.'*

(6:5 – 8:22)

Many scholars believe that various ancient sources lie behind the edition of the text which comes to us in our Bibles. Whether or not this is the case, it is clear that there are certainly different themes which have been woven together to give us the finished text, and which fill out even further the picture of God and his relationships with his world which the earlier chapters of Genesis have painted. We will concentrate mostly on two of these themes which we will call 'sovereignty' and 'intimacy'.

a. Sovereignty

There is a cosmic backcloth to this picture. The story of God's intimate care for Noah and his family, to which we shall turn shortly, is set in the wider context of God's purposes for his whole creation. *And God saw . . .* (6:12). The last time we read these words, what God saw was 'very good' (1:31). Now he not only sees that *the wickedness of man* is *great in the earth* (6:5), but the earth itself is *corrupt* and *filled with violence* (6:11–12). The judgment that will be directed to people is directed also to all living creatures: *everything that is on the earth shall die* (6:17).

The Flood story of these chapters, in contrast to many other flood stories, is depicted not just as the tale of a terrible deluge, but primarily as the narrative of God's activity, as an expression of his sovereign will. God speaks as the Judge in the legal language of 6:13. He is responding as the Sovereign Ruler to the violations of his divine ordering of the world. The cause of the Flood is the wickedness of the human heart. *Every imagination of the thoughts of his heart was only evil continually* (6:5). It is a wickedness which

135

is manifest in violence (6:11, 13) – the 'violent breach of a just order'.[29] It is the culmination of mankind's refusal to live within God-given bounds. We met this first in the Garden, with the sin of disobedience to God's will. It was followed up in the story of Cain's killing of his brother, whose blood belonged to God. Lamech took the theme further in his polygamy, and in his excessive violence which went far beyond the divine boundaries (4:24). We have seen its demonic power in the angel marriages earlier in Genesis 6. Sin has become a transgression of the way things should be in God's world – a violation of God's order, a breaking of his bounds, an abandonment of all God-given natural laws. And in contrast to the ordering work of the Creator in Genesis 1, here in 6:12 we see the author describing a world in which that work is being reversed. Here is a thoroughgoing turning back to corruption, disorder and chaos.

And so the Sovereign God, enthroned as King, 'enthroned over the flood',[30] decrees judgment, and as so often with the judgment of God, he allows the outworking of the results of sin and wickedness to be their own judgment. For what God decreed was to be destroyed (6:13) had already in truth destroyed itself (6:11–12).[31] The Flood itself sets the pattern of creation in reverse. And then the majestic and mysterious creative power of the sovereign God is seen once more making things new.

But first, we pick up another thread woven together with that of God's sovereignty: his gracious and intimate care for Noah.

b. Intimacy

By 'intimacy' I mean those strands in the story which focus on God's personal dealings with Noah. These are the verses in which God is called by his personal name 'Yahweh'. These passages speak of his emotions: he grieves (6:6); he feels sorry (6:6); he gives personal instructions (7:1); he smells the pleasing odour of the sacrifice (8:21). These verses tell of his care: he gives his word that while the earth remains seed-time and harvest will not cease (8:22). These passages also tell us of Noah's faith and obedience (7:5); his consecration and his worship (8:20). Together they fill out a picture of a man who knows his God, because he is intimately known and cared for by him. These are the parts of the story which perhaps the writer to the Hebrews has in mind when he refers to Noah's faith,[32] and to which the author of 2 Peter refers when he calls Noah 'a herald of righteousness'.[33]

---

[29] Cf. von Rad, p. 123.   [30] Cf. Ps. 29:10.   [31] Cf. Kidner, p. 87.
[32] Heb. 11:7.   [33] 2 Pet. 2:5.

By 'intimacy', I mean the *suffering* God. Can there be anything more poignant than the phrase: *the* LORD *was sorry that he had made man on the earth, and it grieved him to his heart* (6:6)? God is affected by what people make of themselves and do with his creation. God suffers. *It grieved him to his heart* could mean 'he felt bitterly indignant' – a mixture of rage and bitter anguish.[34] One of the New Testament parallels might be the picture of Jesus 'deeply moved', snorting with indignation, while also weeping, in the face of the intrusion of death into God's world at the grave of Lazarus.[35]

We commented on Genesis 3 about the risk God took in creating this world with its freedom. Here we see God's vulnerability. Here is the pain of creative love. Here is the wounded spirit of the artist whose work is rejected, the broken heart of the lover whose love is not returned. God makes himself vulnerable. God empties himself in love. God himself enters the world of brokenness and pain. Genesis 6 points us to the suffering God. 'The tears of God are the meaning of history.'[36]

By 'intimacy' I also mean the *gracious* God. There is a richness in the words of Genesis 6:8: *Noah found favour [grace] in the eyes of the* LORD; whose meaning we understand best, as J. A. Motyer has suggested, by reading the translation backwards: 'grace found Noah'. God's initiative of grace towards Noah is mentioned before there is any reference to Noah's faith and righteousness (6:9). And that is important. Between the two – the reference to grace and the reference to righteousness – the editor has given another formula to indicate a development of the story. *These are the generations of Noah* (6:9) – this is the emergent story of Noah. What is the significance of this? Could it be that the author is seeking to highlight the fact that the public life of Noah – who walked before God, who had a family, and who built an ark – *emerges out of* the secret story of Noah as a recipient of God's grace? The editor of this text has very carefully ensured that we read about the grace of God before we read about Noah's obedience of faith. And that is the pattern which again and again the Bible makes clear: 'by grace you have been saved through faith; and this is not your own doing, it is the gift of God.'[37]

The Flood story begins in Genesis 6:5 where the extent of wickedness in the earth causes Yahweh such pain. Here we learn of the grace of God which *despite* such sin *cannot* let man go. We should note, too, the stress that is placed in verses 5–7 on 'man . . . man . . . man . . .'. Noah is part of the world of sinful

---

[34] Wenham, p. 144.   [35] Jn. 11:35, 38.
[36] N. Wolterstorff, *Lament for a Son* (Eerdmans, 1987), p. 90.   [37] Eph. 2:8.

humanity. It was within this sinful humanity that 'grace found Noah'.

c. Grace in judgment and mercy

The Lord decrees that the waters of judgment will wipe out human-kind from the earth, and yet he shuts his man and his family up in an ark. The water which is the means of judgment for the world is at the same time the means of salvation for God's family. In this one action, there is judgment and there is mercy.

And throughout, God's relationship to Noah is one of intimate protecting grace. *I have seen that you are righteous before me* (7:1). Grace holds on to Noah in his faith that God knows what will come to pass, even though all his neighbours are unconcernedly marrying and giving in marriage.[38] Grace holds Noah in his trusting obedience to what surely must have seemed a bizarre command: constructing this great barge in the middle of a dry field! Grace protects him through the storms until the windows can be opened again to let the sunlight in. Does not this speak of a love that will not let me go? Is not this part of the author's concern in retelling this tale? People of God, when things are going well for you, the nation is secure, the king is on his throne, the economics are good, there is money in the bank and food on the table: beware of the temptation to forget the Giver. You are what you are by grace. And when things are hard, when the hand of judgment is heavy around you; when the fountains of the deep burst forth, and all you have is at sea, even then God will not let you go.

Isaiah refers to this story in his emphasis on the everlasting love and compassion of 'the Lord, the Redeemer':

> 'As I swore that the waters of Noah
>   should no more go over the earth,
> so I have sworn that I will not be angry with you ...
> For the mountains may depart
>   and the hills be removed,
> but my steadfast love shall not depart from you,
>   and my covenant of peace shall not be removed,
>   says the LORD, who has compassion on you.'[39]

The story of the Flood is the story of God's sovereign judgment on a world that has lost its moorings. The story of Noah is at the same time the story of God's intimate, compassionate and faithful love. That intimate relationship of a person with God can even

---

[38] *Cf.* Mt. 24:38.   [39] Is. 54:9–10.

now be 'the still point of the turning world' (to borrow Eliot's phrase from *Burnt Norton*). This is the eye of the storm. And it is from this relationship with God that intimacy between people can grow.

d. Intimacy in this world?

The story of the possibility of fellowship in a storm-tossed world is one our world needs to hear again, dominated as we are by pressures of every sort which force us apart from God and so apart from each other. We have all but forgotten what intimacy means. The loss of intimacy: that capacity to relate as a whole person with other whole persons, is a major problem of highly mobile post-industrialized Western men and women. It is becoming a problem elsewhere, too, as urbanization and the lure of capital take a hold. The rural populations of some African villages, where hitherto the intimacy of several generations living together in mutual care and mutual protection are losing out to a situation in which the man moves into the towns in search of quick cash leaving the women, children and older people unsupported. Family breakdown is more likely, as the man takes a 'town wife' to look after him, while keeping a 'country wife' in the village. In the West, marriage break-down, 'serial polygamy', and the increase in television entertain-ment, all militate against intimacy in relationships. And there is a hunger for an intimacy with God. The searching-out of the writings of the Christian mystics which is increasing within the churches, itself points to a deep spiritual void in the hearts of many Christian people.

Part of our problem is the way our culture is dominated by a view of human beings which derives primarily from some aspects of seventeenth- and eighteenth-century philosophy: rational, indiv-idualized, autonomous beings, without purpose, whose values are relative, and whose knowledge of the world is defined by what can be seen and felt and measured.

In William Temple's book, *Nature, Man and God*, he said: 'If I were asked what was the most disastrous moment in the history of Europe, I should be strongly tempted to answer that it was that period of leisure when René Descartes, having no claims to meet, remained for a whole day "shut up alone in a stove".'[40] It was then, we recall, that Descartes made his celebrated attempt to doubt all things, but finding that he could not doubt that he was doubting, affirmed: 'I think, therefore I am.' What Temple thought was disastrous was this retreat into rational self-consciousness which

---

[40] W. Temple, *Nature, Man and God* (Macmillan, 1934, 1964), p. 57.

considerably strengthened individualistic ways of thinking about what it is to be human. This led on to the Enlightenment stress on autonomous human individuality of mind and will, and it is with this that our current lack of intimacy is closely bound up.

We can contrast this with our earlier discussion of 'persons in relation' (see pp. 38–39) as part of the meaning of the image of God. The Velveteen Rabbit, we recall, became Real through being loved. Perhaps we could suggest that, in contrast to Descartes, the Velveteen Rabbit would learn, through relationship, gradually, with pain and struggle, to say, 'I am loved, therefore I am'. That is part of the meaning of grace.

e. The obedience of Noah

We need to begin, as Noah did, with the word of divine grace, and allow the word of God to direct our steps. But the deep relationship between Noah and his God is seen not only in listening to God's voice, but also in the costly obedience of the perplexing duties of building a boat. What qualifies Noah for his inclusion in the list alongside Abel and Enoch in Hebrews 11 is that he, too, is an example of the obedience of faith. 'By faith Noah, being warned by God concerning events as yet unseen, took heed and constructed an ark for the saving of his household.'[41]

As we have said, what a bizarre requirement this must have seemed! Yet twice in the story we are told *Noah did all that the* LORD *had commanded him* (6:22; 7:5). The story of God's protecting love is also the story of Noah's faithful obedience. This is our part in fellowship. Sometimes it can only be learned through pain and struggle, but there can be an intimacy with God even out in the field as we hold the hammer and nails, just as much as at the altar.

In his obedience, Noah also demonstrates his awareness that human life and animal life are all bound up together in the community of creation. Noah the Conservationist takes animals of every sort with him into the ark. Here the divine commission to care for the world is being worked out, as Noah protects animal life alongside his own.

f. The ark

There is no security for Noah anywhere but in the ark. Quite outside his experience, and his expectations, Noah and his family are to be entombed in a place of darkness in order to be saved.

[41] Heb. 11:7.

The three-storey boat, 450 feet long, 75 feet wide and 45 feet high was effectively a prison. And Noah takes on himself the pain and the darkness of the tomb in order to pass safely through the time of divine judgment. By his willing obedience to God, he becomes the saviour of those of his family who trusted in him and his God.

No wonder the ark has featured in Christian thinking as a symbol of salvation in Christ, and as a picture of God's church. The First Letter of Peter uses the salvation through water at the time of the Flood as a picture of the water of baptism. The world outside is judged, as those within are saved.

The delightful touch, *the LORD shut him in* (7:16), as God secures his people within their place of safety, is also a shutting out of everyone else. There comes a time when the door is shut. The picture of God closing the door of the ark reminds us 'that the ark was made secure from the deluge, not by human artifice, but by divine miracle . . . the waters were not restrained from breaking in upon the ark by pitch or bitumen only, but rather by the secret power of God, and by the interposition of his hand' (Calvin). It reminds us also that those who would manage by themselves in rejection of the provision of God will, as some of the stern parables of Jesus tell us, find that the door of salvation is no longer open to them.

The rich man was separated from father Abraham by 'a great chasm'.[42] The unprepared maidens who went out to buy oil when the bridegroom was already on his way, returned to find the door closed.[43] 'Watch, therefore,' says our Lord, 'for you know neither the day nor the hour.'[44]

Noah had to go into this 'grave', had to bury himself in this ark, in order to find safety. He had to seek life through the waters of death. He had to forsake his world in order to find it again. There is life only through death. There is resurrection only by way of the cross. There will be weeping in the night before joy comes in the morning.[45]

Much of the New Testament picks up this theme. There has to be a putting to death of the 'old nature', the life that is lived without reference to God, before we can put on the 'new nature' that is God's gift to us in Christ. In the New Testament, the gift of this new life is symbolized by baptism. Peter links baptism directly with the story of Noah,[46] and goes on to argue that Christian confidence is rooted in the resurrection of Jesus Christ. So in our experiment of faith, in our risk of the unknown, we are helped by the fact that we are not alone in the ark. Baptism into Christ, is

[42] Lk. 16:26. [43] Mt. 25:10. [44] Mt. 25:13. [45] Ps. 30:5.
[46] 1 Pet. 3:21.

141

baptism into a community. It was with his family that Noah went into the ark. The picture for us is of belonging to the Christian church.

We must not make the mistake of thinking that we are saved by baptism alone, or through the church alone. Salvation for Noah began with the word of God to him. Noah believed in God's promise. He took refuge in the place that God had provided, and the Lord shut him in. Christian faith is not faith in baptism, or faith in the church. Nor is it faith in faith itself, as though our believing was what mattered. Christian faith is commitment to Christ himself. He is the word, the promise, the ark; he is also the Obedient Man who through death has saved his family from the storms of divine judgment. 'He opened wide his arms for us on the cross.' He walks out on to the dry ground of the Easter sunrise bringing his family with him.

g. Covenant (6:18)

The twin themes of divine sovereignty and divine intimacy are brought together in a major biblical word which has its first reference in this story (though the reality is there back in the Garden of Eden as we have suggested in our discussion of marriage.) The word is 'covenant'. It is a word which expresses one of the great overarching themes of the whole Bible.

A covenant is a declaration about the future relationship of two parties, a commitment, based on a promise, to enter that relationship, and the growth of the relationship over time. Sometimes covenants are made between friends as equal partners;[47] sometimes between kings and their subjects.[48] When God makes a covenant, he sets the terms and conditions as a sovereign ruler, but his covenant people are invited to share real partnership with him.

We will stand back for a few moments to survey the story of God's covenant relationship. The heart of the covenant of grace between God and his people is most clearly expressed in the Lord's promise to Abraham. 'I will be your God; you will be my people.' That is the divine, sovereign declaration of intent, the divine promise, the divine gift, the divine requirement. God proclaims himself to his people as their God. God declares them to be his people, and in so doing obliges them to a certain way of life. 'You shall be holy, as I am holy' summarizes the obligations of the covenant people. And God offers his grace to enable his people to grow in holiness, for in the Old Testament, as well as in the New, what God requires of us, that he also gives.

---

[47] 1 Sa. 18:3.   [48] 2 Ki. 11:4.

The personal covenant with Abraham, and with his family (Gn. 15; 17), is then reaffirmed and re-angled as a covenant with the whole redeemed people of God.[49] It is given through Moses on Mount Sinai, where the obligations of being the people of God are more clearly elaborated. Blessings and cursings are declared. The law is made known, and sacrifices are instituted. The law is given as a pattern of life for the people whom God has just rescued through the Red Sea. The law, or – as we should more accurately describe it – the fatherly instruction of the covenant God ('torah'), is also a gift of God's covenanted grace. The annual Passover festival developed after the Exodus kept alive in the minds of the people the significance of God's rescue from Egypt, and their status as the people of God. The elaborate sacrifical system provided a way for God's covenant people to remain at one with a holy God.

In time, the people of God lost sight of him. Some of the prophets have to call the kings and the people back to their covenant obligations. The delight of serving God expressed in some of the psalms is always held in tension with the perils of subservience to a code of law – rather different from the fatherly instruction appreciated within the covenant relationship. Religion becomes cold and external, not devoted and alive.

It falls to Isaiah, Jeremiah and Ezekiel[50] to look forward to the day when the covenant shall be renewed – a covenant written on the heart.

'This is the covenant that I will make with the house of Israel after those days, says the LORD: I will put my law within them, and I will write it upon their hearts; and I will be their God, and they shall be my people. And no longer shall each man teach his neighbour and each his brother, saying "Know the LORD," for they shall all know me.'[51]

There will be a day when once again people shall know their God and serve him gladly. That day dawns in an Upper Room in Jerusalem when the words are spoken, 'This is my blood of the covenant, which is poured out for many for the forgiveness of sins'[52] – a day which closes with the cry 'It is finished', called from a criminal's cross when the sun was eclipsed, the earth shook, the rocks were split. That day the curtain of the temple was torn in two from the top to the bottom: a curtain, until then the symbol of God's separation from sinful people, now for ever drawn aside. Men and women may now hear unmistakably the word of warm

---

[49] Cf. Ex. 6:6.   [50] Is. 54:10; Je. 31:33; Ezk. 36:26f.
[51] Je. 31:33–34.   [52] Mt. 26:28.

welcome into fellowship with God their father. The covenant relationship is now restored. In Christ, the family is made new. We are offered adoption as sons and daughters of God himself.

The covenant family is still being drawn together. And in the End-Time, all will be complete. In the new heaven and the new earth there will be a great voice from the throne, saying, 'Behold, the dwelling of God is with men. He will dwell with them, and they shall be his people, and God himself will be with them.'[53]

From Abraham to the coming of Christ's Kingdom, God relates to his people through his covenanted promise and provision.

But the author of Genesis 6 takes us further back even than Abraham. He roots this story of the people of God in an earlier covenant yet. '*I will establish my covenant with you; and you shall come into the ark, you, your sons, your wife, and your sons' wives with you. And of every living thing of all flesh, you shall bring two of every sort into the ark, to keep them alive with you*' (Gn. 6:18–19). A similar promise comes again after the Flood in 9:9–10. The covenant is not only made with Noah and his family, but with *every living creature*. God's commitment is for the welfare of the whole community of creation.

In a world that is devastated by disorder, threatened by destruction, perplexed and confused, and having lost its touch with God, God makes his promise. His world will not be totally destroyed. His creation will be renewed. In sovereignty and yet in intimate love, God is committed to the well-being of all his creatures.

The covenant promise is made here in the context of judgment. '*I will bring a flood of waters upon the earth, to destroy all flesh . . . everything that is on the earth shall die*' (6:17). Noah and his family and his animals are included in that judgment. The judgment of God against wickedness is total. 'I will destroy.' That is verse 17. Then verse 18 says, '*But . . .* '. Within the judgment of God there is the mercy of God. We saw the same pattern a few verses earlier: verse 7, '*I will blot out man . . .* '; verse 8, *But Noah found* [grace] *in the eyes of the LORD.*

The covenant, then, is God's promise of salvation. When God establishes his covenant, he moves into action to save. The word 'establish' means 'stand upon its feet'; God is bringing his covenant to life – putting his promise to work.

And so the waters which fall on the earth in destruction, fall on Noah, secured in his ark, for safety. The water which blots out man is the very water which saves Noah in his ark. Noah, too, has to endure the time of judgment. Yet he is kept safe on the basis of God's gracious provision.

---

[53] Rev. 21:3.

That is not to say life for Noah was a luxury cruise. Shut up for far too long in a dark, doubtless smelly, not to say unhygenic, sepulchre, Noah might well have despaired for his life. Like Jonah in a similarly unenviable aquatic predicament, he doubtless 'remembered the LORD'.[54]

One might guess that Noah rather persistently remembered the Lord, and wondered what on earth was going on. Had God, after all, let him down. Was he saved for this – to live his days cooped up in this prison, eight people and a menagerie, and without even a view. What price obedience now?

h. Innocent suffering?

It may be that there is something rather unfair about Noah's suffering. Though doubtless having his own share of faults,[55] he is also the victim of others' sins. It is at least in part because of the disobedience of others that he is in this predicament now.

As such Noah can serve as a pointer to that deepest of human problems: the suffering of those who don't deserve it. Whether we think of the pre-birth trauma of the unwanted foetus in the womb, explored so movingly, if controversially, by psychiatrists like Frank Lake, or whether we broaden our vision to survey the floods of Bangladesh, the famines of Sudan or the millions of Jewish people who lost their lives in the Holocaust, we are pushed to one of the most powerful arguments for the non-existence of God. How can God allow such things? And in terms of rational argument and deductive logic, there is no reply. We are able to trace hints of an answer in the doctrine of original sin: that in some inscrutable way we all share in the sins and pains of others. We can try to make some sense of the fact that within the human community we all belong to one another, and to some degree share what Old Testament specialists sometimes call a 'corporate personality'. But at the level of our intellect, these carry little weight when we try to hold together a picture which includes a God of love, and photographs of Auschwitz and Hiroshima.

The only answer comes at a different level. It comes as we recall that it is God who provides the ark. It comes most clearly as we gaze at a man nailed to a cross, and allow the shedding of his innocent blood to touch our spirits. For there the perfect man is dying as a criminal; there Innocence is made guilty; there we know that when we stand at the abyss of undeserved suffering and incomprehensible evil Christ stands there with us. At the cross, God himself takes responsibility for the suffering of the world. He

[54] Cf. Jon. 2:7.   [55] Cf. Gn. 6:5–8.

has borne our griefs and carried our sorrows. Though we do not understand, we find that God is there with us. In the depths of our struggle, God does not let us go. The turning-point comes when we reach our hands up from the blackness of the pit, and find that all along God has been holding on to us.

4. God remembered Noah (8:1)

a. The reins of the storm

The turning-point came for Noah with the action of God: *God remembered Noah* (8:1). In fact this short sentence is the turning-point of the narrative. As Wenham has illustrated, the narrative of Genesis 6:9 – 9:19 can be shown to follow a favourite pattern of Hebrew narrative – a palistrophe. He quotes B. W. Anderson's analysis:

> Transitional introduction (6:9–10)
>   1. Violence in creation (6:11–12)
>   2. First divine speech: resolve to destroy (6:13–22)
>   3. Second divine speech: 'enter ark' (7:1–10)
>   4. Beginning of flood (7:11–16)
>   5. The rising flood
>   God remembers Noah
>   6. The receding flood (8:1–5)
>   7. Drying of the earth (8:6–14)
>   8. Third divine speech: 'leave ark' (8:15–19)
>   9. God's resolve to preserve order (8:20–22)
>   10. Fourth divine speech: covenant (9:1–17)
> Transitional conclusion (9:18–19)

As Wenham comments: the structure helps to draw attention to the nature of the flood and the water's rise and fall, and to pinpoint the real turning-point, God's 'remembering Noah'.[56]

Faith is the process – too frequently with pain and struggle – of learning to rest in the providence and rescue of God, even when everything tells us that God has forgotten us. But the God of the covenant, who all too often 'moves in mysterious ways', is the God who does not forget his friends. He is the God 'who rides upon the storm', holding their reins tightly in his hands.

b. Water (7:11–12; 8:1–5)

We have read of the terrifying power of water before. In the first

---

[56] Wenham, pp. 156–157.

creation narrative in chapter 1, God the Creator, who made the waters, blows his wind over them. He separates the water above from the waters below. He makes the dry land appear. In other words, he sets some bound to the water's power. The Creator God is a God of order, who brings some shape to what without his purposeful hand remains chaos, who gives form to what is formless.

And as we saw, the water that is constrained in Eden, in the four rivers of chapter 2, is water that gives life, quenches thirst, and sustains civilization.

But the Flood story shows that this order, established at the beginnings of the world, is breaking down. Now the fountains of the deep are bursting forth, and the windows of heaven are open again. Now the boundaries are broken, and with the unrestrained waters, there is fear and there is threat.

We saw how the sea often functions in the Scriptures as a picture of disorder. The monsters of the deep appear in the psalms;[57] storms and shipwrecks feature in the story of the people of God.[58] After Passover night's rescue from Egypt, the people of God find themselves face to face with the sea. And the storms provoke uncertainty, fear and dread.

How powerful, then, those Gospel stories of Jesus asleep in a boat while his disciples cry out, 'Do you not care that we perish?' How dramatic his stilling of the storm, and his walking over the water. The power of God is not dimmed by the power of the sea.

And in the new heaven and the new earth, along with the end of the rule of death, the end of the pain of sickness, the end of the darkness of the night, we read also, 'And the sea was no more.'[59]

But here in the Flood, the overwhelming powers of the deep are wreaking their havoc. All flesh that is on the earth is destroyed. The sea once again is unrestrained.

But when God remembered Noah, he made a wind blow over the sea, as it did at the opening of creation (Gn. 1, 2; see p. 26), and as later it did at the Red Sea,[60] providing a route for the Exodus out of Egyptian slavery and into a new life. The waters subsided, the fountains of the deep and the windows of heaven were closed, and it stopped raining.

c. A new world (8:1–19)

The salvation of the man and his family, and with them representatives of every living creature, is now presented to us as a picture of a creation restored. God is concerned that life will go on. Life

---

[57] E.g. Ps. 104:26. [58] E.g. Acts 27:39–44; 2 Cor. 11:25.
[59] Rev. 21:1. [60] Ex. 14.

is to be lived in covenant with God in a cleansed world order. Here is a picture that is pointing beyond this age. Here shut up in this ark is a foretaste of what could be. A haven of security when this broken world order ceases. Here there are doves and ravens, expressive of a harmony between man and the animal world. Here the wolf dwells with the lamb, the leopard lies down with the kid, the calf and the lion and the fatling together.[61] Here all animal life is preserved to sing the praises of the Creator. For surely, a new creation is pictured here.

The power of the sea remains in the hand of God. He recalls the waters to their boundaries to establish again the order of his world. The winds blow the rain back into the clouds; the seas are brought back to their shorelines, the banks are rebuilt again for the rivers. Once again the waters separate from the earth, and dry land appears. Once more, birds and animals and creeping things are set free on the earth to be fruitful and multiply. Here again God establishes personal communion with human beings made in his image (Gn. 9:6–8). Those powerful forces, which cause so much fear and devastation, can once again bring life and refreshment. There are echoes here all along of Genesis 1. A new creation is possible! The covenant community can be restored!

Is that not a word of hope to God's people in their troubled times? Does not that bring a word of hope to us?

The story of the salvation of Noah thus has to be seen as part of a bigger cosmic picture. The intimate and gracious God is also Sovereign Lord of all things. It is a picture which begins with the Creator, which traces his blessing despite the rule of death through the generations of world history, which comes to its climax in the provision of an ark of shelter from the destructiveness of divine judgment, which carries the promise of a restored creation,[62] and which points to a new heaven and a new earth in which righteousness dwells. In this cosmic sense, too, Noah is a herald of righteousness.[63]

d. A new promise (8:20–22)

The boat-builder now builds an altar. He steps out of the tomb of his ark into the fresh air and daylight of his Easter morning, kneels down in the mud and says his prayers. Noah's first response is of gratitude, and he expresses this by offering a sacrifice of a *pleasing odour* (8:21). Noah offers his confession of the continuing human need for divine grace. And God is depicted as expressing a new attitude towards the ground, and man and every living creature.

---

[61] Is. 11:6ff. [62] Cf. 2 Pet. 3:6–7, 13. [63] 2 Pet. 2:5.

Why, we may wonder, was a sacrifice appropriate? From the ongoing history of the people of God, we discover that sacrifices kept alive in their corporate memory the significance of one inaugural sacrifice – that of Passover night.[64] That night God's angel moved across the land of Egypt in judgment – and in every household there was a death. In every Egyptian house, the firstborn died. In every Israelite house which was marked by the blood of a lamb, the people were safe: a lamb had died. And as God passed over the people of Israel – keeping them safe in a place of security while his judgments were executed on the world outside – the mark of security, the certainty of protection, was that a lamb had been sacrificed. The people of God thus learned that life-giving was the principle of life. It is through life laid down that life can flourish.

We can assume that the author of Genesis 8 shared this perception of the importance of sacrifice in pointing to the life-giving promise of God. In linking his account of Noah's rescue with the possibility that life can begin again, the offering of a sacrifice is a powerful and appropriate act. Noah offered 'burnt-offerings', which we learn from Leviticus 1 were offerings involving the active participation of the worshipper to make atonement. They also expressed commitment and consecration – nothing is held back.[65] Here is a further underlining of Noah's obedience of faith. The insistence on taking seven pairs of 'clean' animals into the ark (7:2) is in line with the pattern of Israelite sacrifices.[66] It is God who decreed that the clean animals should be taken into the ark, just as it is God who appointed the sacrificial system of Leviticus. The God who remembered Noah is the God who now smells the 'pleasing odour', and promises that there will be no more flood.

We notice, though, that the Flood has not changed the sinful heart of humanity. Surprisingly, here at the end of the story, the author returns to the theme which at the prologue was the very basis for the Flood: *the imagination of man's heart is evil from his youth* (8:21; *cf.* Gn. 6:5). If that were all that could be said, God would have to punish man with daily floods, as Calvin pertinently remarked. But, to quote von Rad,

> The same condition, which in the prologue is the basis for God's judgement, in the epilogue reveals God's grace and providence. The contrast between God's punishing anger and his supporting grace, which pervades the whole Bible, is here presented quite untheologically, even almost inappropriately. It seems almost like indulgence, an adjustment by God towards man's sinfulness.[67]

[64] Ex. 12.   [65] *Cf.* Gn. 22:12.   [66] Lv. 11.   [67] Von Rad, p. 119.

149

What von Rad calls 'indulgence' is in truth the expression of grace and patience. Just as the whole of life in Palestine is ruled by the rhythm of seed-time and harvest, of summer and winter, so the whole of life of which these seasons are symbols is to be kept in being by God. There will be no more flood. This is, for our author, the Last Judgment – a check on the spread of sin, and a revelation that, when all has been said, God is on our side. 'I will never again destroy every living creature.' That is God's commitment to life on this earth. The continuance of the seasons, and the steady way in which day follows night and night follows day, bear testimony to God's faithfulness. As a later writer put it:

> The steadfast love of the LORD never ceases,
>   his mercies never come to an end;
> they are new every morning;
>   great is thy faithfulness.
> 'The LORD is my portion,' says my soul,
>   'therefore I will hope in him.'[68]

In a sermon called 'Surviving with Noah', Moltmann has written:

> What does this mean for us? It means that in spite of all our justifiable mistrust in human history and the history of nature, our fundamental confidence in reality can be greater still. Reality in its deepest foundations is worthy of trust, for it is good. In the abyss of our disappointments we find God's hope. In the deepest depths of appalling guilt we find God's grace. In the bitterness of suffering that offers no escape, we find God's love. At the heart of everything is God's unswerving 'Yes'. And God stands firm.[69]

5. Apocalypse now

It is from this global perspective which the story of Noah heralds for us that we are to understand ourselves – especially in the light of the apocalyptic issues of our times. For we live in a world in which men and women continually try to overstep God-given boundaries. In many areas of life today – nuclear weaponry may be one, bioethics another, sexuality a third – we may be all too willing to stand on ground which properly only belongs to the providence of God. And the effects may be literally catastrophic.

As Richard Bauckham has written, the Noah story assures us, in our nuclear age, of God's commitment to human survival on

---

[68] Lam. 3:22–23.   [69] J. Moltmann, *Power of the Powerless*, p. 11.

earth. The horror of nuclear weapons is their affront to the dignity of human beings and to our commission to cultivate and protect God's world.

To read the Flood narrative with sensitivity to its original import is to acquire a renewed sense of the world in which we live as God's gift to us. As we see its destruction withheld only by God's patience and mercy, we find the world we take for granted becomes once again the world continually granted to us by God's grace.[70]

With all the End-Time features of our polluted and fearful world around us, it is all too easy to forget that all we have and all we are is a gift of Yahweh's grace. If he is committed to the well-being of his creation, can we be any less?

We live in a world which at point after point seems, as it was in the days of Noah, to be busying itself with everything except waiting for the coming of the Son of Man. Yet in this world we are called, like Noah in his generation, to display in our worship and our service, the righteousness of a trusting faith in God. A faith which hangs on to God despite all appearances, and a faith which seeks to translate his word into practice. A faith touched by the words which Jesus spoke to Peter: 'What I am doing you do not know now, but afterward you will understand.'[71] A faith that holds to the cosmic Christ, that in him all God's purposes for his whole creation come to their fulfilment. A faith which believes, as Kuyper put it, that 'There is not an inch of this universe over which Jesus Christ does not say "It is Mine!"' For from him, and through him and to him are all things![72]

But as the enormity of this cosmic perspective begins to overwhelm us, and we begin to feel lost in the vastness of God's dealings with the world, let us hold on to that other more intimate strand in the story of Noah: God is holding on to us. Our Creator is also our Father. He invites us to live in covenant with him, sustained by a love that will not let us go.

[70] R. Bauckham, *Churchman*, 1985, no. 2, p. 154.
[71] Jn. 13:7.   [72] Rom. 11:35.

child
if you could but see
my tears of love

diadems
flowing from the throne
into the crystal sea

wonder
at the new-born lamb
sleeping in the arms of the lion

and feel the freshness
of my gentle rain
renewing and refreshing

cleansing

turn child
turn from the turmoil
of life's storm
and see my bow
scanning the sapphire blue

and know in your heart
that I await you
on my throne

run to me child
and let me hold you

my delight
my joy

for I hold the reins of the storm
in my hands
and I will keep you

fear not
for my bow
outshines the darkest deed.

Be still.
Be still
and let the ears of your soul
hear my love song from the throne.

Elizabeth Stewart

5. Rainbows in a fallen world

And God blessed Noah and his sons, and said to them, 'Be fruitful and multiply, and fill the earth. ²The fear of you and the dread of you shall be upon every beast of the earth, and upon every bird of the air, upon everything that creeps on the ground and all the fish of the sea; into your hand they are delivered. ³Every moving thing that lives shall be food for you; and as I gave you the green plants, I give you everything. ⁴Only you shall not eat flesh with its life, that is, its blood. ⁵For your lifeblood I will surely require a reckoning; of every beast I will require it and of man; of every man's brother I will require the life of man. ⁶Whoever sheds the blood of man, by man shall his blood be shed; for God made man in his own image. ⁷And you, be fruitful and multiply, bring forth abundantly on the earth and multiply in it.'

⁸Then God said to Noah and to his sons with him, ⁹"Behold, I establish my covenant with you and your descendants after you, ¹⁰and with every living creature that is with you, the birds, the cattle, and every beast of the earth with you, as many as came out of the ark. ¹¹I establish my covenant with you, that never again shall all flesh be cut off by the waters of a flood, and never again shall there be a flood to destroy the earth.' ¹²And God said, 'This is the sign of the covenant which I make between me and you and every living creature that is with you, for all future generations: ¹³I set my bow in the cloud, and it shall be a sign of the covenant between me and the earth. ¹⁴When I bring clouds over the earth and the bow is seen in the clouds, ¹⁵I will remember my covenant which is between me and you and every living creature of all flesh; and the waters shall never again become a flood to destroy all flesh. ¹⁶When the bow is in the cloud, I will look upon it and remember the everlasting covenant between God and every living creature of all flesh that is upon the earth.' ¹⁷God said to Noah, 'This is the sign of the covenant which I have established between me and all flesh that is upon the earth.'

(9:1–17)

We have already sketched out the story of God's covenanted relationship with his people, and noticed how God established his covenant with Noah and with 'every living creature' (6:18). Chapter 9 of the Genesis narrative now fills out some of the aspects of covenant life: covenant blessing, covenant law and covenant grace.

The story of God's covenant with Noah after the Flood reminds us that God's covenant blessing is given, and his law provided, in the setting of a disordered and fallen world. Many times in this section of the Bible, we have seen how the life of faith is lived in a world of ambiguity and tension. Genesis 3 comes after Genesis 2: the created world is fallen. Adam is expelled from the Garden, but life goes on. Cain is punished by God, yet protected by God. The story of the Flood itself is a story of mercy and rescue in the very place of judgment and destruction. And now, perhaps more clearly still, in chapter 9, Noah is given God's blessing, but God's law is, so to speak, an 'accommodation' of God's perfect will to the conditions of a very-far-from-perfect world. And, in the rather seedy closing verses of the chapter (9:18–29), even Noah – God's covenant man, the 'herald of righteousness' – is found 'with his trousers down' in a drunken stupor. The Genesis author has no illusions about the ambiguity of the world, and the struggles even for men of faith in living for God. In that context the word of blessing, the provision of God's guiding law, and the reassurance of the rainbow are even more clearly evidences of God's gracious covenanted love and care.

1. Covenant blessing

And God blessed Noah and his sons, and said to them, 'Be fruitful and multiply, and fill the earth' (9:1).

After the destruction of the world by the waters of judgment, man is offered a new beginning. He is again offered a world in which to live, over which to have dominion, and in which to exercise his stewardship. He is again commanded to be fruitful and multiply and fill the earth. So much is reminiscent of the creation story. God remains faithful to his world. God has not abandoned the world he had made. Even though he had seen that 'every imagination of the thoughts of [man's] heart was only evil continually' and was 'sorry that he had made man on the earth' (6:5–6), even despite such disorder in the beauty of creation, the Creator God still gives his creative blessing. Now creation becomes grace: unexpected and undeserved. As Moltmann has put it, 'It was a self-humiliation on God's part when he lent his divine image to a clod of earth. But how much more God lowered himself after the Flood, in the renewal of his blessing!'[1] For now God is giving his creation mandate into the hands of potential evil-doers. Men and women are entrusted with responsibility for creation, even though they have spoiled it all once, and can spoil it again. As Moltmann continues: 'This is the pure, undeserved dignity we have been given. And none of us can sneak away from this responsibility for life on earth.'

It is clear, also, that in this story, God's covenant blessing is given to human beings in general. *Noah and his sons* covers all the human beings there are in the world after the Flood. The picture that is drawn in Genesis 9:1–6 leads again to the affirmation that all human beings without distinction are made in God's image, and when God speaks it is *to Noah and to his sons with him* (9:8). The divine word of blessing – and the renewed creation mandate that we should take responsibility for God's world – is given to all without distinction. It is a mandate that we human beings share *together*.

Life in the fallen world after the Flood is thus a life which is intended to be expressed in a corporate and shared human commitment to show in our relationships and in our mutually accepted responsibilities for the world, that we are 'in the divine image'. We are to be a *community* of creation.

Even in the wickedness which we cause, and through which we suffer, God still accords us the dignity of his image, and still blesses us with the responsibility of being his 'estate manager'.

Yet it is easy for us to evade this responsibility. And one way is by despair. What can I do? What will my small gift count for in the power struggles of the world? I have only a few loaves and fishes, and what are they among so many?

A recent student survey indicated that a growing proportion of undergraduates are becoming resigned to the belief that they will not see out their natural life. The Bomb, they think, will drop within the foreseeable future. So why bother? Why try to recapture the idealism they felt a few years before?

The despair in some reports from famine-torn Ethiopia, plagued by the continuing threats of thousands of deaths by starvation, despite the massive responses to appeals for aid, tells the same story. We tried: but what was the use?

To argue this way is to diminish our humanity. God has entrusted us with this earth. Our choices determine its future welfare. We cannot evade this responsibility by hiding behind a cosmic fatalism of despair. Thankfully, the story of Noah will – as we shall see – point us to rainbows of hope. Before we look at the

---

[1] J. Moltmann, *Power of the Powerless*, p. 4.

rainbow, though, we need to think further about law.

2. Covenant law

Be fruitful and multiply we read in 9:1. So much – as with the ebbing of the Flood itself – reminds us of the creation story in chapter 1. But in verse 2 the tone is different. No longer is the context 'very good' (1:31); rather the world is full of *fear* and *dread* (9:2). So this new start is 'marked from the outset with the stigma of the breach of covenant' (Thielicke). Now, as God re-established the conditions in the world in which life may be lived again, dominion is no longer simply granted: it has to be struggled for (9:2). And now for the first time there are the constraints of a sort of criminal law on the way human life is to be lived.

So in this fallen world after the Flood, even after the drama of salvation, mankind does not go back to Eden. We are still this side of the Garden, living within the tensions of a fallen world. There is continuity and discontinuity. God's creative word is not withdrawn. But it comes to us in a mode that is appropriate for a fallen world. God has not abandoned us, but his law is now given in a way in which it was *not* given in the beginning. Now we read of animals being used for food. Now we read of murder and of capital punishment. God's law is now a law for an abnormal world. His law comes, as it were, refracted through the disordered relationships which mark even this new start.

a. God's provisional will

What we begin to see in this story is a recognition that the Fall of man has to some extent changed the way God deals with us. No longer is his command straightforward, as it was in the Garden. It is accommodated to the needs of a fallen world. This is not something, as it were, forced on God. God in his sovereign majesty calls *every living creature* (9:10) into the covenant of his restored creation, and then he decrees the conditions under which human life shall be lived. God's word, though, comes to us now with this double aspect: there is the divine command expressed often as the covenant rule, that we should be holy as he is holy; and there is a provision of God's law for the restraint of evil in a world that is disordered.

We find this double aspect to God's command elsewhere, and it is important for the use we may wish to make of the divine commands in our moral decision-making. The Ten Commandments, for example, illustrate this double aspect. On the one hand, they require the worship of only one God; on the other hand, they acknowledge the temptation to make graven images. They require the honour of God's name and respect for the sabbath, while acknowledging that both can be disregarded. The negative tone of the commandments against murder, adultery, theft, false witness and coveting have the sense both of obligation and of penalty. The law is occasioned by and relevant to a fallen world. It is, as it were, an 'emergency' provision of God's grace, necessary because of sin.

We can also find a recognition of the double aspect to God's will in the New Testament, most clearly, perhaps, in the narrative of Jesus' discussion with the Pharisees about divorce.[2] Jesus indicated that there was a distinction between the *permission* of God for a bill of divorce granted 'for your hardness of heart',[3] and the *will* of God in the perfection of creation ('from the begining it was not so'[4]). God the Creator in his loving providence makes certain rulings for this fallen world, even though they are at a distance from his creation intention.

This distinction between God's 'creation intention' and his 'provisional will' seems clear from a comparison of Genesis 9 with Genesis 1. It is crucially important in our understanding of God's will for us in this world. If we fail to understand the ambiguity of this age in which God blesses us and call us to covenant allegiance, we may fall over into inaccurate pictures of the way things now are.

We might be tempted, for example, to take the radical demands of the Sermon on the Mount as a new civil law appropriate for all human society. This would be to deal with the present age as though it still existed in its original unfallen state, or as though the coming Day of the Lord had already dawned, and all creation had already been made new. This might lead us into utopian attempts to build the kingdom of God on earth, or to recover a theocratic form of political society. As the Sermon on the Mount itself makes clear, though, it is a pattern of life for disciples,[5] for people of the kingdom[6] and for children of the Father.[7] And without the living relationship with God which these terms imply, and the grace in Christ which can enable such character gradually to grow, it would stand merely as an impossible ideal.

On the other hand, we might be tempted to mistake the 'provisional' expression of the will of God for the fallen world as in fact an expression of his creation intention. Thus we might understand the existence of the State, for example, as an order of creation instead of an emergency provision for the fallen world – a limited providential restraint necessary because of sin. And if we took that

[2] Mt. 19:3–9. [3] Mt. 19:8; *cf.* Dt. 24:1ff.
[4] Mt. 19:8, referring back to Gn. 1:24 and 2:24. [5] Mt. 5:1.
[6] Mt. 5:3, 10, 19–20; 6:33. [7] Mt. 5:45, 48; 6:1, 4, 6, 8–9, 18, 26.

line, we might be led to view war (thought of as an extension of the State's functioning) as an expression of the perfect will of God in some circumstances. This would be the inclination of the militarist crusading tendency in some aspects of 'warlike' Christianity, which sees God as a God of war. A recognition of the distinction between God's creation intention and his provisional will, however, requires us to refuse to call God a 'God of war', while recognizing that it might be possible to justify some war as part of an emergency and 'lesser evil' provision of God for a fallen world.

By way of summary, therefore, we can say that 'covenant ethics' are set in the context of the tension of the fallen world. We cannot simply read off God's creation intention from the way things happen to be in this world – everything is overshadowed by abnormality. Nor can we identify every expression of God's law with his perfect will. But we can be grateful that, as a gift of his covenanted grace, he has given us a law to guide us in loving. For that is what covenant life is ultimately about: learning to express our covenant allegiance to God in ways which show our love to him, and our love to our neighbours. The struggles we have in doing so, the moral conflicts we face, are all symptoms of the disordering effects of sin. We are 'after the Deluge', not 'back in Eden'.

We need to hold on to this tension, this ambiguity, in understanding our own spiritual journeys also. There are themes in the New Testament which remind us that we are new creatures in Christ, rejoicing in the power of Christ's resurrection. There are other themes which remind us of the downward pull of sin, and the need to fight the fight of faith, protected by the armour of God. To concentrate on the first could lead to a triumphalism which pays insufficient regard to the struggles of life. To over-emphasize the second could lead to a denial of the new gift that really is ours in Christ. Romans 5 illustrates the ambiguity. We are still 'in Adam' while we are also 'in Christ'. We live in the overlap of the two ages, waiting for the time when Christ will be all and in all. This side of heaven, both aspects of the truth need to be held in tension. There is healing; there is resurrection; there is freedom from sin, and pain, and sickness and the power of death; but we only receive this gift in part now, its fullness comes only in heaven.

b. Life's sanctity

These verses at the start of Genesis 9 also open up for us a way of understanding the special sanctity that is accorded to human life throughout the biblical traditions. This is of far more than academic interest in our present world. For not only on a global scale do we collude in the deaths through famine, and through civil unrest, of tens of thousands of our fellow human beings, but in the 'civilized world' of the West, the disregard for the concept of life's sanctity is widespread in many debates about the morality of abortion, infanticide or embryo research. Several influential utilitarian philosophers have contributed to debates on medical ethics, for example, by arguing that the concept of life's sanctity is in fact meaningless.

And of course, within an ethical system in which what is good is measured only in terms of 'what produces the greatest overall happiness', the principle of the sanctity of human life seems hard to justify.

Jonathan Glover, for example, writing from the position of a humanist utilitarian, believes that 'the doctrine of the sanctity of life is not acceptable, but that there is embedded in it a moral view we should retain. We should reject the view,' he argues, 'that taking human life is *intrinsically* wrong, but retain the view that it is normally *directly* wrong: that most acts of killing people would be wrong in the absence of harmful side-effects.'[8] Glover then discusses the difficulties of defining life, death, consciousness, personhood, and so on, and bases his moral judgments of such issues as abortion, infanticide, euthanasia and other life-death choices, on 'respect for individual autonomy' and on the slippery concept of a 'life worth living'.

But within the covenant-relationship terms of Genesis 9, in which what is good is defined by the character of God and his concern for what makes for the best for human welfare, the argument is very different.

All life, this author argues, is significant to God. Even animal life may not be needlessly taken. This is illustrated by the restriction of the tendency towards bloodthirstiness implicit in the command: '*You shall not eat flesh with its life, that is, its blood*' (9:4). Animal blood may only be shed within restricted bounds. As von Rad puts it: 'Even when man slaughters and kills, he is to know that he is touching something which, because it is life, is in a special manner God's property; and as a sign of this he is to keep his hands off the blood.'[9]

But more than this: the blood of humans is not to be shed at all. There is thus a distinction between the human species and other animals with respect to the degree of protection appropriate to them. One human being may not decide to take the life of another. God is lord over all life. It is only the utterly serious occasion of murder among fallen humankind which, here in Genesis, can ever require one human being by divine command to take the life of

[8] J. Glover, *Causing Death and Saving Lives* (Penguin, 1977), p. 42.
[9] Von Rad, p. 128.

another. The death penalty in this passage belongs within an over-riding respect for the inviolability of all human life.

There is implicit, therefore, an absolute prohibition against the shedding of innocent human blood. This is a principle which is elaborated elsewhere throughout the Bible: innocent human beings have a right not to be deliberately killed.[10]

This principle has formed the basis for legislation and conventions upholding rights to life. Here, for example, is one source of the doctrine of non-combatant immunity in wartime, and of the criterion of discrimination to which Bishop Bell appealed in the House of Lords in 1944 condemning the Allied saturation bombing of Hamburg and Berlin. This principle is also a central theme, as we have said, in the debates within medical ethics concerning death by choice.

Innocent human beings, Genesis teaches, should not be deliberately killed. And why? *For God made man in his own image* (9:6).

This is a vitally important consideration in the thorny ethical dilemmas surrounding abortion and the sort of embryo research in which human embryos are destroyed. The awful seriousness of taking any human life derives from two important facts. First, human life is in a very special sense God's property. We saw this in Genesis 1. We saw it in the story of Cain and Abel, whose blood cried out to the Lord. We see it again here. Human life is God's gift – or, as Karl Barth puts it perhaps more poignantly: God's 'loan'.

Secondly, as we have seen, every living human being bears the image of God. If our discussion of the divine image in chapter 1 (see pp. 36–41) is on the right lines, it is the relationship God has with such beings – their history before God – rather than any capacity they have within themselves, in which the image of God is seen. And that should lead us to very great caution with respect to those youngest members of the human species – the human embryos. For whatever else we may believe about their 'personality' – their capacities or abilities – they are without doubt living members of the human species, and so in the image of the personal God, and in that sense therefore, 'persons-on-the-way'.

Of course, as we have said before, there are certain human capacities which are involved in the full expression of the image of God in this world. But all of us are called to engage in the process of becoming more fully and truly human – to grow nearer to the image of God we see in Christ. All of us are at a certain stage in that process. It seems entirely consistent, therefore, to believe (with

[10] *Cf.* the prohibition against shedding innocent blood in, *e.g.*, Nu. 35:31–34; Is. 59:7; *cf.* Je. 22:3; Mt. 27:4.

Richard Higginson) that there is already a reflection of that image in the earliest beginnings of embryonic life. Of course the human embryo cannot be anything like a full manifestation of the divine image, but then neither can the foetus, the newborn, nor most of us sinful adults either. Early embryos do not differ qualitatively from the rest of us; they are simply at an earlier stage of the developmental process. God has a history and relationship with them too.[11]

Of embryos, too, therefore – and perhaps especially so since they cannot speak for themselves – it is the case that innocent human beings have a prima facie right not to be deliberately killed. Whether other ethical considerations should override that right is, of course, an area of debate on which many Christian people disagree.

c. Civil Law enforcement

This paragraph in Genesis 9 is also the seed-bed for some preliminary hints which have grown up in later thinking into a theology of the State. For what is important and new here, is that though there are to be divine judgments within history, '*I will surely require a reckoning*' (9:5), in some cases aspects of that judgment are handed over to the human community. '*By man shall his blood be shed*' (9:6).

Human authority is to take a share in the exercise of divine judgment. Here are the beginnings of a doctrine of social order, of the authorities, even of the State.

The principle of ordered government should be a sign that God is still at work preserving a faithless world. Human beings are to order society in a way which expresses something of his character. In particular, the State exists for the provision of a context of order and justice. This is picked up in the New Testament indications concerning the place of the State in the purposes of God, most clearly in Paul's discussion in Romans 12 and Romans 13. In Romans 12 we learn that individuals are never to avenge themselves, for judgment is the work of God. In chapter 13, however, the officers of the State – who in Paul's mind have a limited and provisional role under God – are to be the agents of God's judgment against the wrongdoer.

There are, as we said, hints of this view in Genesis. The human authorities have a divinely appointed, though limited role, under God for the maintenance of order and the punishment of injustice.

---

[11] R. Higginson, *Ethics and Medicine*, 1.2 (1985), p. 10; *cf.* his *Reply to Warnock* (Grove Books, 1986).

d. Retributive justices: capital punishment

Genesis 9:6 has often been used as a biblical basis for the justification of capital punishment.

Philosophers have tended to answer the general question 'Why punish?' in one of three ways. Two of the answers follow a 'utilitarian' approach, looking to the future good which might be achieved, either in reforming the criminal, or removing him from society and perhaps deterring others. The other answer looks back towards the past crime, and argues that because of what he did, the criminal deserves to be punished. These are, of course, not exclusive approaches to the meaning and purpose of punishment: there must be justice in the practice of punishment, as well as justice in the decision to punish at all.

In the case of capital punishment, it is not clear what reformative effect it could be thought to have, except perhaps eliciting repentance while on Death Row. Further, from most of the studies available, the view that capital punishment is a deterrent to others to commit crime is very difficult to establish. The case for capital punishment would need to rely heavily, therefore, on the concept of desert.

The idea of 'desert' – of punishing someone because it is deserved – has often been described in terms of 'retribution', an idea which is not acceptable to some modern minds. And yet, as many have argued, would it not be immoral to punish anyone who did not deserve it? 'Retribution' does not need to be primitive, vengeful or retaliatory. It can stand positively for the view that to transgress against the laws which are essential to the well-being of society requires that society takes measures to uphold its laws.

The notion of retribution is clear in Genesis 9, where the principle of capital punishment for shedding innocent human blood is laid down. '*Whoever sheds the blood of man, by man shall his blood be shed*' (9:6).

For some Christians, this has not only confirmed the importance of retribution as an essential part of the meaning of punishment, but has also led to the view that capital punishment is *required* for murder, a view which we need to treat which some caution, for a number of reasons.

First, the law against eating 'flesh with its blood' a few verses earlier is clearly not applied as an absolute law throughout the Scriptures. Indeed Jesus himself 'declared all foods clean'.[12] As with this law, we Christians need to read Genesis 9:6 in the light of the gospel of Christ, and decide how it then looks.

[12] Mk. 7:19.

162

Secondly, it seems clear that capital punishment in the practice of ancient Israel was linked to the laws of the Decalogue. In the Pentateuchal legislation, capital punishment was prescribed for striking a man so that he dies, for wilful murder, for striking father or mother, for stealing another man, for cursing father and mother, for harming a woman with child as a result of a brawl in which someone loses their life,[13] for being a sorceress, or for bestiality,[14] for various other sexual offences which broke the seventh commandment,[15] and for a number of other crimes. The laws were given to enforce the identity of Israelite society as the people of Yahweh. And clearly they were maximum penalties – we do not know when or how often they were exacted. Even by the time of Hosea, it is clear that capital punishment was not routinely required for adultery.

Thirdly, we need to set the practice of punishment in the social context in which justice is to be administered. In the desert community in Ancient Israel, with no top security prison on hand, the need for immediate and definite action to prevent further crime was clearly best served by the death sentence in some cases. It does not necessarily follow that justice is always served in this way. For even though Genesis 9 specifies the death penalty for murder precisely because it is the dignity and sanctity of human life as the image of God which has been violated, the question for us – this side of the cross and the empty tomb, and in a culture in which other forms of punishment are available – is how best to order our practice of punishment so that the same dignity and sanctity of human life is upheld.

Some Christians believe that the death penalty is still an appropriate means of upholding justice in the face of murder. Some would say that this is so especially in the case of terrorist murder. They argue that Jesus did not repudiate the death penalty, as he did the food laws, and that St Paul taught that the magistrate who carried the sword of justice is God's servant.[16] Others, however, believe that, in the ambiguous fallen world in which we have to bring our human justice into line as far as we can with the justice of God, but in which motives are often blurred, responsibility sometimes diminished, and cases of mistaken identity and miscarriages of justice in the complexities of modern society more possible than we would wish, the irreversible decision of depriving another person of life should be replaced by other forms of punishment which can more effectively be seen to honour the Genesis 9 principle of the

[13] Ex. 21:12–14. [14] Ex. 22:18–19.
[15] Lv. 20:10, 13–14; 21:9. [16] Rom. 13:1–4.

163

sanctity and dignity of human life.[17]

e. Distributive justice

Human authorities, we said, have a God-given, if limited, role under God for the maintenance of order, the establishment of justice and so the punishment of injustice. Since that role is set in the context of the creative purposes of God for his world, and since, as we have seen, the creation mandate is something we human beings share *together*, and, further, as this section in Genesis leads into the covenant promise in which Noah is bracketed with his descendants and with every living creature, we must include in the concept of justice that 'distributive justice' which is seen in an equitable sharing of earth's rich resources. The State is not only a 'minimal' provision for 'law and order', but also has a responsibility for social justice more widely. Doesn't our understanding of human persons as essentially 'persons in relation' point in the same direction? Justice covers the relationships of men and women with each other, and with the rest of the created order, within the community of creation.

The covenant God who orders the seasons is also concerned with seed-time and harvest.

3. Covenant grace

There can be few sights more moving and powerful than the dazzling brightness of a full rainbow, set against the threatening blackness of the thunder clouds. The Hebrew term used to describe the rainbow in Genesis 9 is the term normally used for the bow of a warrior. How pointed, then, is this particular sign from God at this particular time. *I set my bow in the cloud* (9:13) is the sign of the covenant which God makes with Noah and with all living creatures. The hostility is over: God hangs up his bow! The covenant is nothing man-made. In its spectral beauty, it tells us only of the Creator – and that the light of his beauty shines through even the reminders of his watery judgment. The weapon of war itself is transformed into a delight. Here is the Creator's overarching care: the Creator God is the Covenant God. He who made us still loves us.

The only other references to the rainbow in the Bible are found in Ezekiel 1:28, and in Revelation 4:3 and 10:1. In Ezekiel, the rainbow is part of the 'appearance of the likeness of the glory of

---

[17] *Cf.* the excellent discussion in O. M. T. O'Donovan, *Measure for Measure: Justice in punishment and the sentence of death* (Grove Books, 1977).

the LORD'. In Revelation 4:3, it forms a halo round the throne of God – a picture of the final consummation of the Covenant when the whole company of heaven worships 'him who is on the throne': 'Worthy art thou, our Lord and God, to receive glory and honour and power, for thou didst create all things, and by thy will they existed and were created'.[18] In Revelation 10, the picture is of a strong angel, robed in a cloud with a rainbow about his head – he is the warrior angel speaking the judgment of God.

Salvation, we saw in the Flood story, is grace and judgment. The rainbows of Revelation tell the same story. The covenant promise is of God's gracious and never-failing steadfast love – his hostility towards us is over. The covenant man has been kept safe in the ark, and can now live freely under the rainbow. But God still needs his warrior angel. He is still at war with evil, his rainbow, as it were, holding back the threatening black clouds which could, unrestrained, unleash the waters of judgment once more.

The rainbow in Genesis 9 reminds us that the world is held in being by God's promise. '*I will remember my covenant*' (9:15), he said to Noah. There is no cosmic fatalism here. No grounds here for saying, 'Let us eat and drink for tomorrow we die'. The world is held in being by God's commitment that it shall be so. The rainbow, then, is a sign of hope. To quote Moltmann once more:

> The promise never again to destroy all flesh because of its wickedness is an unconditional promise on God's part. It is God's indestructible 'Yes' to his creation. The history of nature, with its changes and chances, and the uncertain history of humanity, both rest on the foundation of God's unconditional will. Natural catastrophes and the human catastrophes of history cannot annul this divine 'Yes' to creation and to the human person. Not even human wickedness can thwart the creator's will towards his creation. God remains true to the earth, for God remains true to himself. He cannot deny himself.[19]

For God, this means the suffering of divine love, awaiting the Prodigal's return. For us, it means the confidence that despite all the chances and changes in this uncertain life, God 'has the whole world in his hands'. We need such hope today. In a world in which so many of our contemporaries are given over to a cosmic fatalism – perhaps overshadowed by the Bomb, or by the apparent intractability of political disputes, ideological conflicts or the mutual hatred born of generations of mistrust – we need to find ways of making known the fact that, despite all appearances, God has not

[18] Rev. 4:11.   [19] Moltmann, *Power of the Powerless*, p. 10.

and will not give us up.

For the covenant points back to creation. This colourful imprint in the heavens of God's purposes of love, point us back to the order and patterns of creation. The rainbow in its vivid splendour indicates to us a *natural* order, which depends on the physics of light and refraction. But the beauty of that natural order also serves as a 'signal of transcendence' (Berger), pointing beyond itself to the God of creation and covenant. The light shines in the darkness, and the darkness does not overcome it. The natural order of the physical world is a visible counterpart to the moral order of the covenant God.[20] We live in an ordered moral universe of which the rainbow is a sign. This many-coloured arch stretches back unmistakably to the themes of creation, providence and covenant faithfulness. In its majestic sweep across the skies, it points us on to the Lamb on the throne, and the fulfilment of creation in the covenant community. The rainbow is a sign of hope. It also, as Delitzsch remarks, in originating from the effect of the sun upon the dark mass of clouds, 'typifies the readiness of the heavenly to pervade the earthly'.[21] 'Heaven' and 'earth' can come together. The rainbow is also a sign of grace.

Notice what this passage is doing: it is interpreting the apocalyptic questions of the present – the meaning of continuing life in the light of God's judgment in history – by referring back to the God of creation, providence and covenant.

Is that not another theme to comfort the people of God?

Is that not a word for our contempories also? Part of our task as Christian people is to interpret the apocalyptic questions of our day in such a way that we point beyond them to God. When we engage in discussion of bioethics, or nuclear deterrence, we may not stay only with questions concerning the genetics of the foetus or the theories of military strategy. In these and other areas, when not only the lives of men by the humanity of man are at stake, we are standing on holy ground. We are to be witnesses to the holiness of God in these so important questions. We are to bear witness to the God who keeps his promise, the God who will not let us go. Our witness should also lead us to the social task of so ordering our society – and holding the leaders of society accountable to God – that our social order and justice may reflect something of his character of holiness, goodness and love.

There is an individual dimension to this, too. For the covenant sign of the rainbow was given to an individual: *God said to Noah* (9:17). The rainbow serves not only as a reminder of God's commit-

---

[20] *Cf*. Ps. 19.
[21] Quoted in C. F. Keil and F. Delitzsch, *Biblical Commentary on the Old Testament*, vol. 1 (Eerdmans reprint, 1971), p. 155.

ment to his world; it strengthens Noah's faith in God's promise.

That is the way with covenant signs. The sign of circumcision, sealing the covenant between God and Abraham and his descendants[22] is also given to an individual – to Abraham himself as a strengthener for his faith. It is a sign that God has made a promise, and a summons to the obedience of faith which God henceforward expects. The sabbath, also, is a sign of God's promise to sanctify his people, and of their obligations to order their lives in accordance with his creation pattern.[23] In the New Testament, baptism – which corresponds to the Old Testament sign of circumcision[24] – is likewise not only the sign of initiation into the Christian community, but is particularly the sign that God's promise of grace has been made especially to this individual person, to strengthen their trust and to commit them to the obedience of faith.

The signs of the covenant, some of which we now call 'sacraments', are outward and visible signs of an inward and spiritual grace. They are given as a means of grace to both individual and community life, for at one and the same time my individual commitment to God is also my involvement in the community of his people,[25] his Body, his church. To be a member of the covenant community is to be obliged in individual and in social life to living as the people of God.

And our strength for doing so, our confidence for doing so, and our motivation for doing so, come from the promise of God, 'Behold, I establish my covenant with you . . . I will never again curse the earth.' God's promise (as Moltmann puts it) 'gives us all the chance to live'.

4. The drunkenness of Noah

The sons of Noah who went forth from the ark were Shem, Ham, and Japheth. Ham was the father of Canaan. [19]*These three were the sons of Noah; and from these the whole earth was peopled.*

[20]*Noah was the first tiller of the soil. He planted a vineyard;* [21]*and he drank of the wine, and became drunk, and lay uncovered in his tent.* [22]*And Ham, the father of Canaan, saw the nakedness of his father, and told his two brothers outside.* [23]*Then Shem and Japheth took a garment, laid it upon both their shoulders, and walked backward and covered the nakedness of their father; their faces were turned away, and they did not see their father's nakedness.* [24]*When Noah awoke from his wine and knew what his youngest son had done to him,* [25]*he said,*

[22] Gn. 17:10.   [23] Ex. 31:13–17.   [24] Col. 2:11–12.
[25] *Cf.* 1 Cor. 10:14–17.

> 'Cursed be Canaan;
>> a slave of slaves shall he be to his brothers.'

[26]He also said,

> 'Blessed by the LORD my God be Shem;
>> and let Canaan be his slave.
> [27] God enlarge Japheth,
>> and let him dwell in the tents of Shem;
>> and let Canaan be his slave.'

[28]After the flood Noah lived three hundred and fifty years. [29]All the days of Noah were nine hundred and fifty years; and he died.

(9:18–28)

Why on earth didn't the editor of these chapters take a blue pencil to this nasty little paragraph? After the salvation story of the Flood, and the reassurance of the divine promise given in the rainbow, why come back now to this story of drunken stupor, sexual immodesty, family embarrassment and the curse against Canaan? It really seems to lower the tone.

Some of the allegorical interpretations of the early church have tried to rescue the story, and sanctify it, with the suggestions that Noah is here a type of Christ. The Holy Trinity is figured in the farmer who prepares the soil. Christ drinks the cup of salvation; his nakedness is his self-exposure to evil on the cross; Ham stands for the unbelieving Jews who deride and mock him, Shem and Japheth are the converts to Christ, Jew and Gentile, on which God now builds his church, the dwelling place of his Spirit.

Alternatively, the paragraph was used by some as a moral lesson, to guide subordinate clergy in their obligation to 'cover over' the faults of their bishops! However important that may be, it is surely pressing this particular text a little far!

We need, first, to look at the text as it stands.

Verses 18–19 link the story of Noah with the ongoing life of his sons, from whom *the whole earth was peopled*. The 'developing story' formula comes again in chapter 10:1. We are being led into an account of the spread of civilization throughout the earth after the Flood. And it is in that context that this episode with Noah is placed.

Noah, we are told, was a tiller of the soil. There are unmistakable echoes of Adam in the Garden in Genesis 2:15. After the Flood, civilization has to be rebuilt. Noah planted a vineyard. There is nothing particularly wrong with wine; indeed some biblical authors recognize that wine may 'gladden the heart of man'[26] – and is to

[26] Ps. 104:15.

168

be received as a gift from the Creator. However, even in the world after the Flood – as we have seen several times before – life is lived in tension. What is given as a blessing can become a source of temptation. The vine which Noah planted eventually takes control of him. Even the man of faith can be overtaken by temptations which become too strong to handle.

It seems clear from this text that Noah was lured into the immodesty of nakedness – often regarded as a disgrace and source of shame in the Bible. The Noah who walked with God, who did all that the Lord commanded him concerning the ark, who trusted the Lord in faithful obedience when all around was disorder, who offered the burnt offering of consecration, and who received the Lord's covenanted promise – this God-fearing man is now described as a drunk lying uncovered in his tent. Many commentators have thought that the picture is so incongruous that it must come from another hand. But could it not be that it is precisely the incongruity that is important for us to notice? We were reminded in Genesis 8:21 that even after the Flood 'the imagination of man's heart is evil'. God has saved Noah and his family, but salvation is not the same as transformation. People of faith still fall into sin. To be declared in baptism to be a member of the Christian community is not a guarantee of instant holiness, it is but the beginning of a pilgrimage journey of sanctification and growth. The life of faithful obedience has its pitfalls. The fall of Noah is another story which engages with us all. And the chapter ends with a reminder that he, too, was mortal! (9:29).

But whatever we say of Noah, it seems that the major problem lies with his son Ham. In contrast to the modest response of Shem and Japheth, Ham is pictured as dishonouring his father presumably by impurely looking at his father's nakedness, by doing we know not what, and then by broadcasting the indecency around. In the ancient world, honouring one's parents is one of the highest virtues, and Ham, it appears both from his brothers' response, and from Noah's own reaction, had violated another aspect of the divine order.

But we need to move beyond the text as we have it to our prior question: Why was it important that this paragraph was included in the edition of Genesis which we now have? What message did this incident carry for the people of God?

Perhaps our answer lies in the way Canaan, the son of Ham, is cursed for Ham's sin (9:25–27). For, according to many parts of the Old Testament, the Canaanites are one of the greatest sources of temptation to the people of God. The sexual perversions of the Canaanites, often associated with their religious drunken orgies, were held up to the people of God as behaviours to avoid. 'You

169

shall not do as they do in the land of Canaan,' says Leviticus 18:3 – and then follows a list of sexual malpractices which are not consistent with the life of the people of Yahweh.

By contrast, Noah blesses God for being the God of Shem, and prays that Japheth may dwell in his tents. These verses, full of difficulties, their precise meaning obscure, may possibly indicate that Noah is looking forward to a time when the people of Japheth (perhaps the Philistines?) will dwell in the tents of Shem, within the land of Canaan. Is there a hint here that despite all the comings and goings of the nations (described in Gn. 10), God still has his hand on world history – and that one day even 'outsiders' will be welcomed among the people of God? What is clear, though, is that Genesis 9 is telling us in this vivid story of how the father of the Canaanites was guilty of ungodly behaviour – towards his own father. It serves as a reminder to the people of God how easy it is to be led astray from the patterns of life appropriate to covenant people. Even the 'herald of righteousness' is not immune to temptation. The sins of one (Ham) can set the course for succeeding generations (Canaan). And beware, people of God, lest you, too, be led astray by the Canaanites at your door.

How good that before we read of this continuing struggle for the man of faith against ignorance, weakness and failure, symbolized by the fall of Noah, we were told of rainbows of hope.

HOPE

Hope means to keep living
    Amid desperation
And to keep humming
    In the darkness.

Hoping is knowing that
    There is love.
It is trust in tomorrow.
    It is falling asleep
And waking again
    When the sun rises.

In the midst of a gale at sea
    It is to discern land.
In the eyes of another
    It is to see that
He understands you.

As long as there is still hope
There will also be prayer.

And God will be holding you
    In His hands.

Henry J. M. Nouwen

6. God is our hope and strength

These are the generations of the sons of Noah, Shem, Ham, and Japheth; sons were born to them after the flood.
²*The sons of Japheth: Gomer, Magog, Madai, Javan, Tubal, Meshech, and Tiras.* ³*The sons of Gomer: Ashkenaz, Riphath, and Togarmah.* ⁴*The sons of Javan: Elishah, Tarshish, Kittim, and Dodanim.* ⁵*From these the coastland peoples spread. These are the sons of Japheth in their land, each with his own language, by their families, in their nations.*
⁶*The sons of Ham: Cush, Egypt, Put, and Canaan.* ⁷*The sons of Cush: Seba, Havilah, Sabtah, Raamah, and Sabteca. The sons of Raamah: Sheba and Dedan.* ⁸*Cush became the father of Nimrod; he was the first on earth to be a mighty man.* ⁹*He was a mighty hunter before the* LORD; *therefore it is said, 'Like Nimrod a mighty hunter before the* LORD.' ¹⁰*The beginning of his kingdom was Babel, Erech, and Accad, all of them in the land of Shinar.* ¹¹*From that land he went into Assyria, and built Nineveh, Rehoboth-Ir, Calah, and* ¹²*Resen between Nineveh and Calah; that is the great city.* ¹³*Egypt became the father of Ludim, Anamim, Lehabim, Naphtuhim,* ¹⁴*Pathrusim, Casluhim (whence came the Philistines), and Caphtorim.*
¹⁵*Canaan became the father of Sidon his first-born, and Heth,* ¹⁶*and the Jebusites, the Amorites, the Girgashites,* ¹⁷*the Hivites, the Arkites, the Sinites,* ¹⁸*the Arvadites, the Zemarites, and the Hamathites. Afterward the families of the Canaanites spread abroad.* ¹⁹*And the territory of the Canaanites extended from Sidon, in the direction of Gerar, as far as Gaza, and in the direction of Sodom, Gomorrah, Admah, and Zeboiim, as far as Lasha.* ²⁰*These are the sons of Ham, by their families, their languages, their lands, and their nations.*
²¹*To Shem also, the father of all the children of Eber, the elder brother of Japheth, children were born.* ²²*The sons of Shem: Elam,*

Asshur, Arpachshad, Lud, and Aram. ²³*The sons of Aram: Uz, Hul, Gether, and Mash.* ²⁴*Arpachshad became the father of Shelah; and Shelah became the father of Eber.* ²⁵*To Eber were born two sons: the name of the one was Peleg, for in his days the earth was divided, and his brother's name was Joktan.* ²⁶*Joktan became the father of Almodad, Sheleph, Hazarmaveth, Jerah,* ²⁷*Hadoram, Uzal, Diklah,* ²⁸*Obal, Abimael, Sheba,* ²⁹*Ophir, Havilah, and Jobab; all these were the sons of Joktan.* ³⁰*The territory in which they lived extended from Mesha in the direction of Sephar to the hill country of the east.* ³¹*These are the sons of Shem, by their families, their languages, their lands, and their nations.*

³²*These are the families of the sons of Noah, according to their genealogies, in their nations; and from these the nations spread abroad on the earth after the flood.*

(10:1–32)

Genesis 10 opens with the literary formula we have met several times before: *These are the generations of the sons of Noah.*

From the single origin of Noah and his family in the ark, the earth is to be populated again, and the narrator now presents us with another genealogy, a table of the nations. As Genesis 5 told us of chronology – the development of the primeval families through time – Genesis 10 concentrates on geography: the territorial spread of the nations across the lands.

The genealogy of chapter 10 stands in our Bibles as a sort of preface to chapter 11. We have seen this pattern before. Genesis 5 acts as a genealogical preface to the salvation story of the Flood. And as we mentioned earlier, genealogies preface the salvation stories of two of the New Testament Gospels. They remind us that the story of God with particular people is a story set within a larger context of God's concerns with history and with the world.

Especially is this true here. The individual concerns of the story of Noah and his sons, and soon of Abraham and his family, are set into the international context of many peoples, many groups, many nations. 'Be fruitful and multiply, and fill the earth' was God's word to Noah (9:2). Chapter 10 tells us that he had a pretty good try.

A key word is 'spread'. *From these the coastland peoples spread* (10:5); *the families of the Canaanites spread* (10:18); *the nations spread abroad on the earth after the flood* (10:32). The narrative spells out the families descended from the sons of Noah, who form the nations known to the people of Yahweh. First Japheth (10:2–5). Then a much larger section concerning the descendants of Ham (10:6–20) – with an additional comment about Nimrod (10:9), who probably stands as 'an archetype of Mesopotamian ideals of kingship' (Wenham) – signifying pride in their achievements as fighters and hunters as well as builders; and then a paragraph about the important Canaanites (10:15–20; *cf.* 9:25). Finally, 10:21–31 refers to the sons of Shem, including a reference to the days of Peleg when *the earth was divided* (perhaps looking forward to chapter 11:1–9).

Here is a picture of international growth, of national diversity, yet all descended from one man – a sort of second Adam: Noah. God's covenanted blessing to Noah is being confirmed. God's providence encompasses all the nations. Indeed, seventy peoples are included here – a numerical symbol of fullness and wholeness. God's blessing covers the whole earth.

This is the theological significance of this table of nations. Before the Genesis story moves into the particular election of one man, Abraham, and the election of one people descended from him, Israel, we are told of the universal extent of God's purposes. The line from Noah to Abraham moves out first to cover the whole known world. The family tree of the nations begins with Noah, the man rescued by grace from a humanity that was doomed. It is *his* family that now spreads through time and space. This family tree thus tells us that God's blessing to Noah means in reality God's blessing on the whole of subsequent human history.[1]

All human people, even of different national and cultural identities – as chapter 10 itself accepts – are of the same origin, have the same dignity, and belong in the same world. This undercuts all human divisiveness based on nationality, culture and race. However good, however rich national and cultural diversity can be, it should never be allowed to cloud the more fundamental fact that all human people share the same nature, breathe the same air, live on the same earth, and owe their life to the same God. In Gandhi's words, 'All men are brothers.' Or, as St Paul put it standing in the middle of the Areopagus in Athens: 'He made from one every nation of men to live on all the face of the earth, having determined allotted periods and the boundaries of their habitation.'[2]

Another implication of Genesis 10 is that the people of God belong within a whole world of nations which are part of God's purposes and equally express his blessing to Noah. This chapter gives a very significant context to the word to Abraham in Genesis 12:3, 'by you all the families of the earth shall bless themselves.' The particular calling of Abraham is to be a source of blessing to all. Likewise the particular calling of Israel is to be a light to the nations.[3] The election of God is always to be an election for service

[1] *Cf.* Westermann, *Genesis 1 – 11*, p. 529.
[2] Acts 17:26.   [3] Is. 42:6.

and a means of bringing divine blessing to others.

However, if in chapter 10, placed here as a preface to chapter 11, the spread of the people points to God's blessings, in verses 1–9 of chapter 11 the scattering of the people points us to God's judgment.

So here, once more, in the juxtaposition of these chapters, we are faced with the tension, the ambiguity of life, to which Genesis 1 – 11 has so often drawn our attention. On the one hand the nation is part of God's providential ordering of his world; on the other, it may also be under his judgment.

That judgment now focuses down on to one particular group who migrated from the east and came to the land of Shinar (11:1–2).

1. The scattering

Now the whole earth had one language and few words. ²And as men migrated from the east, they found a plain in the land of Shinar and settled there. ³And they said to one another, 'Come, let us make bricks, and burn them thoroughly.' And they had brick for stone, and bitumen for mortar. ⁴Then they said, 'Come, let us build ourselves a city, and a tower with its top in the heavens, and let us make a name for ourselves, lest we be scattered abroad upon the face of the whole earth.' ⁵And the LORD came down to see the city and the tower, which the sons of men had built. ⁶And the LORD said, 'Behold, they are one people, and they have all one language; and this is only the beginning of what they will do; and nothing that they propose to do will now be impossible for them. ⁷Come, let us go down, and there confuse their language, that they may not understand one another's speech.' ⁸So the LORD scattered them abroad from there over the face of all the earth, and they left off building the city. ⁹Therefore its name was called Babel, because there the LORD confused the language of all the earth; and from there the LORD scattered them abroad over the face of all the earth.

(11:1–9)

We have been caught up into the stories of earlier chapters of Genesis, and have seen ourselves in Adam, in Cain, in Noah. We are caught up into this picture, too. But now the theme is not the dealings of God with an individual. Rather, the question of destiny is now being explored in much more than individual terms. Now we are invited to see what happens to community life when whole communities step outside the ways of God.

This story, which forms the last of the stories of the primeval history before Abraham comes on stage, shows the further spread of disorder within God's world. Its careful literary pattern

175

illustrates the crescendo and diminuendo of the story-teller in a way which parallels the rising and dying away of the waters of the Flood. We begin with a community with one language (11:1). This leads us into a journey and a settlement in the land of Shinar (that is Babylonia, 11:2). The people make bricks and start to build a tower (11:3–4). The high point is reached in verse 5 when the Lord *came down to see*, and forms his opinion of what is going on (11:6–7). Then all begins to subside again, and the pattern is reversed. The building ceases and the peoples are scattered (11:8). We end up not with a community bound together with one language, but with the confusion of tongues.

Gordon Wenham helpfully depicts this diagrammatically:

> The whole earth had one language (v. 1)
>   there (v. 2)
>   each other (v. 3)
>   Come let us make bricks (v. 3)
>   let us build for ourselves (v. 4)
>   a city and a tower
>   the Lord came down . . . (v. 5)
>   the city and the tower
>   which mankind had built
>   come . . . let us mix up (v. 7)
>   each other's language
>   from there (v. 8)
>   the language of the whole earth (v. 9)[4]

From one perspective, the whole tale is told to lead up to verse 9: 'Therefore . . . '. It is intended, that is, to give a meaning to the word 'Babel', and the significance of Babylon before God. Now Babylon, as we know, was the centre of the civilization of the ancient world. The *Enuma Elish* refers to the building of Babylon and its temple tower. Von Rad says that 'Babylon in ancient times especially in the second millenium B.C., was the heart of the ancient world and its centre of power.'[5] The mighty towers of the Babylonian ziggurats were widely known. From the perspectives of human achievement, Babylon was the summit. The word 'Babel' for the Babylonians meant 'the gate of the gods'.

How ironic, then, this story in Genesis 11! For a Hebrew word sounding like 'babel' means 'mix up'; and to the narrator of Genesis 11:9, the significance of 'Babel' – the significance of the great Babylon from the perspective of God's heavenly court – is merely 'mixed up': 'confusion'.

---

⁴ Wenham, p. 235.   ⁵ Von Rad, p. 146.

There is more irony in this paragraph, too. The tower is not the gate of the gods: it is so small that God has to come down even to see it (11:5)! And as for the building materials themselves, perhaps there is a disparaging scorn suggested in verse 3. As if to say: 'Where we use stone and mortar, these Babylonians only have brick and bitumen!' The very materials they used were bound to decay.[6]

So Genesis 11 is inviting us to reflect on the meaning of human community, human achievement, human pride from the vantage point of God's purposes for human well-being, and God's judgment against yet another human attempt to cross from 'man's place' to God's.

The story of the tower of Babel is a sad description of the fracture of community, of a breakdown of fellowship, of a failure in communication, of a growth in isolation and confusion. It all results from a communal failure to live in dependence on God, an insistence on striving to reach the heavens, and from giving way instead to pride in human achievements and power, and from human beings' determination to be the source of their own security. Does that carry a social health warning which the world, then and now, needs to hear?

Let us look at the story in a little more detail.

a. 'Come let us make' (11:1–4)

The picture is of the coming-together of a nomadic group from the east into a settlement. Here, in a continuation of Genesis 4:17, are the beginnings of what we call 'civilization'. The other marks of civilization are there also – the development of technical skills, presumably of sufficient architectural and mathematical knowledge for the building of a tower, and of a city, and the political will needed for such a corporate endeavour. As Westermann puts it, 'Genesis 11:2–9 in essence anticipates the possibility of a development that would be realized only in the technical age in a way that would affect the whole of humanity.'[7] Here there are hints of political power and technological achievement. Allied with both, and motivated also by a sense of corporate insecurity ('lest we be scattered') is a striving for fame: 'Let us build ourselves . . . Let us make a name for ourselves' (11:4).

And the focus of their ambition is this tower. 'Come, let us build ourselves a city, and a tower with its top in the heavens' (11:4).

But as we have learned earlier in Genesis 1 – 11, the prerogative of 'making a name' belongs with God.[8] And as we have seen several

---

[6] Cf. Wenham, p. 239; von Rad, p. 144.
[7] Westermann, Genesis 1 – 11, p. 554.   [8] Cf. Is. 63:12; cf. Wenham, p. 240.

times, 'heaven' is God's place and not that of human beings. Here, once again, as in the Garden of Eden, as with Cain and with Lamech, as with the marriage of the sons of God and the daughters of men, God-given boundaries are being crossed; human beings are trying to grasp at what does not belong to them and to assert that no longer are they bound by the limits which God has set. Here is a communal rejection of the necessary separation between the heavenly and the earthly. Our human sin is that we fail to recognize that God is God, and we try, both individually and corporately, to take God's place.

How easy it is to fall into the temptation to grasp at divinity. The root of sin is rebellion – rebellion against God's lordship; an assertion of human autonomy without God; a refusal to live in dependence on the Creator who is the Covenant Lord, Yahweh.

This tower is a sort of architectural symbol of humankind's asserted greatness. *With its top in the heavens* is an idiom for impregnable security. But it is another symbol and picture of a violation of the limits God sets to human life and to human behaviour, for the sake of human well-being.

God scatters the proud in the imagination of their hearts, and puts down the mighty from their thrones.[9] Isaiah made the same point when against the king of Babylon he wrote:

> You said in your heart,
>   'I will ascend to heaven;
> above the stars of God
>   I will set my throne on high;
> I will sit on the mount of assembly
>   in the far north;
> I will ascend above the heights of the clouds,
>   I will make myself like the Most High.'
> But you are brought down to Sheol,
>   to the depths of the Pit.[10]

As the rest of our story makes clear, the proud ambition of the men in the land of Shinar is 'brought down' also. But before we come back to the Genesis text, let us pause with the ragged edges these verses expose on the monuments of human technological achievement.

b. Technological pride

In his book *Begotten or Made?*, concerned with the medical ethics

---

[9] Lk. 1:51–52.   [10] Is. 14:13–15.

of in-vitro fertilization, Oliver O'Donovan discusses a theme that Jaques Ellul, Hans Jonas and others have explored, namely the way our culture is to a very large extent a 'technological' culture.[11] What he means is not only that we have developed technical skills in many areas of life, but that the way we *think* of ourselves is affected by technology, that study of science governed by and restricted to its practical and industrial uses.

We tend to understand ourselves as constructionists, as makers, as interveners, as those whose relationship to the world is primarily one of technical intrusion: as those whose relationship to what is not ourselves is described in terms of what the Jewish philosopher Martin Buber called 'I-It'.[12]

Now, of course, there are many technological interventions for which we can thank God. There are many advances in medical and agricultural technical skills which save lives. And many other areas of technological progress are life-enhancing. That is not in dispute. What is troubling is technological pride. To think of ourselves primarily as 'constructionists', as 'technical interveners', can lead us to believe that what we *can* do (rather than what we *may* do) is the touchstone of what we *will* do. If we see the world outside of ourselves simply as something we make, it then becomes subject to our will and at our disposal. (This is sometimes happening in connection with work on human embryos and fertilization techniques. It is this which has led Oliver O'Donovan to urge us to think again about the importance of seeing children as 'begotten' – with part of the story including all the wonder, contingence and unpredictability of God's life-giving providence – rather than as 'made' by our human will, and so at our human disposal.) By living so much with an 'I-It' way of thinking, asserting our autonomy and our power, we can very easily find ourselves crowding out other much more personal and relational ways of living – what Martin Buber calls 'I-Thou'. If technological pride takes over, personal and social values can be forgotten.

Several times we have noted in Genesis that part of the meaning of the image of God is 'persons in relation'. Human community under God is meant to harness the rest of the created order in a way that enables personal communion and harmony within creation, to flourish. In that setting, technology can be an important servant to us, as part of our service for God.

But notice the contrast between the humility of the writer in Genesis 1, and the proud story in Genesis 11. There, in Genesis 1, we were offered a picture of an ordered, contingent world – the

[11] O. O'Donovan, *Begotten or Made?* (OUP, 1985).
[12] Buber, *I and Thou.*

sort of world which science has to assume in order to be science at all. There we had a picture of men and women granted the task of being stewardly estate managers in God's world. In that light, the scientist can see her or his role as a sort of 'priest' of nature: standing before the silent world of God's creation and bringing 'its mute rationalities into such articulation' (Torrance) that they with us may sing the praise of the Creator. In that light, the technologist is God's servant, harnessing the resources of the world for mankind's good and God's glory.

In Genesis 11, however, the tower in the land of Shinar is a monument to ambitious technological man who has lost touch with the ways of God. The bricks and the bitumen are there for us to build up power structures of our own. It reminds us that when technology ceases to be our servant, it very quickly becomes our master, and human communities and human values are all too often the casualties.

'Science', as a quest for truth, is now frequently getting swallowed up by 'technology'. 'What is truth?' gets taken over by 'what is useful?' Research money is provided for particular projects which fit in with certain political ideologies. 'Technique' and 'skill' become more important than understanding or wisdom.

And then what becomes of science?

The research chemist Walter Thorson wrote some years ago:

Having finally understood that scientific truth is a source of power, man has made the crucial decision that from now on the will to power and the uses of power should dictate the relevance and value of that truth. Because of that decision, 'pure' science, the science of the past four hundred years, will begin to be altered in subtle ways, and will eventually disappear.[13]

If Thorson is right in this, it means that what we are often seeing in our scientific research programmes is effectively a cost-benefit manipulation of truth for the sake of practical or political usefulness. 'The fusion of science and technology means that increasingly the moral decision as to the uses of truth will be made pre-emptively before the truth itself is even sought; we shall seek only truth which fits our purposes.'[14]

Technological pride, coupled with political will, and an abandonment of the ways of God is not only a tale told in Genesis 11. It is part of our world, too, and we are part of the story. 'Let us build *ourselves* a city.' 'Let us build *ourselves* . . . a tower with its top in the heavens.' 'Let us make a name for *ourselves*.'

[13] W. Thorson, 'The Spiritual Dimensions of Science', in C. F. Henry (ed.), *Horizons of Science* (Harper and Row, 1978), pp. 217f.   [14] *Ibid.*

And for us, too, one danger is the same: the loss of community.

c. The loss of community (11:5–9)

There is one supreme danger in the sort of technological thinking where God is no longer the centre, and where constructionist man tries to place his autonomy at the centre. The danger, as Thielicke illustrates so powerfully in *How the World Began*, is the loss of any centre at all. For in this community in the land of Shinar, as for any community in which God himself is banished from the centre, people very soon discover that there is nothing left to bind them *to each other*. 'I–It' eventually squeezes out 'I–Thou'.

The people themselves, it seems, sensed the hidden presence of what Thielicke here refers to as a 'centrifugal force'. Their frantic building, motivated by ambition, is also spurred by anxiety, as they fearfully say, ' . . . *lest we be scattered abroad*' (11:4). Thielicke's comment is once again worth quoting in full:

> Long before the judgement of dispersion fell on them, men already had a premonition, a dim fear that they might break apart and that even their languages might be confused. They sensed the hidden presence of centrifugal, dispersive forces.
>
> This arises from the fact that they have suffered something that might be called the 'loss of a center' and that now that they have banished God from their midst they no longer have anything that binds them to *each other*. Always the trend is the same: wherever God has been deposed, some substitute point has to be created to bind men together in some fashion or other. You start a war, perhaps, in order to divert attention from internal political dissensions and thus create a new solidarity by making people feel that they are facing a common threat. Or you build a tower of Babel in order to concentrate people's attention upon a new center by rallying them to united and enthusiastic effort and this way pull together the dispersive elements. Or you whip together by terror those who will not stay together voluntarily. Or you utilise the powers of suggestion, 'propaganda', and 'ideology', in order to generate the feeling of community by means of psychological tricks and thus make people want precisely what you want them to want. All these are substitute ties, conclusive attempts to replace the lost center with a synthetic center. But this attempt – this *experimentum medietatis* – is doomed to failure. The centrifugal forces go on pulling and rending and a hidden time-fuse is ticking in the piers of all the bridges.[15]

[15] Thielicke, p. 281.

When God, the Lord, disappears from the centre of community life, then the seeds of dispersal, of fragmentation, of loss of communication are sown. There is no unity of fellowship in human community endeavours, unless they are bound together around a centre outside themselves. Human societies which organize themselves without reference to God, and build up power structures of their own in the place of God, are always prey to the demonic. The end of that road is the totalitarian Beast of Revelation 13. Taking to itself what properly only belongs to God, the Beast rising from the sea[16] is the awful monstrous power of the self-absolutization of the creature. It is chaotic; it is a revolt against natural order;[17] it is an ideological tyranny which makes war on the ways of God.

For Genesis, the break-up of community is not merely the inevitable outworking of human pride. There is also in this fragmentation of human society something of the judgment of God.

Verse 5 is the mid-point of the story: God now steps in to frustrate human ambition. From God's perspective in heaven, things are different. The people are building a tower up to heaven, struggling to the heights. Then we read the irony of 11:5: God *came down to see!* Like the psalmist of Psalm 2: 'Why do the nations conspire, and the peoples plot in vain? . . . He who sits in the heavens laughs!'[18] This picture is even of some divine amusement between God and his heavenly court: '*Come, let us go down*' (11:7).

And God in judgment decrees that the centrifugal forces will have their way. If you will live without God as the centre, you will have no centre at all. The judgment is expressed in verse 7: '*Come, let us go down, and there confuse their language, that they may not understand one another's speech*'; it is carried out in verse 8, as the Lord scatters the people over the face of the earth, and the city remains half-built.

For a society which breaks the bounds of God-given order, and which tries by itself to reach the heavens, the results are only disintegration and frustration.

But verse 6 seems to indicate something more. There is not only judgment in this divine action. There is also preservation. Earlier in Genesis, in the story of Adam, the sending-out of the Garden was both judgment and preservation. The mark of Cain also illustrated the same thing: there was judgment, but there was preservation. So too the story of the Flood spoke both of judgment and preservation. And the same is true here. For the Lord saw that the attempt to build the tower was *only the beginning of what they*

---

[16] Rev. 13:1.   [17] Rev. 13:2.   [18] Ps. 2:1, 4.

will do (11:6). The demonic dangers of mob rule, crowds united in their energies, striving for power but directed to goals which can only lead inexorably to destruction, are perhaps not too far from the thoughts of this author, nor is humankind's determination to be its own salvation. In C. S. Lewis' masterly fantasy *The Great Divorce*, he depicts hell as a town constantly growing in size but also in emptiness, for everyone is constantly moving out.

So in order to prevent things getting worse in Shinar, God's judgment in dividing the community is also a restraint. His purposes for human co-operation, communion and fellowship will not be achieved by allowing the city in Shinar to be built. Heaven is not to be grasped at by human ambition. Heaven, we have discovered before, is found as a gift of grace. We will need to wait till chapter 12, for the story of God's gracious covenant dealings with his people in history, before a God-centred community can be built.

Much of our contemporary culture has centrifugal forces at work. The Enlightenment heritage, building on Newton's picture of a 'world-machine', in which everything works by physical cause and effect, is still powerful in our minds. The mechanization of our culture – the depersonalizing of medicine, the careless exploitation of the environment for economic gain, the loss of the 'person' in much contemporary social and psychological science – these are symptoms of our loss of a centre. And the more they are indulged, the further from each other we are thrown.

Personal values, and the interpersonal communion facilitated by and symbolized by language, easily get flung to the edges. We find it hard to talk with each other about what really matters.

Thielicke writes:

On my trip to Asia, the word 'Coca Cola' was the one word I understood in every language; it sprang out familiarly from signs written in the most alien characters. What's wrong with a world in which this is the only word that has survived the Babylonian confusion of tongues? We can still talk to one another about Coca Cola, but not about freedom, not about God, not about what a neighbour is.[19]

What a sober warning these verses offer to the people of God, that in their good times they do not lose sight of their God. What a warning that they shun the temptation, from whatever source – political, economic, ideological, technological – to build up power-structures of their own, towers with their tops in the heavens,

[19] Thielicke, p. 285.

grasping for themselves what properly belongs to God. The social fragmentation which inevitably results is a sign of the judgment of God.

2. The hope of a restored community

We have become used to various themes in these eleven chapters. After the initial opening poem of creation in chapter 1, and its emerging story in chapter 2, in which we read of the majesty and mystery of the Creator, the glory of humanity made as the image of God and placed in a Garden with the tasks of stewardship and the gifts of fellowship, we have read story after story of disorder, destruction and death. Many times the disorder has been related to human beings trying to become as gods, grasping at a divinity which is not theirs, and flaunting an autonomy which is actually illusory. Adam, Cain, Lamech, the sons of God, and the nomadic settlers in the land of Shinar, each in their own ways tried to bring earth up to heaven and cross the boundaries God had given for human well-being.

Throughout these stories there is a pattern. Sin leads to punishment, the results of sin become clear, but there is then a word of divine grace so that in the punishment there is also restraint and preservation. Finally, there is a promise of hope for the future.

In the Garden, Adam and Eve fell into sin, God's word of judgment was spoken against the serpent, against the ground, and against them, then he made them garments of skins and allowed their life to continue outside the Garden. There was grace, and there was hope.

In the story of Cain, we read of Cain's murderous sin, and God's word of judgment. Cain was sent away as a fugitive, but in grace God put a mark of protection on him. Civilization began, and once again there was a hint of hope.

In the narrative of the Flood, after God saw the wickedness of mankind in the earth, he brought his deluge as a judgment on evil, but in grace he shut up Noah in an ark of safety. He held on to the reins of the storm and gave the promise of a new creation and a new beginning. The covenant of grace was sealed with a rainbow of hope.

In each case the story leaves us open to God, with the possibility that faith and hope and love might still grow.

But, in the story of the Tower of Babel, we seem to be left with disintegration, scattering, separation and confusion. Once again there has been sin and there has been judgment. There was even a measure of restraint and protection. But where is the hope for the future? How can life now go on?

The genealogies, we have noted, often preface a story of salvation, and we might have expected the same with the genealogy of chapter 10 leading into some saving action of God in the land of Shinar. But where is the salvation here?

It is when we have appreciated this pattern of sin and judgment and then grace and hope, that we realize all the more forcefully that this story in chapter 11 leaves us just with sin and judgment. We are effectively pressed to ask, 'O Lord, what now? Will you, O Lord, leave the people whom we believe are the fruit of your gracious blessing to Noah, will you leave them scattered, confused and separated from you and from each other? O Lord, what now?'

It is when we come to ask *that* question, that we are ready for what now follows in chapter 12. Now the primeval story has ended. The account of the people of God in history – a salvation history ultimately centred in Christ – can begin. For now God begins to reverse the judgment of Babel. A new community is being built as the family of Abraham. Through Abraham, we are told, *all* the families of the earth will again receive blessing (12:3). Through Abraham the covenant story of sacred history begins.

The descendants of Shem

These are the descendants of Shem. When Shem was a hundred years old, he became the father of Arpachshad two years after the flood; [11]*and Shem lived after the birth of Arpachshad five hundred years, and had other sons and daughters.*

[12]*When Arpachshad had lived thirty-five years, he became the father of Shelah;* [13]*and Arpachshad lived after the birth of Shelah four hundred and three years, and had other sons and daughters.*

[14]*When Shelah had lived thirty years, he became the father of Eber;* [15]*and Shelah lived after the birth of Eber four hundred and three years, and had other sons and daughters.*

[16]*When Eber had lived thirty-four years, he became the father of Peleg;* [17]*and Eber lived after the birth of Peleg four hundred and thirty years, and had other sons and daughters.*

[18]*When Peleg had lived thirty years, he became the father of Reu;* [19]*and Peleg lived after the birth of Reu two hundred and nine years; and had other sons and daughters.*

[20]*When Reu had lived thirty-two years, he became the father of Serug;* [21]*and Reu lived after the birth of Serug two hundred and seven years, and had other sons and daughters.*

[22]*When Serug had lived thirty years, he became the father of Nahor;* [23]*and Serug lived after the birth of Nahor two hundred years, and had other sons and daughters.*

[24]*When Nahor had lived twenty-nine years, he became the father*

of Terah; [25]*and Nahor lived after the birth of Terah a hundred and nineteen years, and had other sons and daughters.*

[26]*When Terah had lived seventy years, he became the father of Abram, Nahor, and Haran.*

[27]*Now these are the descendants of Terah.. Terah was the father of Abram, Nahor, and Haran; and Haran was the father of Lot.* [28]*Haran died before his father Terah in the land of his birth, in Ur of the Chaldeans.* [29]*And Abram and Nahor took wives; the name of Abram's wife was Sarai, and the name of Nahor's wife, Milcah, the daughter of Haran the father of Milcah and Iscah.* [30]*Now Sarai was barren; she had no child.*

[31]*Terah took Abram his son and Lot the son of Haran, his grandson, and Sarai his daughter-in-law, his son Abram's wife, and they went forth together from Ur of the Chaldeans to go into the land of Canaan; but when they came to Haran, they settled there.* [32]*The days of Terah were two hundred and five years; and Terah died in Haran.*

[12:1]*Now the* LORD *said to Abram, 'Go from your country and your kindred and your father's house to the land that I will show you.* [2]*And I will make of you a great nation, and I will bless you, and make your name great, so that you will be a blessing.* [3]*I will bless those who bless you, and him who curses you I will curse; and by you all the families of the earth shall bless themselves.'*

(11:10 – 12:3)

The bridge between the story of Babel and the history of Abraham is the family tree of Shem. After the opening formula, *These are the descendants of Shem* (11:10), we are taken through the generations to Terah, the father of Abraham (11:26). The life-spans are gradually shortening; children are being born when the father is quite a young age. We need to know this when we come to read later that the promise to Abraham that he would have a son came to him at the then-unexpectedly-great old age of a hundred years.[20]

In this genealogy, the spread of the nations across the world, of which we read in chapter 10, is now narrowed down to the single line of Shem, the son of Noah's blessing. All the while the world is experiencing the confusion described in 11:9, God is quietly, secretly, undramatically working out his purpose. The God who is concerned for all the nations (ch. 10), is the God whose purposes for all the nations are to be worked out through his covenant with one particular man and his descendants (ch. 12). This is the riddle of divine election. This is the mysterious particularity which is part of the story of God's grace. God's plan for *all the families of the*

[20] Gn. 17:17.

earth (12:3) is linked to his blessing of one man, Abraham, who came from the line of Shem, Arpachshad, Shelah, Eber, Peleg, Reu, Serug, Nahor and Terah. Their importance is not only their link backwards through Noah and Seth to Adam, but onwards through Isaac and Jacob, down the generations to David, and on through David's family tree to one called Joseph who was espoused to Mary who gave birth to her first-born son in Bethlehem in the days of Caesar Augustus.[21]

This genealogy provides the link between the primeval history of Genesis 1:1 – 11:9 and the actual sacred history of the patriarchs and their families with which the rest of Genesis is concerned.

The family history of Terah, Abraham's father, is told in 11:27–32. It mentions Abraham's brothers, nephews, and some of the women of the family. The only one for whom there is an important aside is Abraham's wife Sarai: *Now Sarai was barren; she had no child* (11:30). The narrator, almost in passing – but how significantly! – is not only preparing us for the surprise of the promise to Abraham that he would be blessed as the father of a great nation (12:2), but also for the later miracle story of the birth of Isaac,[22] through whom that blessing would come.

a. Abraham

At the end of the story of the Tower of Babel we were left without hope. These first eleven chapters of Genesis have stressed again and again that there is no hope for sinful human beings outside the gracious blessing of God. But now the story of Abraham begins. And it begins with the blessing of God. Five times in 12:2–3 God speaks again of blessing. There are unmistakable echoes of the first blessing on human beings at creation (1:28), and the blessing on Noah and his sons when creation began again after the Flood (9:1). Here is another new beginning.

Furthermore, the blessings to Abraham seem to counterbalance some of the judgments and curses we have also heard through chapters 1 – 11.[23] The ground was cursed in 3:17; Abraham is promised land to possess (15:7). Cain was cursed and became a wanderer in 4:11, 14; Abraham the wanderer is given a home. Cain, and the Nephilim, and the builders of Babel all sought for themselves a name; God says to Abraham, '*I will . . . make your name great*' (12:2). Cain, who built a city in the land of restlessness, and the migrants from the east who tried to build one at Shinar all discovered the 'here we have no continuing city';[24] Abraham, we

[21] Lk. 3:23–38.   [22] Gn. 17:17ff.; 18:10–14; 21:1–2.
[23] *Cf.* M. W. Poole and G. J. Wenham, *Creation or Evolution: A false antithesis?* (Latimer House, 1987).   [24] *Cf.* Heb. 13:14.

187

are told, 'looked forward to the city which has foundations, whose builder and maker is God'.[25] The families of the nations were scattered at Babel; in Abraham all the families of the earth will be blessed (12:3).

So Genesis 12:1–3 is about blessing, and 'blessing' as we have seen before in the Old Testament means creativity, fruitfulness and vitality. The Lord of life is at work in Abraham. Through him all the families of the earth can receive life. So these verses sound forth the opening chords of the great oratorio of salvation history. It is also the coda and recapitulation at the end of the overture we have heard played through chapters 1 – 11. For many of the themes of these eleven chapters are taken up and played through again in the story which begins with Abraham, though now in a different key.

From the perspective of Genesis 12, and the later stories of the covenant history of God with his people, we can now see that (to change the musical metaphor for a literary one), Genesis 1 – 11 serves as a prologue and an explanation. The story of salvation history is the answer to a question posed by the prologue: what hope can there be for a world as beautiful and yet as ugly, as structured and yet as disordered, as full of potential for brotherly love, and yet as poisoned with envy and hate? What hope is there for a people who have abandoned God, and have thereby abandoned each other? Can 'the creation community' be restored?

b. Jesus Christ

The remaining chapters of Genesis, and beyond, tell us that there is indeed hope for God's world: it is through Abraham and those who like him trust in the covenant promises of God that the world will be made new. The story of Abraham is a story of God's faithfulness and of the restoration of faith, individual and corporate. It is a story which spans the centuries. It takes us to Egypt and the Exodus, through the times of the judges and the kings, into exile and back to the land of promise. It reaches high points in its spirituality (the psalms), its wisdom (the proverbs), its oracles (the great prophets like Isaiah and Micah). It goes through the bleaker times of rebellion and judgment, suffering and loss.

This is a story which comes to its climax when Jesus Christ is affirmed as Lord. He is the Second Adam, the one whom Luther called 'The Proper Man'. In him the promise to the woman that the head of the serpent should be crushed comes to its fulfilment.[26] In him God's vulnerable, self-emptying love is embodied:[27] his is

---

[25] Heb. 11:10.   [26] *Cf.* Col. 2:15.   [27] Phil. 2:7.

the self-giving sacrifice of the Lamb of God.[28] His shed blood is 'more eloquent' than that of Abel.[29] In Christ the law of retaliation seen in Cain and Lamech is set aside. He bears the storm of God's judgment, and the alienation of his curse.[30] He knows the desolation of separation.[31]

And yet the New Testament tells us that it is in Christ that the security of God's ark of salvation is provided. In him the covenant of God's grace is sealed,[32] and the gift of God's fellowship is freely offered.[33] Indeed, in him all created things come to their fullness,[34] and will rejoice in the glorious liberty of the sons of God.[35] In him, the things of earth and the things of heaven come together,[36] not by our graspingly stretching upwards, but in God's gracious condescension in love bringing heaven down, to make us 'partakers of the divine nature'.[37] In Christ, our Creator is willing to be known as our Father.[38] In him the blessing of Abraham comes upon all the nations.[39] And the fellowship of person with person, man with woman, human being with the rest of creation, and all with God, can be made new. In him the vision of a new world of harmony,[40] peace,[41] healing and liberty[42] comes to its completion – for he is the centre of the new creation,[43] the new heaven and the new earth 'in which righteousness dwells'.[44]

Here is what some have called a 'cosmotheandric' vision: the vision of a restored creation centred on the Man who is God, the Cosmic Christ, Jesus our Lord.

He is the image of the invisible God, the first-born of all creation; for in him all things were created, in heaven and on earth, visible and invisible, whether thrones or dominions or principalities or authorities – all things were created through him and for him. He is before all things, and in him all things hold together. He is the head of the body, the church; he is the beginning, the first-born from the dead, that in everything he might be pre-eminent. For in him all the fullness of God was pleased to dwell, and through him to reconcile to himself all things, whether on earth or in heaven, making peace by the blood of his cross.[45]

This cosmic restoration is not a natural process. The world will not simply evolve to its Omega Point, as Teilhard de Chardin believed.[46] The new creation is itself a gift of grace; it comes only

---

[28] Jn. 1:29.   [29] Heb. 12:24.   [30] Gal. 3:13–14.   [31] Mk. 15:34.
[32] Mt. 26:28.   [33] Rom. 8:14–16.   [34] Eph. 1:9–10.   [35] Rom. 8:19–21.
[36] 1 Tim. 2:5.   [37] 2 Pet. 1:4.   [38] Mt. 5:45; 6:9–13.   [39] Gal. 3:14.
[40] Is. 11.   [41] Mi. 4:1–5.   [42] Is. 61:1–3.   [43] Mt. 19:28.
[44] 2 Pet. 3:13.   [45] Col. 1:15–20.
[46] Teilhard de Chardin, *The Phenomenon of Man* (ET, Collins, 1959).

by the power of Christ's resurrection from the dead. And in the power of that risen life, there is healing.

When Christ is again at the centre, there is healing for lives, for communities, and around the tree of life, there is healing for nations.[47]

There is even healing for language; and that for a particular purpose.

The prophet Zephaniah looks forward to the coming Day of the Lord, of which he says: 'At that time I will change the speech of the peoples to a pure speech . . .'. And why? ' . . . That all of them may call on the name of the LORD, and serve him with one accord.'[48]

The Pentecostal birth of the church is the beginning of that Day. The gift of the Holy Spirit, poured out on the church, begins to bring the potential of the whole of creation towards God's kingdom of glory. The many nations in Jerusalem hearing in their own tongues the mighty works of God[49] is the sign, too, of the possibility, when Christ is Lord, of a new 'I–Thou' community even in this ambiguous world.

So the birth of the church is the sign that the judgment of Babel is closed. That is the hope to which the story of Abraham will point us – and it points beyond even that. For God's restoration of community will be seen in its fullness when once again men and women from every tribe and tongue and people and nation gather, together with other living creatures from earth and heaven, around a throne overarched by the light of a rainbow. And they gather with one voice to sing the praise of the Lamb:

> Worthy art thou, our Lord and God,
> to receive glory and honour and power,
> for thou didst create all things,
> and by thy will they existed and were created.[50]

That, too, is our hope and strength.

[47] Rev. 22:2.   [48] Zp. 3:9.   [49] Acts 2:11.   [50] Rev. 4:11.